NEWSPAPERS AS ORGANIZATIONS

TO

CHRIS, LARRY AND MY
OTHER FRIENDS IN
NEWSPAPER COUNTRY

Newspapers as organizations

LARS ENGWALL

University of Uppsala

Gower

© Lars Engwall 1978

All rights reserved. No part of this publication may be reproduced, stored in a retrieval system, or transmitted in any form or by any means, electronic, mechanical, photocopying, recording, or otherwise without the prior permission of Gower Publishing Company Limited.

First published 1978 by SAXON HOUSE, Teakfield Limited
Reprinted 1981, 1983, 1986 by
Gower Publishing Company Limited,
Gower House,
Croft Road,
Aldershot,
Hampshire GU11 3HR,
England

British Library Cataloguing in Publication Data

Engwall, Lars
   Newspapers as organizations
   1. Newspaper publishing
   I. Title
   338.4'7'0705   PN4734 .E5

ISBN 0-566-00262-0

Printed and bound in Great Britain by
JFB Printing Limited, Camberley, Surrey

CONTENTS

LIST OF FIGURES ix

LIST OF TABLES xi

PREFACE xii

PART I: FORWARD!

    CHAPTER ONE.   TRAVELS IN NEWSPAPER COUNTRY

        1.1 Introduction   2
        1.2 An Organizational View   3
        1.3 Some Observations from the Field   6
        1.4 Characteristics of Newspapers   8
        1.5 The Main Outline   10

        Appendix to Chapter One. Five Case Study Descriptions:

        1A1. "Suddenly the Ground Started to Shake . . ."   11
        1A2. The Pankab Bankruptcy   18
        1A3. In the Field   22
        1A4. The Neartown Car Dealer   26
        1A5. The Policy Discussion   28

    CHAPTER TWO.   THE RESEARCH METHODS

        2.1 Introduction   33
        2.2 Written Material on Newspapers   34
        2.3 Interviews   34
        2.4 Allocation Data Analysis   38
        2.5 Participant Observation   40
        2.6 The Research Strategy   42

PART II: NEWSPAPER COUNTRY

    CHAPTER THREE.   NEWSPAPER TECHNOLOGY

        3.1 Introduction   46
        3.2 The Case Studies Reconsidered   46

	3.3 A Paradigm for Analysis	51
	3.4 The Collection Phase	54
	3.5 The Processing Phase	57
	3.6 The Reproduction Phase	60
	3.7 The Distribution Phase	63
	3.8 Concluding Remarks	65
CHAPTER FOUR.	NEWSPAPERS' ENVIRONMENT	
	4.1 Introduction	69
	4.2 Customers	69
	4.3 External Providers I: Suppliers	73
	4.4 External Providers II: Financiers	75
	4.5 External Providers III: Governments	79
	4.6 Competitors	83
	4.7 Concluding Remarks	95
CHAPTER FIVE.	NEWSPAPER PERSONNEL	
	5.1 Introduction	96
	5.2 Differentiation	96
	5.3 Integration I: Hierarchy	103
	5.4 Integration II: Lateral Contacts	109
	5.5 Integration III: Environmental Communication Links	114
	5.6 Concluding Remarks	121
	Appendix to Chapter Five. Organization Structures in Six Newspapers:	
	5A1. Introduction	122
	5A2. The Boston Globe	122
	5A3. The New York Post	123
	5A4. The New York Times	124
	5A5. The Washington Post	126
	5A6. The Daily Mirror	128
	5A7. The London Times	129

PART III: FOUR ISSUES IN NEWSPAPER COUNTRY

CHAPTER SIX.	FLOW		
	6.1	Introduction	133
	6.2	Buffering	140
	6.3	Leveling	142
	6.4	Forecasting	147
	6.5	Rationing	149
	6.6	Human Relations Aspects on the Flow Issue	151
	6.7	Concluding Remarks	154
CHAPTER SEVEN.	TECHNOLOGY		
	7.1	Introduction	157
	7.2	The Pressure for New Technology	159
	7.3	The Procedure of Introduction	166
	7.4	The Distribution of Benefits	174
	7.5	The Demarcation Problem	178
	7.6	Human Problems	182
	7.7	Concluding Remarks	184
CHAPTER EIGHT.	ALLOCATION		
	8.1	Introduction	188
	8.2	Allocation of Financial Resources	188
	8.3	Provider Allocation	194
	8.4	Allocation of Space	201
	8.5	Concluding Remarks	208
	Appendix to Chapter Eight. Variables Used		213
CHAPTER NINE.	PUBLICATION		
	9.1	Introduction	215
	9.2	The Conflicts Involved	215
	9.3	External Rules of the Game	222
	9.4	Selective Recruitment	225

	9.5 Socialization	229
	9.6 Some Results of Publication Decisions	237
	9.7 Concluding Remarks	241

PART IV: NEWSPAPER COUNTRY, AU REVOIR!

CHAPTER TEN.	CONCLUSIONS	
	10.1 Introduction	246
	10.2 A Quick Guide to Newspaper Country	246
	10.3 Implications Outside Newspaper Country	253
	10.4 One for the Road	255

REFERENCES[1] 256

SUBJECT INDEX 272

---

[1] The reference list also serves as an author index. For each reference is indicated the pages of the book on which the reference in question can be found.

LIST OF FIGURES

1:1	The Organization Model	5
3:1	A Flow Chart of the Events in "The Pankab Bankruptcy" and "The Neartown Car Dealer"	48
3:2	The Reproduction Phase in Traditional Newspaper Production	49
3:3	The Technology of Newspapers	50
3:4	Technology Profiles of the Collection Phase	57
3:5	Technology Profiles of the Processing Phase	59
3:6	Technology Profile of the Reproduction Phase	63
3:7	Technology Profile of the Distribution Phase	64
3:8	Manufacturing-Service Paradigm	66
4:1	Number of Newspapers in Sweden During the Period 1947-1971	85
4:2	Average Weekly Circulation Among Swedish Newspapers During the Period 1946-1971	86
4:3	Trends of Weekly Circulation in the Tabloid Group 1946-1971	87
4:4	A Summary of the Circulation Spiral Model	89
4:5	Trends of Weekly Circulation in the Örebro-area	90
4:6	Trends of Weekly Circulation in the Gävle/Sandviken-area	91
4:7	Trends of Weekly Circulation in the Borlänge/Falun-area	91
4:8	The Development of Cable Lines During the Earthquake	94
5:1	An Interviewee's Perception of the Relation Between Business and Journalistic Goals	97
5:2	Four Groups of Personnel	98
5:3	Lateral Contacts in Newspapers	113
5:4	External Communication Links	120
5:A1	Organization Chart of The Boston Globe	122
5:A2	Organization Chart of The New York Post	123
5:A3	Organization Chart of The New York Times Co.	125
5:A4	Organization Chart of The Washington Post	127
5:A5	Organization Chart of The Mirror Group	128
5:A6	Organization Chart of Times Newspapers Ltd.	130
6:1	Flow Conflicts Between Groups	135
6:2	Day-to-Day Variation in Number of Pages in a Provincial Swedish Newspaper	136

6:3	Le Monde: Average Number of Pages Allocated to Different Categories per Month, 1974	138
6:4	The Advertising Volume in Dagens Nyheter 1965-1973 Plotted on an Index Basis	139
6:5	Number of Pages to Be Made Up at Given Points in Time in a Swedish Provincial Newspaper	143
6:6	Flow Into and Out of the Composing Room one Day at The Record	144
6:7	A Summary of the Strategies Used in Newspapers to Handle Variations	155
7:1	The Development of Web Offset Printing in Scandinavia	157
7:2	The Development of Composition Technology	165
7:3	The Transition of Employees into New Jobs in a Swedish Newspaper	177
7:4	Technology Conflicts between Groups	184
8:1	Journalistic Share of Financial Resources in 1968 and 1972 Plotted Against Circulation in Semi-Logarithmic Scale	192
8:2	Share of Journalistic Employees in 1972 Plotted Against Circulation in Semi-Logarithmic Scale	196
8:3	Number of Persons in Editorial Office Plotted Against Circulation in Double Logarithmic Scale	199
8:4	The Outcome of Space Allocation in The Record During a Month in 1974	204
8:5	Journalistic Share of Space in 1968 and 1972 Plotted Against Circulation in Semi-Logarithmic Scale	206
8:6	Allocation Conflicts Between Groups	209
8:7	Share of Journalistic Resources for Different Groups of Newspapers in 1972	211
9:1	Publication Conflicts between Groups	221
9:2	Different Processes Involved in the Publication Issue	243
10:1	A Map of Newspaper Country	247

LIST OF TABLES

3:1	A Summary of the Aspects to Be Investigated in the Present Chapter	53
3:2	A Summary of the Technology of Newspaper Production	55
4:1	The Distribution of Votes in Le Monde	77
7:1	Average Annual Growth Rates in Costs, 1968-1972	161
7:2	Mean Growth Rates of Prices Charged by Fourteen Swedish Newspapers, 1968-1972	161
7:3	Mean Growth Rates in Circulation and Advertising Space in Fourteen Swedish Newspapers, 1968-1972	162
7:4	Steps in Introducing New Technology in Times Newspapers	169
7:5	Economic Compensation to Leaving and Remaining Employees of Dagens Nyheter	177
7:6	Employment in Composing and Printing at Different Levels of Automation	185
8:1	Percentual Distribution of Resources in Samples of Swedish Newspapers	190
8:2	Share of Total Revenues Allocated to the Journalistic Group in 1968 and 1972	193
8:3	Costs per Copy (SCr) in the Two Groups in 1968 and 1972	194
8:4	Costs per Column-meter (SCr) in the Journalistic and Business Groups in 1968 and 1972	194
8:5	Share of Employees in the Three Groups	197
8:6	Average Difference in Number of Employees Between Pairs of Newspapers in the Same Distribution Area	197
8:7	Parameters in the Regression Equations for the Number of Journalists on Circulation in Double Logarithmic Scale	200
8:8	Space in Per Cent Allocated to the Journalistic Group in 1968 and 1972	207
8:9	Annual Average Growth Rates in Space in the Period 1968-1972	207
8:10	Values of the Rank Correlation Coefficient between Three Allocation Variables	210
9:1	Topics of Front-Page Stories in The Record and its Main Competitor	239
9:2	Topics of News-Bill Items	240

PREFACE

Dear Chris, Larry and my other friends in Newspaper Country:

I have dedicated this report to you as your cooperation has been crucial to my pursuit of my research interest in newspapers. You have all been very helpful to my efforts to understand your country. In addition to your cooperation I am also grateful to colleagues in my own "University Country", who have provided me with a great deal of knowledge through their exploration of newspapers and other organizations. I have also benefited from discussions with colleagues in various seminars.

As you know from your own work, funds constitute an important prerequisite for most projects. My own research is no exception, and I should like to express my gratitude for a grant from The Swedish Council for Social Science Research which has been most important to the project.

Cordially,

Lars Enqwall

PART I: FORWARD!

                                            "The die is cast"

                                            (Julius Ceasar,
                                            when crossing the river
                                            Rubicon, 49 B.C.)

CHAPTER ONE.   TRAVELS IN NEWSPAPER COUNTRY

1.1   Introduction

Daily newspapers are accorded a great deal of importance in most nations. In Western democracies the press is even referred to as "a fourth branch of government", and the need for a free and responsible press is stressed by politicians of all parties. In many countries this public interest in newspapers has been manifested in government support, direct or indirect, to the press in order to counteract declining trends in the number of daily newspapers (cf. e. g. Smith, 1977). The purpose of these subsidies has been to avoid the closing down of existing newspapers in order to maintain "a free political debate" between different political opinions. In some instances, as in Sweden, subsidies have also been provided to stimulate the publication of new titles.

In this situation of public support for the press it seems important to try to find out more about the conditions under which newspapers work. If we are spending public money on the press, we should know what we can expect from newspapers, and what can be done to improve their performance, in an economic as well as a communications sense. In order to acquire such knowledge we must penetrate newspapers, i. e. explore a territory which will be referred to here as NEWSPAPER COUNTRY.

Another reason for undertaking TRAVELS IN NEWSPAPER COUNTRY is the apparent need for in-depth studies within different industries to further the development of organization theory. Many studies have been made of business firms involved in "normal" industrial production, particularly manufacturing. These findings have then been used as a basis for generalizations concerning "organizations". Research findings in recent years, however, suggest a need for theory based on contingencies, i. e. theory taking particular organizational conditions into consideration.

The main purpose of the present study is thus <u>to investigate the conditions under which daily newspapers work</u>. In order to provide a basis for such an analysis this initial chapter offers a description of an organization model. It then uses this model to stress some of the specific characteristics of newspaper organizations. The conclusions are partly based on five case study descriptions which are summarized in Section 1.3, and which are reproduced *in extenso* in the appendix.

1.2 An Organizational View

There are number of approaches to organizations; the choice of approach in any given study is often a result of the background of the researcher. This is the case with the present study, as earlier contacts with the work of Barnard, Simon, Cyert and March, Lawrence and Lorsch, Thompson, and Hall, have been prime influences.[1]

The basic approach used in the present study is the coalition concept of organizations.[2] According to this view, the organization is looked upon as an open system, in which different interest groups interact. The three main components of the model are

        A. TECHNOLOGY
        B. ENVIRONMENT
        C. PERSONNEL

The first of these three concepts, TECHNOLOGY, refers to processes by which different kinds of input are transformed to output. The inputs can be different kinds of raw material, financial resources, labour, etc. and the output is different kinds of products for customers.

Concerning the ENVIRONMENT, three main groups can be identified: 1) *external providers*, 2) *customers*, and 3) *competitors*. They differ from PERSONNEL in that they are not employed by the organization. Nevertheless, some of them may be fairly well integrated into the

---

[1] Cf. Barnard (1938), March & Simon (1958), Cyert & March (1963), Lawrence & Lorsch (1967), Thompson (1967) and Hall (1972).

[2] For a more extensive discussion of the organization model, cf. Engwall (1974 b, particularly Chapter Three).

organization.

The external providers are the groups in the environment which provide different kinds of external input. In this group we can include a) financiers (lenders and owners), b) governments (local and national), and c) suppliers (of material and services). While the external providers furnish the organization with input, the customers buy its output. Concerning both groups, however, the organization has to compete with competitors that may offer more attractive benefits, i. e. higher revenues for external providers and lower costs for customers. Competition also concerns the personnel group, i. e. those employed by the organization, since other organizations may offer better conditions.

The relationships between these organizational components are summarized in Figure 1:1, which demonstrates how input is provided from the ENVIRONMENT by external providers, and is operated on by PERSONNEL employing the TECHNOLOGY of the organization. In this way output is produced for customers (the physical flow), for which they pay a price. The revenues obtained are then distributed among providers, i. e. among personnel and various external provider groups (the financial flow). The model thus looks upon the organization as a place for the exchange of goods and financial resources.

A basic criticism raised against the coalition model of organizations is that it neglects conflicts. This criticism has some validity for some of the applications of the model, but it is not valid for the model per se. In point of fact, the model includes strong elements of conflict. In the exchange with the environment there is a conflict between the interests of providers and customers -- the former striving to increase revenues per output unit, and the latter to cut the expenditure per purchased unit. There are also conflicts between different provider groups concerning the distribution of the sales revenues. Finally conflicts may arise from the competition for customers and providers.

The model described above will be used for the analysis in the following chapters and constitutes a basic point of departure for the present study.

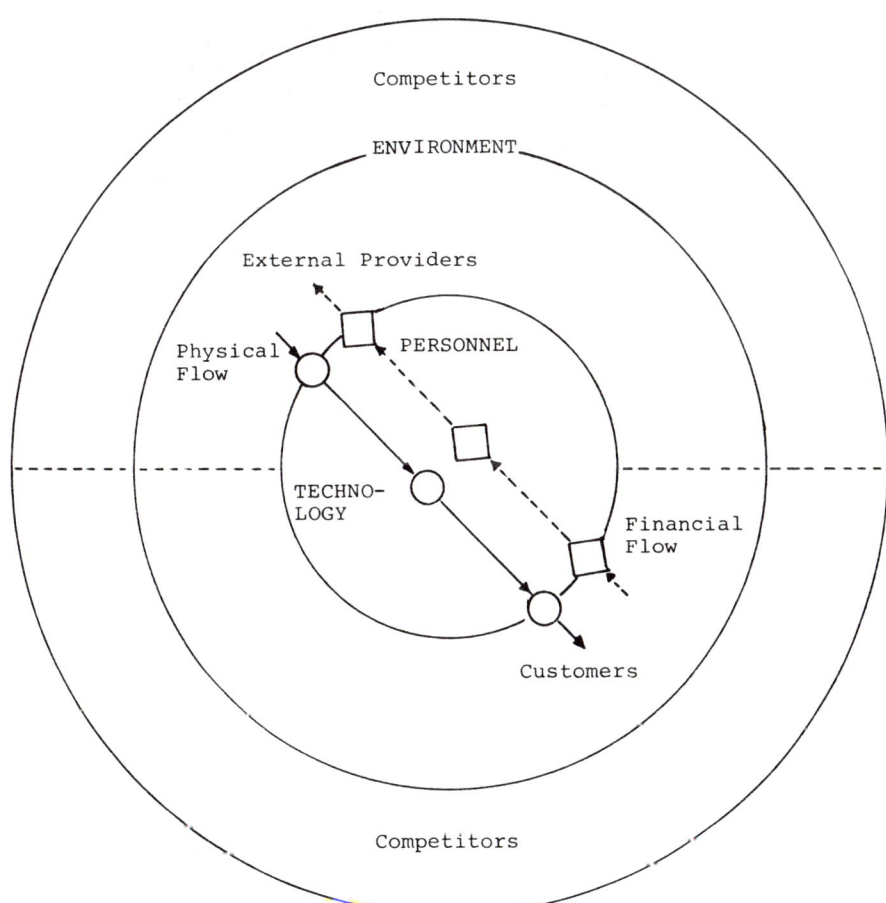

Figure 1:1. The Organization Model.

1.3   Some Observations from the Field.

Chapter Two will provide a closer description of the different methods used to explore newspapers. Among these methods is a participant observation study of one Swedish local newspaper, The Record, which produced five case study descriptions (cf. Appendix to this chapter). I summarize them here in order to provide some insights into NEWSPAPER TECHNOLOGY, NEWSPAPER ENVIRONMENT and NEWSPAPER PERSONNEL.

In the first case study (Section 1A1 : "Suddenly the Ground Started to Shake . . .") news about an earth quake in Italy was received on the teleprinter just before the final deadline. Action had to be taken by the staff in the newsroom to change the contents of the paper. This work of redesigning the paper included not only journalists but also compositors and printers. The news story which could be included was not very extensive. It was followed up on the following day by stories based on news agency material as well as interviews with Swedish locals returning from the earth-quake stricken area. The case stresses four basic points:

- 1a) the uncertainty that prevails for the input of news with respect to both content and timing

- 1b) the need for cooperation between specialized employees in different phases of the production process

- 1c) the disadvantages of a minor newspaper: even when the personnel of such a newspaper do their utmost, they are beaten by the major newspaper!

- 1d) the efforts of a local newspaper to find a local touch in the presentation of international news

The second case study (Section 1A2 : "The Pankab Bankruptcy") describes the work of a journalist on a story concerning a bankrupt company. In the case study the story is followed from the assignment at the morning news conference to the point of printing the story. During this period the reporter tried to acquire information on the company from several different sources. He had some difficulties in obtaining all of the information desired due to the unwillingness of the managing director to provide information.

After this article was printed the latter even protested against the news story, filing complaints with the Ombudsman of the Press.

In summary the case:

- 2a) provides an illustration of the successive steps in the newspaper production process
- 2b) points out the time pressure under which reporters work and how successive postponements in writing can result in heavy time pressure at the end
- 2c) highlights pressures from the environment, both before and after publication
- 2d) shows how the work of copy-editors can produce irritation not only of readers but of reporters as well

The third case study (Section 1A3 : "In the Field") summarizes the work of two reporters during a single day. It describes the coverage of a light motor cycle competition at a local school and the events of a press conference arranged by a local community. This case points to:

- 3a) the continuous pressure information sources exert on newspapers. Various organizations and authorities are very eager to communicate favourable information about their activities. At the same time they also want to pass on "accurate" information.
- 3b) collegial relations between journalists of different mass-media organizations and between journalists and a press relations officer
- 3c) the jumping of journalists between different routine assignements.

The fourth case study (Section 1A4 : "The Neartown Car Dealer") describes the flow of an advertisement from the advertiser to the printed product. It includes the administrative processing, the production of artwork, and the reproduction work in the composing room. It also provides an account of the problems encountered when errors creep into advertisements. The case study description stresses:

4a) the specialization and differentiation of employees in the production process (manifested through statements such as "I'm not really supposed to do this," and "Whenever there are problems, the compositors always put the blame on us").

4b) the dominance of negative feedback. A good job is very seldom acknowledged, whereas errors cause immediate reactions.[1]

The fifth and final case study (Section 1A5: "The Policy Discussion") concerns a policy discussion in the newsroom. The meeting was arranged in order to develop new editing policies due to a scarcity of space. Several proposals were made during the meeting but no decision taken due to differences in opinion. The case points to:

5a) the difficulties encountered in undertaking product development in newspapers (a contributing factor in this context is the limited knowledge of the preferences of present, as well as presumed, readers)

5b) the dependency of daily newspapers on advertisements (the inflow of advertisements constitutes an important factor influencing both circulation and the volume of news the paper can carry)

1.4 Characteristics of Newspapers

The case studies described above, brought together with other types of evidence in Chapters Three to Nine, will make it possible to conclude that NEWSPAPER TECHNOLOGY is characterized by

- a short production cycle
- a chain of tasks, with different technological characteristics, which have to be integrated
- variations in input

---

[1] The same was true in the first case study: the journalists and compositors were not praised for managing to print the story, but were scolded for being bested by The Record's main competitor.

Second, it can be stressed that NEWSPAPER ENVIRONMENT is characterized by:

- the existence of two types of customers -- readers and advertisers -- of which the latter provide most of the revenues in quality papers
- difficulties in developing the product and in changing reader habits
- relatively great interest on the part of newspaper owners in influencing the mix of the product
- a tendency on the part of various other groups in the environment to try to influence what is published by feeding as well as the withholding information

Third, we can conclude that the group of NEWSPAPER PERSONNEL is characterized by:

- a high degree of differentiation between, as well as within, personnel groups
- a pronounced need for contacts between the various groups as well as between individual groups and the environment

It is also possible to see that the characteristics of newspapers mentioned above lead to a number of ISSUES. With reference to the organization model presented in Section 1.2, it can be noted first that an <u>issue</u> <u>of</u> <u>flow</u> arises from the fact that the product has an extremely short production cycle; it is crucial that the product hits the distribution system at the right time. The physical flow through the various parts of the organization is, therefore, of particular importance.

Second, it can be shown that a <u>technology</u> <u>issue</u> has moved into newspaper organizations as computer and photographic technology have drastically changed printing methods. These technological changed have caused, and will cause, organizational changes which, in turn, engender a number of problems.

Third, newspapers face the <u>issue</u> <u>of</u> <u>allocation</u>, i. e. a need to resolve questions such as: "How large a share of total revenues can different groups obtain?" and "How are the revenues to be distributed within a provider group?". In addition to these allocation decisions, which newspapers have in common with other organizations, there is an additional one in newspapers: that decision concerns the mix of the product, i. e. the space devoted to different types of material in the newspaper.

Fourth, newspapers have to resolve an issue of publication, i. e. to decide what material should be included in a particular number. Here, newspapers deviate from most other organizations, because the daily mix of the product may cause conflicts among personnel as well as between employees and persons or groups in the environment.

1.5 The Main Outline

The present and the following chapter set the scene and describe the different research methods employed. They are followed by eight chapters which are arranged in three parts: NEWSPAPER COUNTRY; FOUR ISSUES IN NEWSPAPER COUNTRY; and NEWSPAPER COUNTRY, AU REVOIR! The first of these parts includes three chapters devoted to the three basic components of the organizational model presented in Section 1.2, i. e. TECHNOLOGY, ENVIRONMENT and PERSONNEL.

The succeeding part, Chapters Six to Nine, will focus on the four issues identified in the previous section: the ISSUES of FLOW, TECHNOLOGY, ALLOCATION, and PUBLICATION, respectively. The final part of this volume presents the conclusions drawn from the study. These conclusions concern newspapers in particular, but implications for other organizations will also be discussed. In addition, the last section discusses topics for future research.

APPENDIX TO CHAPTER ONE. FIVE CASE STUDY DESCRIPTIONS.

1A1. "Suddenly the Ground Started to Shake . . ."

It's late Thursday night in the composing room of The Daytown Record. The clock is nearing twenty minutes past midnight as I stand talking with Jack and Dick, the engravers.[1] They have had a hectic time since midnight, when the last pages of The Record were composed. Eight pages had been delivered almost simultaneously for photographing and engraving. But, the process is rather quick, and it took Jack and Dick no more than about twenty minutes to deliver the eight pages to the press room.

Our conversation, which has focused on printer's errors, is suddenly interrupted by Larry, the night editor, who rushes into the composing room carrying a news telegram in his hand: "This thing about the earthquake is developing. I think we should do something about it."[2] The time is 0.25 a.m.

By the time Larry arrives with the news telegram, all the compositors have left the composing room, since they are permitted to leave when all pages have been composed. So, he runs up to the cafeteria to see whether there are any compositors left in the building. In a couple of minutes he returns to the composing room, tells us that all compositors are gone, and walks back to the newsroom. After a short while Larry returns to the composing room, this time accompanied by Chris, a copy-editor, and another news telegram. - "It's clear now we've got to do something. Jack, can you and Dick handle the composing machines?"

It turns out that the two engravers are not able to handle the composing machine for the text of the story. Fortunately, however, they do know how to handle the composing of headlines, and they also tell Larry and Chris that the engraving can be done from typewritten text on a piece of paper.[3]

---

[1] Naturally, all names used here are fictitious.

[2] The news telegram in Larry's hand from the Swedish news agency (TT) provided information on an earthquake in Central Europe. It was based on information from the German news agency DPA and mentioned that the earthquake was felt in Berlin. The strength of the earthquake measured 6.5 on the Richter scale.

[3] The Record employs photo composition and offset printing.

As we hear the printing start in the printing room, further items on the earthquake come in on the teleprinter. Hectic activity ensues in the composing room. The journalists, Larry and Chris, work quite fast. They ask Dick to compose the headline "EXTRA EXTRA EXTRA EXTRA EXTRA EXTRA". Then, they examine the photos of the different pages to see which one will be easiest to change. They rough out a short story on the earthquake as well as the headline.

Chris hands the headline text to Dick and runs for fresh wires. They are very vague, but it is now quite evident that the story is developing. Larry, the night editor, tries to find a typewriter with good enough type for the message on the earthquake. He starts writing a story based on the information in the wires that have arrived. Jack and Chris come up to him. Jack, an engraver rejects the typewriter's print: "Take the electric one instead!" Larry moves and starts writing again. - "Hell, the carbon is red!" - "It doesn't matter, I can take it anyway," Jack answers calmly. In the meantime, Chris has been working on the wire items and is now able to dictate the story to Larry. In the middle of the story they are interrupted by yet another wire. It provides information from a radio amateur, who reports three deaths and hundreds of injured.

The three-paragraph story is delivered into the darkness of the camera room for photographing. Standing there with the engraving men, I happen to ask: "Are you going to change the news-bill, too?" - "That's a good question," Dick replies and runs up to Larry, relaying my question to him. - "Is it possible?" - "I'll ask the circulation man," Dick replies and runs out of the composing room.[1] Just one minute later we hear him again: "It's OK!" Chris rushes into the news-room and returns almost instantaneously with a manuscript for the news-bill.

In the meantime, the film of the new text has been processed in the developer. Jack cuts the photo of page nine, which has been selected for the story. As Dick is composing the text for the news-bill, Jack goes on to engrave a new plate. In about five minutes

---

[1] My intention was not to engage in action research. Sometimes, however, innocent questions have unforeseen consequences.

the plate is ready. He opens the door to the printing room and
whistles loudly to the printers. They respond immediately, and
we hear them slow down the printing press.

About five minutes later the change of plates has taken place,
and the printing starts again. Three minutes later, the "revised"
paper is delivered into the news-room. We read the message
together and think it looks rather good, despite some typographical errors which crept into the story as it was rushed away.

At about the same time, the plate for the news-bill is ready
and is sent to to the printing room. It is now 1.15 a.m., and
Jack and Dick leave The Record. I sit down and talk with Larry
and Chris in the news-room. They relax, quite happy about having
been able to respond to the late-breaking story. Chris says: "A
day like this is a Hell of a lot of fun. I like it when there's
a lot going on. At other times, it is easy to fall asleep."

We discuss the make-up of page one, life in general and newspaper
life in particular. We also discuss the news-bill, and Chris and
Larry think they will be the only ones in town to have the earthquake story on the news-bill. Our discussion is interrupted by a
man from the day shift who has a bone to pick with Chris. After
arguing with Chris about half an hour he disappears just as the
circulation man enters with copies of The Record's main competitor, The Chronicle. We pounce upon the delivered copies and find to
our dismay that The Chronicle has the earthquake in the upper
righthand corner of its front page.

Chris and Larry are crestfallen:"Hell! They have it on page one with
a continuation on page six." - "I don't even want to look at it."[1]
They decide to leave for home, whereas I prefer to stay in the
printing room. In addition to the four printers, there are also
circulation people, all working hard to deliver piles of printed
papers to waiting cars.

---

[1] Before we left, Larry received an additional copy of The Chronicle from Martin, a printer. Martin does not usually deliver copies to the news-room, and it was quite evident to Larry that this particular delivery was meant as criticism, as Martin is generally critical to the news-room.

Printing finished and most of the piles of newspapers having been handed over to the cars, I start talking to two of the printers, Peter and John. They too, are disappointed. They had hoped The Chronicle would have missed the story. At least, it shouldn't have had better coverage. - "But, that's the life of a smaller paper. The major paper has the resources and thus the means of producing better coverage," Peter concludes.

My first contact with the earthquake story the following day, a Friday, is the 1.00 p.m. radio newscast, in which the newscaster reports "a severe earthquake with 300 deaths, 1.000 injured and damages at a value of 10.000 million lira." On my way to The Record I also learn that The Record was not alone in featuring the earthquake story on the news-bill. The Chronicle has it too, on the upper half of the news-bill, whereas The Record filled the bill with the earthquake: "EARTHQUAKE LAST NIGHT. Houses damaged - casualties."

As I arrive at The Record, I learn from Bill, one of the news editors, that the people in the news-room have been discussing the earthquake coverage during the morning. Some **detective work** has been undertaken to find out why The Chronicle had better coverage than The Record and what percentage of the copies distributed had carried the story. Again, the staff expresses disappointment at having been beaten by The Chronicle. "The story ought to have been on page one, and it should have been more extensive," Bill complains.

During the day the **news-room** follows the development of the story by means of radio and teleprinter in order to gather background information for the stories for Saturday's paper. - "But, you can't do very much during the day," Bill tells me. "You know that more up-to-date wires will arrive in the evening, and that pictures will be available from the consolidated bureaus. What you can do **is** try to do a local follow-up."

By afternoon, a tip regarding a local follow-up has arrived. At noon-time a local correspondent of a Stockholm evening paper phoned Bill, telling him about three local citizens who are expected to return from the earthquake area the same night. In return for the tip-off, the evening paper journalist is promised pictures of the arriving locals, an arrangement which is part of an informal agreement between him and The Record.-"Our relations are quite good. There is no formal agreement behind it. It all depends on the person. His predecessor wasn't cooperative at all." Bill says to me.

In response to the tip-off, Bill has called his own local correspondent in the prospective interviewees' hometown, asking him to do an interview. Bill then receives a call from the local correspondent, who has learnt that the three men are due to arrive at the local airport by five o'clock. Bill sends a reporter and a photographer to the airport to do the job.

It is 4.30 p.m., and I am sitting in at the news conference. It opens with a discussion on the earthquake story. Bill tells the night editor and the copy-editors that he has learnt that the story was not included in all copies distributed locally in Daytown. The staff also discuss possible reasons why The Chronicle should have a better coverage than The Record. In this context it is mentioned that Al, the second news editor, heard about the story on an extra newscast at 11 o'clock the previous night.

Larry and Chris (night editor and copy editor, respectively) describe the situation, telling about the gradual arrival of diffuse telegrams from about midnight on. They also voice their suspicion that The Chronicle has access to a teleprinter from the international news agency, Associated Press. - "Their story carries 'AP' at the top, and the text is completely different from the one we received. It seems as though they received the story before we received it."[1]

---

[1] There was certain uncertainty concerning the existence of an Associated Press printer in the news-room of The Chronicle. But, some days later it was determined that The Chronicle does indeed have such a printer.

-"Funny," Chris adds, "they didn't flash it. Earlier last night they flashed a story on an airplane crash in Germany where three Swedes were killed. - "What's more, the first item about the earthquake came on the printer carrying sports news!"[1]

After the discussion of the earthquake coverage in Friday's paper, Bill turns to his memo to the night editor, in which he outlines a follow-up of the earthquake on page one. The coverage will involve compiling wire-service stories, plus the intended interview with the three local eye-witnesses. In addition, he has planned a number of local stories for the Saturday paper.

Immediately after the news conference the tipster calls the news-room, eager to hear how things are working out. He is assured that everything is all right: "The reporter and the photographer just returned from the airport. The photographer thinks that he has some good art."

After the call Nick, the reporter, tells his colleagues about his experiences at the airport. The three men had been rushed away by a driver who was in a hurry. Nick could only put a few questions and exact promises to be allowed to call later in the evening. Nick seems confident that he will obtain the necessary information: "They seem OK. I think they'll talk on the phone. I'll call them by seven o'clock. And, I think I have a good story. They told me they had been sitting in a restaurant and suddenly heard a roaring sound. First, they thought it was a truck, then a tank, then they started running .... "

After a while, Bill, the news editor, enters the news-room and starts talking to Larry, the night editor. -"I think we should play up the local angle today. They were in the middle of the catastrophe. That's something. Local people in the area stricken by the earthquake." They also discuss the design of page one and the layout of the page carrying the earthquake coverage. Their discussion ends with some comments on the order of pictures from a syndicated bureau.

---

[1] A "flash story" breaks all other stories and is announced by ringing bells.

The Record has two teleprinters, one of which, the reporters feel, carries predominantly sports news. Any such "division of labour" is denied by the news agency, however.

A fresh wire from the Swedish news agency gives the figure of 450 dead in the quake. Like the rest of the wires, however, it is short, and those at the copy desk agree that the material is useless as it stands. Rewriting will be necessary, but an alternative might be to wait for the summarizing story from the news agency. As time goes by, further short telegrams arrive, and Chris exclaims: "This story may get awfully long. We have to keep to the essentials!"

Nick calls the men who have returned from Italy, and they feed him further details of their experiences. In the middle of the call Bill walks up to his desk and hands him a paper telling him he should go to a local Red Cross meeting by half past seven, i.e. within twenty minutes.

The telephone interview goes on until 7.25 p.m., at which time Nick comes up to the copy desk and starts talking to the copy editors. They consider the interview most important, and tell Nick to give it priority. -"But I have to go to the Red Cross meeting," Nick explains. "Being new here, I can't just skip a job." He rushes away to the meeting.

By 8.00 p.m. the pictures of the returning local people are on Larry's desk. They look fine. He has barely had a chance to look at them when the journalist from the evening paper (the tipster) calls to check up on the situation. This call is followed by new discussions on the order of pictures from the syndicated bureau and the formulation of the news-bill. The pictures are ordered and received by telephoto. They are not very good, a circumstance which makes Chris exclaim, "It doesn't exactly make you jump for joy. It looks like and old boa gone to pieces. I think it might look more dramatic if I remove a strip along the bottom."[1]

By 9.00 p.m. the discussion at the copy-desk on the formulation of the news-bill becomes heated. Chris smiles at me and says: "You see, it's really _too_ good. You have three local guys right on the spot!" - Finally, they agree on the following formulation for the news-bill:

"DAYTOWNERS back from Italy:- SUDDENLY THE GROUND STARTED TO SHAKE..."

---
[1] Chris did cut out the lower portion of the picture, thus removing some houses which had not been destroyed in the earthquake. The Chronicle used the same picture, but the copy-editors there had not cut the picture.

1A2. The Pankab Bankruptcy

Phil, a reporter specializing in the labour market, arrives in the news-room of The Record a few minutes after 9.00 a.m. At this point there has been activity in the composing room and at the non-newspaper press room the past two hours or so. At 9.30 people start gathering in the upper end of the news-room for the news conference, a meeting during which the news editor distributes assignments for the paper of the following day. Phil has been working on a story about the bankruptcy of a local firm, Pankab, since yesterday, and Bill, the news editor, tells him: "Go on working on your story today. But count on publication tomorrow. Today's a weak news day."

After the news conference we all congregate at the coffee table, and by 10.00 Phil has started working on his story. He works mainly by telephone. He is interrupted several times by in-coming phone calls about other matters. Among these are two calls from a very talkative man who frequently calls Phil to talk politics. These calls give Phil an opportunity to go through some of the magazines he is supposed to read.

At 11.15 Phil puts a paper into his typewriter, upon which he is immediately interrupted by more phone calls. He then makes some calls in relation to his story. He is also approached by the copyist, who asks him to choose some photos for the story. Phil asks the copyist to make prints of four frames in the film and then rushes away to look up earlier stories about Pankab in past issues of The Record. He also picks up some coffee and snacks, which will constitute his lunch.

By 1.00 p.m. the prints of the photos are ready, and Phil decides to use two of them. He tells me he has decided to phone the President of Pankab despite an earlier decision not to do so. The President is apparently most unwilling to talk to journalists and breaks off the conversation several times in order not to reveal too much. He even urges Phil not to write the story on Pankab, a request which later prompts, Bill, the news editor to comment: "That's just the way to be sure of publication!"

It is now 2.30 p.m. Phil makes some phone calls to regional authorities and decides to go downtown and see them in order to look at some documents. Before he leaves, he tells me: "I have an appointment at six o'clock, and I won't be home until half past nine. So, I have to deliver the story before six. I haven't written a line of it yet." He walks out of the news room.

Phil's downtown visit lasts until 4.15. Returning to the news-room, he informs me that the regional authorities practically urged him to write the story. He also points out to me once more that he is short of time. He adds, jokingly: "The advantage of postponing writing a story is that you then _have_ to write it." Phil smiles wryly and goes over and sits down in front of his typewriter. It is 4.20 p.m.

As before, Phil is interrupted in his work several times by phone calls. At 5.25 Phil tells me he has three manuscript pages, but he is not content: "I haven't got any real kick into the story yet."

Around 6.00 journalists start leaving the news-room. Phil is still writing his story. Ten minutes past six he delivers four manuscript pages to the copy desk. He also hands over the photos and a lead for page one. Chris, the copy editor, asks: "What's the gist of the story? Who wins, who loses?". Phil gives him a quick run-down and rushes away to his meeting.

The lead for page one is handed over to Larry, the night editor, the pictures are delivered to the engravers, and the story temporarily rests in a box marked "To Edit". Larry starts working on the headlines for page one. He types out one idea after another for Phil's story but throws them away. Consulting Chris, he decides on: "Pankab -- fiasco where EVERYBODY loses."

About 7.00 p.m. the headlines for page one are handed over to the composing room, and Chris starts to work on the body of Phil's story. In just a few minutes he has a suggestion for the headlines over the main story: "Soon gone: a company given 315.000 in sub-sidies/Left: 50 jobless". He turns to Larry, and they joke a bit

about some of the tentative headlines. Their conversation is
interrupted by the messenger, who delivers the latest mail
and takes orders for hot-dogs and French fries.

Chris goes back to the story. He decides to put it on page nine
and then turns to editing the copy, i.e. brushing up the language,
adding sub-heads and giving style instructions to the composing
room.

Larry delivers the lead for page one to the composing room, while
Chris turns to the dummy of page nine and starts drawing up the
page. He puts Phil's article at the top of the page. In the meantime Larry starts working on the news-bill: Phil's story is put
on the bottom half of the bill.

By 8.15 Chris has written a lead for page nine and drawn the
article into the dummy. His colleague Mary comments: "I hope you're
not blowing it up like it was a new world war!" A remark followed up
by some joking. Chris then delivers the edited manuscript to the
composing room and turns to another story on page nine.

In the composing room the night shift has been working since 4.30 p.m.
The have had a half-hour break at 7.30 and will take another break
at 9.00. Phil's story arrives just in time to allow Barbara to
key-punch it before the 9.00-break. She passes the cassette on to
Jeremy, one of the proof-readers, who stores it in a rack. Returning
from his break, at 9.30 he can start proofreading it on the video
screen. As he has gone through the full article, having paused
now and then to check details, the contents of the cassette are
fed into the computer. After a while Jay, one of the compositors,
is able to take the story out of the composing machine. He walks a
few steps and puts it into the developer. When the article emerges
from this latter machine, it is in readable form again. Jay removes
excess margins and puts the story on a rack of material ready for
paste-up. It is not long before Tim, another compositor, fetches
it and places the Pankab story on page nine. Although, the Pankab
story is ready around 10.30, it is not until 11.47, just before
midnight, that the rest of the page is filled and can be delivered
to engraving. This delivery has been preceded by joint consultations
between Tim and the journalists, Larry and Chris.

Five minutes past midnight, page nine returns to the composing room as a developed photo. Jack, one of the engravers, adds the pictures and brings the page to plate-making. The latter is a relatively rapid process, and it is not long before Jack can deliver the plate to the printing room, where the four printers, Bob, Martin, John and Peter, have been busy since 10.00 preparing the presses for tomorrow's paper. At 0.30 a.m. Bob can press the the button and the presses start rolling. In a few minutes I am able to read Phil's article in print.[1]

The following afternoon I talk to Phil about his story. He tells me that he was somewhat irritated when he opened up the paper and found the word "fiasco" in the headlines: "It wasn't in the story. But, after a while, I decided it was OK, anyway." He also feels he left out some points, since he had been in a hurry: "If I'd had the time, I would have worked overtime to fix it up a little more. Among other things, the story is about one manuscript page too long." Another consequence of the time shortage was that Phil hadn't been able to phone a labour leader and read the article to him as promised.

Phil does not expect any problem with the labour leader, which turns out to be a correct judgement. But, one other person is annoyed: Pankab's President. He phones Herb, the Editor-in-Chief, and threatens to bring The Record before the Press Ethics Review Board (Pressens Opinionsnämnd) unless the paper carries a correction on page one. Both Phil and Herb chuckle at the phone call: "Even if he did bring us before the Board, there'd be no problem He doesn't have a chance."

Pankab's President did in fact raise the issue with the Ombudsman for the Press in a letter, in which he particularly complained about certain formulations in the article and the headlines.[2]

---

[1] The usual procedure upon receiving finished copies of the paper "hot off the presses" is to sit down in the news-room for a relaxed chat. This particular evening was an exception: Just after the presses had started to roll, the news of the Italian earthquake started to break.

[2] The Ombudsman sent a copy of this letter to The Record for comment. The conflict was then resolved by The Record's publication of a "letter-to-the-editor" by the Pankab President. (The complaint was dismissed.)

1A3. **In the Field**

Upon his arrival at work in the morning Larry receives a short note from Bill, the news editor, on a light motorcycle competition at a local school. Larry calls the school, and we drive out, finding a crowd of youngsters on a school ground. Jerry, *The Record*'s photographer, has already arrived and is busy taking pictures. As we arrive, Larry starts noting the names of the people on Jerry's pictures, a vital detail.

After a while we are approached by the man in charge of the event. He hands over a press release and volunteers to phone later in the afternoon concerning the results of the competition. It is quite evident that he is very interested in receiving publicity. He comes from the national organization's headquarters in Stockholm and will be arranging many similar competitions in the region in the near future. He volunteers to phone *The Record* at regular intervals during his tour of surrounding communities.

Larry glances through the press release as he smokes a cigarette. He turns to me and says: "A good job, where you get all the information you need." Jerry, the photographer, then comes up to tell us he thinks he has enough pictures. He then leaves for another job.

We are approached by a local employee of the sponsoring organization. Larry interviews him briefly and then gets som final information from the man in charge. We leave. The whole assignment has taken about half an hour.

Back in the news-room Larry immediately sits down to bang out his story. About a quarter of an hour later Larry hands the story to me. It is one and a half manuscript pages long and gives the highlights of the event. Much of it is based on the press release issued at the school. Some space is left for the results, which are to arrive later in the afternoon.

Larry leaves the news-room again to go to the regional authorities in order to check their incoming mail, while I join Phil, who is scheduled for a press conference at the Town Hall.

We arrive at the Town Hall somewhat in advance and are taken care of by the Press Relations Office. He furnishes Phil with some additional material on the meeting of the previous day. They then talk casually about some of the items on the agenda but are interrupted by the arrival of a reporter from the Swedish Broadcasting Corporation.[1] After mutual greetings all three casually discuss the agenda.

It is now ten minutes after the time set for the press conference. The reporter from The Chronicle hasn't arrived yet. -"How long do you usually wait?" the P.R.O. asks. - "Not more than ten minutes," one of the reporters responds, and they start a more organized discussion than before.[2]

The P.R.O. relates some information unrelated to the meeting of the board. The township is going to start a drive for the collection of newspapers, and a visit from the Swedish Navy is planned. The journalists take notes. They then turn to the agenda, questioning the P.R.O. in relation to various items on it.

- "How about economic compensation for committee members?"

- "Did they say anything about the compulsory membership to the student union?"

---

[1] A corporation jointly owned and controlled by representatives of the Government, of finance and industry, labour and the "popular movements" (consumer cooperation, the temperance movement, evangelical churces, etc.) enjoys monopoly rights to non-commercial radio and TV broadcasting in Sweden. Local broadcasting is in its infancy, and Sweden lacks the flora of local radio stations common in the U.S.A., Canada, the U.K., and in many other Western countries.

[2] "It has never before happened to me during ten years on the job that a paper misses a press conference," the P.R.O. told me afterwards.

The P.R.O. answers their initial questions rather formally, and the journalists are disappointed. They haven't got anything substantial yet. Suddenly, the radio correspondent exclaims: -"Let's look at number eighteen. There's something for a small story. Tell us about it!" -The P.R.O. gives some information and concludes that he will have to call the City Manager if they want to know more. The journalists are content with his story.

Further questions down the agenda: nineteen, twenty-one, twenty-three, twenty-five. -"Oh, that's about the school where the parents were demonstrating the other day. Tell us about it!" The P.R.O: gives a short briefing and suggests that they go on to the other issues and that he then call the City Manager. The journalists agree to his proposal.

Twenty-nine, thirty-two, thirty-four. -"Oh, number thirty-six. There it is. The construction of a vocational training centre in town." -"Well, you've carried that story before. The question is whether I have anything more to give you." -"The basic issue is whether there will be any centres left in the smaller communities." - "Well, you have already answered that question in an earlier broadcast," the P.R.O. responds. The radio correspondent looks surprised and digs into the manuscript, which a colleague had produced for the broadcast in question. He can't find anything to the effect mentioned by the P.R.O., and they agree to call on the staff member who has been dealing with the issue.

The P.R.O. calls the person in question, and after som negotiation he tells the two journalists: "He will come, I hope." They then turn to the four remaining issues, the last of which interests the radio correspondent very much. -"That one will top your broadcast!" Phil remarks. Their joking is interrupted by a secretary, who says that the official they are waiting for will be with them in just a minute.

He enters, and the journalists start interviewing him as he stands there. He answers with some reluctance, and the interview is concluded by clearing up a misunderstanding on the part of both journalists. -"You're confusing this issue with the other project," he responds. -"Oh, I see. It is all quite clear, then," Phil says.

The radio correspondent adds: "I thought the same as you did, Phil." The official leaves.

-"Well, then, we have the City Manager. When he comes, I think you should ask him about the last paper in the handout. It is not on the agenda, but I think it is an interesting issue," the P.R.O. says. He turns to the phone and calls the City Manager.

During his telephone conversation the two journalists start commenting on the press conference. -"This is pretty slim. Nothing, really, to build a story on." As the P.R.O. tries to protest from the telephone table, the radio correspondent tells him: "Ah, come on. You've been a journalist yourself." And, to me he explains: "We were colleagues at the Townville Station."

The City Manager enters, and at the request of the P.R.O. he starts talking about the issue concerning the school. He does it in a somewhat bureaucratic, but very clear way. -"That was a fast response to the parents' demonstration," Phil comments. -"Well, we had been making calculations long before that. And, long before you had your story in The Record. It's sheerly a question of money."[1]

-"Then, we have the issue on the last page in the handout," the P.R.O. says. Again, the City Manager starts a concise briefing on the issue. The briefing leads to some discussion with the journalists. Phil then starts to gather together the printed handouts. He has to go to another meeting. -"I haven't anything more for you," the P.R.O. concludes. We thank him and rush away.[2]

---

[1] The article referred to was published in The Record Tuesday, the week before.

[2] On the following day we learn from The Chronicle that the reporter assigned to the press conference had forgotten about it as he was also responsible for covering a meeting of a county council. As a result, The Chronicle did not carry any story on the meeting of the community board. The Record carried two stories related to the press conference: one on the building of the vocational training centre, the other on the construction of the school. The radio carried bulletins on the same topics.

1A4. The Neartown Car Dealer

One afternoon a car dealer in Neartown meets with Laura, the branch office representative of <u>The Daytown Record</u>, and places an order for an ad. Jotting down the information from the car dealer on a form, Laura learns that he wants a lay-out similar to the ad of another advertiser, also a car dealer. She therefore cuts out a sample from an earlier issue of <u>The Record</u> and attaches it to the order form. The order is mailed to the head office, where it arrives the following morning. It is received by Joan, one of the four women in the advertising booking office, who puts the ad on the booking schedule and makes space estimates.

The ad is not ready-made, nor is material available from earlier ads. Therefore, the order is forwarded to Ron, the lay-out man, who is able to start working on it at 3.00 p.m. Until then he had been occupied with other ads. He starts by roughly sketching the ad, and he scratches his head as he notices the advertiser's desire to have his ad resemble that of another car dealer: "I think that would be unfair. We can't do it like that. But, I may be able to reverse the black-white composition, remove some of the cars and make some slight changes in lay-out. Then it will be all right with the other dealer, and this advertiser should be satisfied, too."

Ron picks up a fresh piece of paper and starts a new sketch. He then takes the logotype from the advertiser and uses attachable letters to produce the basis for the reversal. He tells me: "I'm not really supposed to do this. It's the compositor's job. But I like to do it to make sure the ad turns out the way I want it. It's hard to explain my ideas to the composing room, otherwise."

We take the material he has produced and walk into the darkroom, where Ron makes the reversal using a camera. He develops the picture and looks dissatisfied: "It doesn't look good. But, I'd better go to the men's room and pour water on it." He returns five minutes later to print the reversed film. Having done this, he concludes that his suspicions as to quality were well founded: "I'll have to do it over again."[1]

---

[1] I can hardly see that the letters are fuzzy, but being a professional, Ron takes pride in doing a good job.

Ron repeats the procedure. He is not really satisfied this time either, but decides to use the second print anyway. He returns to his desk to make a more careful lay-out of the ad. He measures the photo of the car dealer, computes the degree of decrease, and draws the picture into the lay-out. Ron tells me that it is important that size computations be accurate: "Whenever there are problems, the compositors always put the blame on us."

Ron takes some ready-made clichés and glues them onto his lay-out. He then turns to his sketch and composes the ad. By 4.00 p.m. we can admire the finished sketch, which he passes, together with the order, on to the ad booking office. He walks down to the composing room and hands the pictorial material to Will, the foreman in the composing room.

Joan in the ad booking office forwards Ron's sketch to the composing room, where Will does the coding with respect to typographical style. The ad is then transferred to the rack of manuscripts for key-punching. After key-punching, proof reading and composing, the different parts are stored again. By about 9.00 p.m. Mac, one of the compositors, places the ad on page twelve, and 30 minutes later he delivers the page to engraving. By about 10.00 the plate for page twelve has reached the printing room.

In the course of this process an accident occurred which caused the ad to feature a black square instead of the photo of the car dealer. He was rather annoyed when he contacted Laura the next day, but things cooled down as he was promised a free ad on the following day. This promise was communicated to the advertising office, and an order was sent to the composing room for a new ad. This time coding, punching and proof reading were not necessary, since the original ad could be used again.

In addition to re-ordering the ad for the Neartown car dealer, the women in the ad booking office also had some other contacts with it: they measured its size and stamped an invoice number in a copy of the paper, prepared the key-punch manuscript for the invoice, and sent a copy of The Record to the car dealer. Their final contact with the ad occurred a couple of days later, when the key-punch manuscript was filed.

1A5. The Policy Discussion

-"What's this about? Betty exclaims, as she stands at the bulletin board, "here's a note on a policy discussion next Wednesday afternoon at five. Does anybody know anything about it?" Some journalists gather at the bulletin board to read the message. It is news to all of them. The subject of the meeting is "copy-editing". Exchanging a few comments on the note, they all return to their work.

Wednesday at five only a few members of the news staff are gathered round the table where the meeting is supposed to take place. But, by 5.10 Al, one of the news editors, can call the meeting to order. He briefs those present on the purpose of the meeting. The background is that The Record has been forced to cut down its number of pages due to economic problems. The news staff must now decide how to handle the situation. The issue has been discussed at an earlier meeting, and Al has also had a meeting with his local correspondents.

-"I don't want to tire you with figures," he says, "but I have some statistics on the number of pages we've turned out during the past three weeks." He goes through the weeks day by day, and it turns out that the volume has been somewhat greater than would have been the case, had the two-page cut been effective. -"But, this is due to the unexpectedly large inflow of advertisements." - "As a result," Bill, a fellow news editor adds, "Sam [the Managing Director] has been much more flexible these days with regard to format. He relates how he and Al have been running up to the Managing Director with piles of manuscripts to ask for more space.

Al continues his briefing and concludes that the decrease in format hasn't been too painful, thanks to careful copy-editing and the increased inflow of ads. -"The cut in format," Herb, the editor-in-chief (and editorial writer) comments, "has mainly hit the national and foreign news. I have had several calls from readers to that effect." The participants in the meeting simply agree with his comment, and Al goes on to suggest some rearrangements of the features in the paper. He has clipped some articles out of earlier issues which he now goes through, making comments. A basic issue is a merger of the page for soft news and the Radio & TV columns. Al also suggests the relocation of "Letters to the Editor".

Herb asks what the advertising people had to say about shuffling these features. He is told that they were asked to think it over, but that nothing has been heard from them. The position of the different pages in the production flow is also brought up: -"As produced now, the 'soft page' fits well into the flow. But, one advantage to moving it back would be that we could use colour," Bill comments.

The floor is now open for discussion, and Mary, a reporter, starts it off with some comments on the news editors running up to the Managing Director. She then makes some suggestions on the use of other typographical styles. The discussion quickly turns to the use of colour. One argument is the paper could save money using less colour. -"But, you can't go without colour on Wednesdays. With 16 pages you have to cheer the pages up with colour. But, we should think twice about using four-colour". Al's comments are met with big laughs from the journalists: -"Think twice! Noone could be more careful than we are. We use four-colour three or four times a year - at the most."

The colour discussion fades, to be followed by speculations as to readers' preferences. Do they read ads on Saturday mornings when they have time, or do they prefer ads on weekdays so they will be able to contact advertisers?

It is more or less agreed that the soft material and the TV & Radio material can be relocated. -"The problem is the advertising department," Bill rounds off the discussion. -"I think we could try the change and discuss it further with the people up there."

The discussion then turns to the proposal to move "Letters to the Editor" to the editorial page. This is apparently a much hotter issue. Herb, the editor-in-chief, disagrees: "I don't think it's a good idea. We need space for articles on cultural activities. It is not good esthetically, either. There's also a risk that readers will confuse the editorials and 'Letters'". Al and Bill present some counter-arguments, which causes Sibyl to warn them that page two is likely to become an extremely dull page. Herb welcomes this point and underlines it, pointing to the dullness of the editorial page of another Social Democratic paper which has tried this combination.

The arguments go back and forth. The discussion gradually moves to concern page three, the present location of "Letters to the Editor".-"Page three just has a lot of odds and ends. I think the 'Letters' column is the only thing on the page that makes sense. Otherwise it is just rubbish. Elk getting run over, etc.," Sibyl comments. Her colleagues agree, but Mary exclaims" "I really don't think The Record should print rubbish. If that's the case, we are not short of space." - "Oh, it's not rubbish," Bill replies, "I don't think that's the word for it. It happens to be the material left over from the previous day."

After a few comments on the need to publish more detailed stories from local correspondents, the discussion returns to the location of "Letters to the Editor". - "I consider the proposal to put the 'Letters' column on page two as a good one," Al states. Herb objects almost instantaneously, repeating the arguments regarding the problems with cultural articles and the risk that the page will become less attractive from an esthetic point of view. Al looks somewhat disappointed: "I thought we were ready to make the change, but that doesn't seem to be the case."

Nobody really responds to his comment. Instead, the discussion turns to focus on the quality of "Letters to the Editor". Several comment on the inability of letter writers to write concisely. Someone suggests more intensive editing of the letters. -"We can't do that," Herb replies. "We got big headlines in a national paper because we cut some sentences in one letter. So, that's out of the questions."

The journalists start joking about the "Letters" column. Laughter. -"Take the letters on elk hunting for instance," Sibyl puts in. "You don't dare touch those letters. You never know what they're trying to say. Is the guy for or against?" Laughter. Bill and the sports editor start a private conversation, which brings the other journalists to break off their discussion.

A new round of the general discussion opens up. Somebody asks about what the advertising people think about moving the "Letters" column. Al replies that they say it alters the whole basis for their work. He then adds: "Do you think we should vote Herb down?" -"I'm not the only one who's against the idea," Herb retorts. "Well, I thought our arguments ought to convince him," Bill adds. "We'll just have to go home and sharpen them up."

Al concludes the meeting by asking the rhetorical question: "What have we decided?". The basic decisions seem to be some changes in the soft page and the typographical style. The meeting breaks up as Bill remarks: "I still think it would be a good idea to move 'Letters to the Editor' to the editorial page."

I walk over to the copy desk, where Chris is doing copy-editing. He sat in at the meeting for a while, but left quite early. Since the meeting has taken place in the news-room, he has been able to get the main arguments of the discussion anyhow. -"I couldn't stand sitting there. I've heard the arguments over and over again. Nothing happens. They always discuss the wrong things," he says. In response to my asking what should be discussed, he says the most important thing is how the newspaper should be marketed. What should be done in order to increase circulation?

I sit down at my corner of the copy desk. After a while Herb comes up to me, and talk about a story in an evening paper. I make some remarks related to the points made in the policy discussion. We agree that changes in newspapers have to be taken step by step. We then turn to the question of marketing. Herb tells about an advertising campaign of a couple of years ago, when The Record used posters with the picture of the general manager of a local industrial company. -"In the ad he said that although he disagreed with the opinion of the paper, he read it, and it kept him very well informed. In response to the ad, three subscribers cancelled their subscriptions. They couldn't stand having the same paper as their general manager. But, I have subsequently heard that many officers in the company started subscribing to the paper because their general manager did."

-"Well, he could easily make that statement in the spirit of repressive tolerance," Chris intrudes. "I didn't like that ad at all. I think it was all wrong. We should have had a poster with a company manager saying our paper was awful. Then readers would trust us. You have to define your profile." Herb and Chris start a long and intensive discussion, Herb arguing in favour of the poster. Chris is definitely against. After a while Herb terminates the discussion and walks to his room.

CHAPTER TWO. THE RESEARCH METHODS.

2.1 Introduction

The participant observation study, from which the five case study descriptions in the previous chapter derive, constitutes but one step in a longer process of research into the organizational aspects of newspaper production, which commenced with a study of structural changes in the Swedish newspaper industry (cf. Engwall, 1975).

Intitially, the project consisted largely of "desk research", except for some interviews with top management in four large American newspapers. This first phase of the study produced a frame of reference for the study of newspapers, which was then confronted with empirical data obtained through semi-structured interviews with different types of newspaper employees in Swedish newspapers. These interviews suggested revisions of some features of the frame of reference.

A third phase of the project involved an analysis of how a sample of Swedish newspapers allocated financial resources, employees and space. Although this analysis yielded a great deal of information, it also pointed to the need for penetrating formal figures, to relate the research to individual newspapers. Hence, the participant observation study mentioned above was undertaken. It was preceded by a series of interviews in the United Kingdom and France.

To summarize, the results presented here are based on a number of sources, and the information obtained from these sources, has been analyzed using a variety of methods. In order to provide further insights into the approaches chosen and to put the data into perspective, the following sections will provide information on the sources and methods used in this study.

2.2 Written Material on Newspapers

Many different kinds of material have yielded relevant information throughout the project. One basic group of references comprises reports of other research projects on newspapers. Since newspaper activities are related to issues discussed in a variety of traditional disciplines, the choice of literature has been interdisciplinary, with a certain bias toward sociology, political science and business administration. Another important class of literature is the memoirs and accounts written by figures in the newspaper world (cf. Nycop, 1970 & 1971; Talese, 1970; Tingsten, 1971 a & b; Woodward & Bernstein, 1974, i. a.).

A third approach leading into newspaper country has been the professional journals Grafia, Journalisten and Pressens Tidning, which have made it possible to follow the various arguments in relation to different issues as well as to develop a "feel" for the language used in newspaper country.[1] Novels set in newspapers also offered bits of an "inside" perspective.[2]

2.3 Interviews

Interviews with employees in newspapers yielded a great deal of information. As noted above, the first such interviews were undertaken in December 1973, in four large American newspapers: The Boston

---

[1] The three journals are published by the Swedish National Graphical Association, the Swedish Federation of Journalists and the Swedish Newspaper Publishers' Association, respectively.

Attendance at discussions held in one of the professional organizations (The National Press Club) constituted another important source of information.

[2] Cf. e. g. Gustafson (1968), Sandgren (1968) and Böll (1974).

<u>Globe</u>, <u>The New York Post</u>, <u>The New York Times</u> and <u>The Washington Post</u>.[1] They constituted pilot interviews with top management.

During the Fall of 1975 interviews were then conducted in a number of Swedish newspapers with different types of newspaper employees. This round of interviews included metropolitan as well as community papers, morning as well as evening papers, and newspapers in different competitive situations.

Finally, some interviews were undertaken in late 1975 and early 1976 with management in the French newspaper <u>Le Monde</u> and the British newspapers <u>The Times</u> and <u>The Daily Mirror</u>. My inquiries at <u>The Times</u> also included a seminar discussion with editors. Some interviewing was also undertaken with officers of the National Graphical Association.

Semi-structured interviews were used in all cases. The interviewees were engaged in conversation and were given quite some opportunity to stress what they considered important. Some structuring was provided through the frame of reference mentioned earlier (Section 2.1). So that top management people were confronted with questions such as:

- What are the main events in the newspaper during a normal twenty-four hour period?
- Do you have any organization chart?
- What positions do you have in the organization?
- Do you have job descriptions?
- What's your estimation of the degree of cooperation between different groups of employees?

---

[1] All four newspapers have a long tradition of publication and are basically politically independent (cf. Editor & Publisher, 1973). They each have a weekday circulation of around half a million copies.

(For further information on the four papers, cf. Chapter Five, Sections 5A1-5A4).

In all interviews the structuring implied that the following questions were raised:

- Which is your present position and what earlier jobs have you held?
- What is the schedule of your working day?
- Which are the important problems in your job?
- How are those problems solved?
- What professional contacts do you have inside and outside the newspaper?
- How is decision-making undertaken in the newspaper?
- What is your opinion of reader reactions?
- What do you feel is the task of a newspaper?
- What are the characteristics of a successful newspaper?

The interviews were often concluded by asking the interviewee for suggestions as to prospective interviewees.[1]

A record of each completed interview was made up as soon as possible. This record was typed out, a copy being sent back to the interviewee for corrections and comments. The revisions made by the interviewees were seldom very extensive, but they were nevertheless often quite significant.[2]

The employment of the feedback technique was not a result of any extensive evaluation of alternative approaches. Rather it proved to be a feasible means as the research project proceeded. In retrospect a number of advantages can be identified, however.

First, of course, the feedback technique permits the removal of misinterpretations and errors. Second, it permits relatively high accuracy of information without requiring more than one interviewer or a tape recorder. Third, it produces an edited version of the interview. Fourth, and finally, it is a good "opener", establishing a link by which the researcher may feed back his research results to his interviewees.

---

[1] For a description of this "snow-ball" sampling technique, cf. Mitroff (1974).

[2] Once in a while interviewees made remarks like: "I might have said that, but it is a little too strong." This happened not only among administrators but also among journalists (even those with a reputation of "tough" reporting).

With respect to the first point, it might be argued that the records may be tapped of interesting information, since the interviewees are likely to be anxious to avoid passing on disadvantageous information. This, of course, is a risk, but since the use of the data to a great extent depends on the confidence of the interviewee in the interviewer, such "laundering" of the material is not only advisable but necessary. Moreover, it is not unusual that persons intend to say one thing but fail to express themselves accurately. Therefore, it may be to advantage that the material be "laundered" before use.

As for the second point, limiting the interview staff afforded great convenience. In most cases I thus performed the interviews alone, the exception being the interviews in the United States and the United Kingdom, where I was accompanied by a colleague.

Minimizing the number of interviewers has one advantage in that difficult appointment scheduling is simplified. Moreover, it seems as though a more intimate relationship with the interviewee can be established.[1] Similar arguments speak against the use of tape recorder, which is often considered an alternative to the use of an interview team. The presence of a tape recorder is very likely to make an interviewee uncomfortable and less inclined to speak freely.[2] This might often have been the case in the course of this project, since many of the interviewees got on to sensitive issues.[3]

A third advantage with the interview method employed is that it enforces relatively careful editing of the interview, since the summary is to be read by people outside the research team. In this way related remarks in different parts of the conversation can be brought together, which in turn facilitates the use of the interview data in subsequent analyses.

---

[1] Of course, this advantage has to be assessed against the inability to discuss the interview with co-interviewers afterwards.

[2] Cf. Argyris (1970), whose own experience implies that "the recorder has been most helpful with upper-level executives, especially those who are quite verbal. In most other cases, the recorder seemed to make the respondent uncomfortable". (Op.cit., p. 295; emphasis mine)

[3] A usual cue in this context was: "How are you going to use this?" And, when I guaranteed anonymity, the person went on with his story. I doubt this would have been the case had I used a tape recorder.

The opportunity to establish a relationship with interviewees was mentioned as a fourth advantage. Feeding back the records from their own interview, it is then more natural to show how the material was used by the researcher. Such feedback seems a vital means by which to confront research results with reality. Referring to Berger & Luckman (1966), it is a question of matching the researcher's construct of reality with those of the interviewees. Such matching seems extremely important in working with qualitative data. Therefore, it must be very appropriate that the research results be continuously examined for credibility. Such examination should not only be limited to interviewees, however. The building up of rapport with interviewees also has the disadvantage that continuous joint discussions may well produce a cross fertilization so that not only is the interviewer influenced by the comments of the interviewee, but the interviewee may adopt the views of the interviewer. Therefore, the research results should continuously be fed back not only to interviewees but also to different "fresh" persons. This can be achieved either by sending research reports for comment or via feedback sessions, in which research results and certain interview data are presented. In most cases the latter approach is probably to be recommended, since academic research reports tend to be tough reading for people outside research institutions.

2.4 Allocation Data Analysis

The study of allocation outcomes was based on data from fourteen Swedish newspapers. These newspapers were subjectively selected from a sample used in one of the studies carried out by the 1972 Parliamentary Commission on the Press (SOU 1974:102).[1] They were selected, first by picking circulation areas having competing newspapers. Among these, a further selection was made to obtain a wide geographical distribution over the country. This selection procedure resulted in

---

[1] For a reproduction of the questionnaire, cf. SOU 1974:102, pp. 167-171. The questions referred to revenues, costs, prices, number of employees, etc.
For further information on the original sample, cf. SOU 1974:102, pp. 29-32.

a sample of seven circulation areas (of a total of 70), which implied a sample of 14 of the 82 Swedish newspapers published more than five days a week.

The questionnaire asked for information for the period 1968 to 1972, i.e. a period covering years before and after the introduction of production subsidies. Consequently, a short time series is available for most variables, the exception being employees.

It should be stressed that the selection procedure has subjective elements. But, it can be mentioned, that the indicator, average weekly circulation, suggests that the sample used is not too far off from the total population. Using data from Engwall (1974 a), we thus find that the total population had an average weekly circulation of about 266 thousand copies in 1970. The corresponding figure for the "allocation" sample is 247 thousand copies.

The questionnaire data for the fourteen newspapers were confidential. But, through the courtesy of Karl Erik Gustafsson, who conducted the study, and the managing directors of the newspapers, access to the questionnaire material was obtained.[1] The presidents were assured however that "as was the case with [the original] study, the results will be published in such a way that identification will not be possible."[2]

The analysis of the described data employed such methods as Spearman's rank correlation coefficient and regression analysis.

---

[1] The reliability of the data is another vital issue in the present case, since the data have been collected by someone other than the analyst, thereby leading to what March & Simon (1958, p. 165) term "uncertainty absorption". The reliability of the data has therefore been discussed with Karl Erik Gustafsson, who judged the data to have good reliability, as in addition to the collection of questionnaire data he also undertook face-to-face interviews with the newspaper executives.

[2] For this reason some of the diagrams in Chapter 8 have no scales on the axes.

2.5 Participant Observation[1]

The participant observation portion of the project was performed in a provincial Swedish newspaper subjectively selected on the basis of its accessability. The contact was obtained through the Managing Director of what shall be known as The Daytown Record, but the study was also discussed and approved by the labour unions of The Record. My letter of introduction was discussed in the works council, and, although some were critical of the study I was accepted.

The Record is published in a relatively large Swedish town, the seat of regional authorities. The political orientation of The Record is Social Democratic, whereas its rival, The Daytown Chronicle, is bourgeois. Both papers are published six days a week, but in terms of circulation The Record is far outnumbered by The Chronicle, which is also the elder of the two papers.[2] Earlier considered to have "coloured" or slanted reporting, The Record nowadays maintains a clear distinction between reporting and editorials. Like The Chronicle, it stresses sports and uses pictures to a high extent. Both these features seem to be a result of efforts to compete with its larger rival.

Both The Record and The Chronicle use photo composition and offset printing, which enables them to print black/white, plus three colours (FLT, 1976). The change of technique was made a couple of years ago quite smoothly, despite some implementation problems.

The study at The Record lasted ten days and included visits to the composing room, the press room, the news-room and various commercial departments. In addition I joined reporters in the field and accompanied the errand man on one of his downtown tours.[3] Finally, a sight-

---

[1] Important predecessors using participant observation in newspapers are Matejko (1967), Rühl (1969), Sigal (1973) and Tuchman (1973).

[2] The Record was founded in the beginning of the present century.

[3] The errand man, it appeared is a very important man at the newspaper. He transports all sorts of material to and from the newspaper and for the night shift in the news-room he is the source of food. As the night editor put it when we had given our orders for hot dogs and french fries: "He is the only guy here you miss when he's on vacation. He is very important."

seeing tour was made to the rival <u>Chronicle</u>.

During my sojourn at <u>The Record</u> it was apparent that the information about my study left a great deal to be desired, as it happened now and again that people asked me what I was doing there.[1] Once I had assured them I was neither a time-motion engineer nor hired by the Company, people were happy to talk. As a matter of fact my experience was much that of Mitroff whose "respondents were more than willing to talk; it was as if they not only wanted to talk but that they needed to talk." (1974, p.41 f.)

Although I circulated in the newspaper building, my usual location was at the copy-desk in the news-room, where I sat working on my research notes. This location also made it possible for me to survey the flow of events in the news-room and the adjacent composing room.

My aim was to follow the processes going on in <u>The Record</u>. Two basic case studies were made: one concerning the flow of a news story through the building (cf. Section 1A2), the other concerning the flow of an advertisement (cf. Section 1A4). In addition I made various case studies in relation to some occurences.

I took continuous notes, on the basis of which I then produced records of the course of events. These records were then handed over to the persons involved for comments and corrections.[2]

---

[1] This was particularly the case outside the news-room. In the news-room, on the other hand, I was hardly noticed as a newcomer. A journalist explained: "There are always a lot of people walking in and out of the news-room. There are irregular working hours, and several people working on a free-lance basis. So, it's hard to keep track of all the new faces. On the other hand, you don't miss a person when he quits, either."

[2] In terms of Pearsall's (1970, pp. 341-343) classification my study may be characterized as "observer-as-participant".

2.6 The Research Strategy

Based on many different sources and kinds of data, the multi-method approach of the present research has been used in order to obtain a better understanding of newspapers. In accord with the terminology of Habermas (1968) the interest of knowledge of this study should, therefore, probably be classified as hermeneutical, i. e. a "development of knowledge through a <u>tacking</u> procedure or dialectics." (Radnitzsky, 1970, Part II, p. 23). This employment of the "hermeneutical circle" means that the research process has been a continuous process of dialectics -- a dialectics between different types of data as well as between a derived theory, and empirical (quantitative as well as non-quantitative) data.

An important feature of the social science studies, which facilitates the application of the described research approach is the possibility of communicating with the people who are the objects of the research. In this way the latter may comment on the results obtained, so that early interpretations can be challenged and refined. In the present project the possibilities for communication have been exploited through the feedback of interview results (cf. Section 2.3) and progress reports. Another technique of challenging old interpretations has been to reanalyze old material in light of new insights.[1]

The research approach described here implies that the researcher has acquired a better understanding of newspapers. But the reader may justifiably ask, to what avail? What can the further results of the present study be? What are the possibilities for generalization? Such questions appear relevant in light of Karl Weick's

---

[1] Cf. here the experience of "Woodstein", the two Washington Post reporters uncovering the Watergate story. One of their informants, Z, adviced one of them to re-read carefully their own stories: "There is more truth in there than you must have realized -- many clues." (Woodward & Bernstein, 1974, p. 212).

critic of "anecdotal evidence as the empirical base" (Weick, 1969, p. 18), which read in the introduction:

> "Any discipline will rise or fall depending on the reliability and validity of the observations on which its theories are based. Few fields have made so much of so little as has organization theory. The large number of theories, concepts and prescriptions in this field far outdistances the empirical findings on which they have supposed to be grounded. For instance, considerable use has been made of anecdotal case studies. Even though case studies have a richness of detail, they have at least four drawbacks: they are (1) situation-specific, (2) ahistorical, (3) tacitly prescriptive, and (4) one-sided. These four items are drawbacks because of their effect on theory construction." (loc. cit.)

These critical remarks on anecdotal evidence have a great deal of relevance. No doubt there is a great risk of falling into the same trap as the one the former Vice President of the United States, Spiro T. Agnew, fell into when he responded to an invitation to visit a ghetto by the words: "Once you have seen one, you have seen them all!" As the reader may recall his remark generated a number of counter-remarks. It was quite evident that a problem of generalization existed. The same problem also occurs often in organizational research where research is done on one specific organization and wide conclusions are then drawn regarding the characteristics of other organizations in the same industry, of organizations in other countries and of organizations in a very general sense.

The hard-data oriented Aston-studies (cf. e. g. Hickson et al., 1969) by providing an analysis of formal data for a large number of organizations were one response to this problem. In addition to the empirical results obtained from these studies, however, they also demonstrated that research on organizations require in-depth-studies as well.

The present work is an attempt to provide such an in-depth-study of the organizational aspects of one particular industry. In so doing it has tried to avoid the criticism voiced by Weick by using observations from a relatively large number of newspapers as well as statements from a wide range of newspaper employees. In addition the present research has not been pursued in a vacuum: as has been demonstrated above it takes into account earlier research works.

Concerning the question of generalization it has to be admitted that, for practical reasons, data from the Swedish scene dominates the research. There are, however, several reasons why data from Sweden may be of interest also outside this country.

1. Sweden has one of the largest newspaper consumptions per thousand inhabitants in the world (411 morning papers and 154 evening papers per thousand inhabitants, i. e. 565 copies per thousand. Cf. SOU 1975:79, p. 53 f.)

2. Sweden has for several years had a system of government subsidies to the press.

3. According to the terminology of Bell (1966), Sweden is, in terms of standard of living, moving toward a "post-industrial state", something which may be expected to happen several nations in the near future.

4. Sweden has in recent years had quite an intensive debate on industrial democracy, something which is particularly touchy in mass media companies.

PART II: NEWSPAPER COUNTRY

"Some people argue that one characteristic of an organization is that its members strive toward a joint goal. If so, this is not an organization!"

(A newspaper executive)

CHAPTER THREE.   NEWSPAPER TECHNOLOGY

3.1   Introduction

The core of the organization model presented in the previous chapter is technology, i.e. the processes (or set of tasks) by which input is acted on in order to produce output. The importance of these processes for organizational design has been stressed by many authors, among whom Perrow has pointed to technology as "the defining characteristic of organizations" (1967, p. 194 f.). In other words: in the dyad technology -- structure, Perrow looks upon technology as the independent variable and structure the dependent one.[1]

The present chapter aims at penetrating different parts of the newspaper production process in order to explore its eventual effects on organizational structure. First, we shall recall some of the accounts from the case studies presented in Chapter One in order to identify four parts of the work flow. These are then treated in four sections, using a paradigm suggested by Hickson et al. (1969).

3.2   The Case Studies Reconsidered

Recalling the accounts of the processes going on at The Record presented in Chapter One, we may first of all note that a significant feature of the production process in a daily newspaper is the very short production cycle, for most activities a twenty-four hour period. During this period news items as well as advertisement orders are acted on in different ways. The basis of the news story is an event, a process or a situation. Information about the event, process or situation is communicated to the newspaper organization, where a decision is taken to act, or not to act, upon it. If the item is deemed worthy, one or more journalists are assigned to the story and start gathering information.

---

[1] Perrow (1967) suggests a framework for the comparative analysis of organizations. By way of introduction he mentions four characteristics of this perspective: (1) technology is the defining characteristic of organizations, (2) technology is the independent variable, (3) organizations are conceptualized as a whole, and (4) technology offers a better basis for comparing organizations than other factors (p. 194 f.).

This can take some time and effort or be a rather short process (cf. Sections 1A2 and 1A3, respectively). The final step for the journalist is to write the story, which may be fairly intensive work. Then, the story is handed over to copy editors, who edit it, decide on its location in the paper and add headlines. This is the last stage of "creative" production. From this point on the contents of the story remain unchanged.[1] It is simply transferred to other media in order to facilitate reproduction onto newsprint. Finally, the newspaper is distributed to readers.

The processing of advertisements is similar to that of news, as was illustrated in Section 1A4 ("The Neartown Car Dealer"). The exception is that for the majority of advertisements no decision is taken inside the newspaper concerning its publication. In addition, not infrequently the advertisements themselves are produced outside the newspaper: not all advertisements are designed inside the company like that of the Neartown car dealer. The "creative" part of the production of ads is thus often more limited than is the case with news. The same is true of the reproductive phase of production when no composition is required.

Figure 3:1 summarizes the production flow in two of the case studies. The technique indicated here is photo composition with offset printing, whereas Figure 3:2 describes traditional technology. There are, of course, variations on both themes.

---

[1] The exceptions being cases when stories have to be cut in order to fit into a page, but that is just shortening. Formulations are very seldom changed.

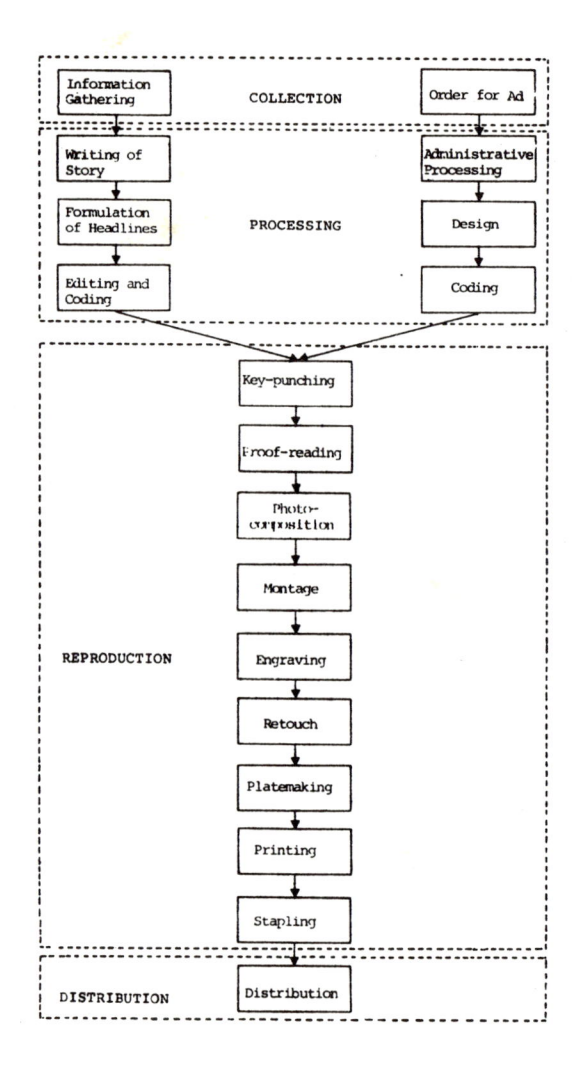

Figure 3:1. A Flow Chart of the Events in "The Pankab Bankruptcy" and "The Neartown Car Dealer".

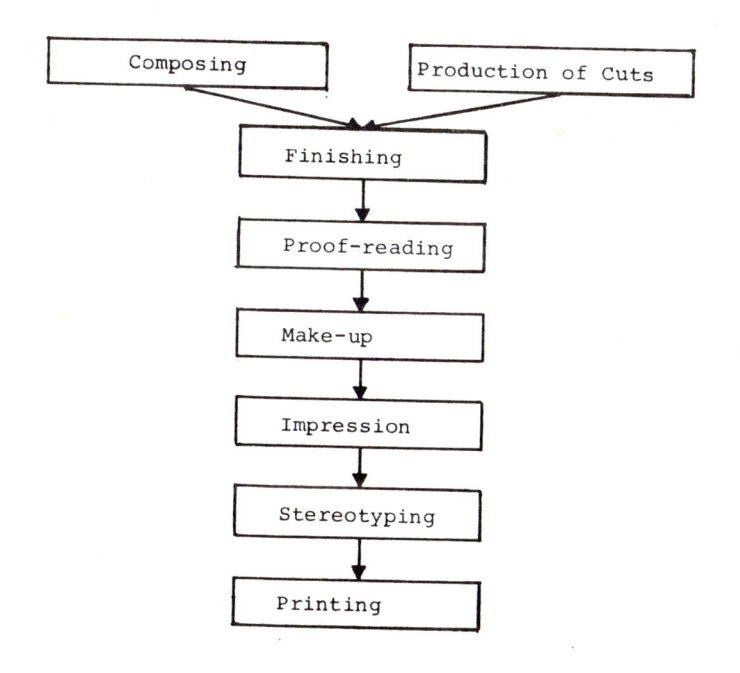

```
┌─────────────┐         ┌──────────────────┐
│  Composing  │         │ Production of Cuts│
└──────┬──────┘         └─────────┬────────┘
       │                          │
       └────────────┬─────────────┘
                    ▼
            ┌───────────────┐
            │   Finishing   │
            └───────┬───────┘
                    ▼
            ┌───────────────┐
            │ Proof-reading │
            └───────┬───────┘
                    ▼
            ┌───────────────┐
            │   Make-up     │
            └───────┬───────┘
                    ▼
            ┌───────────────┐
            │  Impression   │
            └───────┬───────┘
                    ▼
            ┌───────────────┐
            │ Stereotyping  │
            └───────┬───────┘
                    ▼
            ┌───────────────┐
            │   Printing    │
            └───────────────┘
```

Figure 3:2. **The Reproduction Phase in Traditional Newspaper Production.**

As Figure 3:1 shows, we may identify four different phases of production. These concern the <u>collection</u>, <u>processing</u>, <u>reproduction</u> and <u>distribution</u> of information.[1] This four-phase model enables the construction of Figure 3:3, which summarizes the production flow, indicating different types of information in the collection and processing phases. The latter two phases

---

[1] Parallel to these four phases, in newspapers, like in all other business firms, administrative processes with longer cycles than one day are also going on.

comprise the handling of: (1) news items for news stories, (2) news items for editorials and (3) advertisements. These three types of information are brought together in the reproduction phase in a joint product, which is distributed to readers.

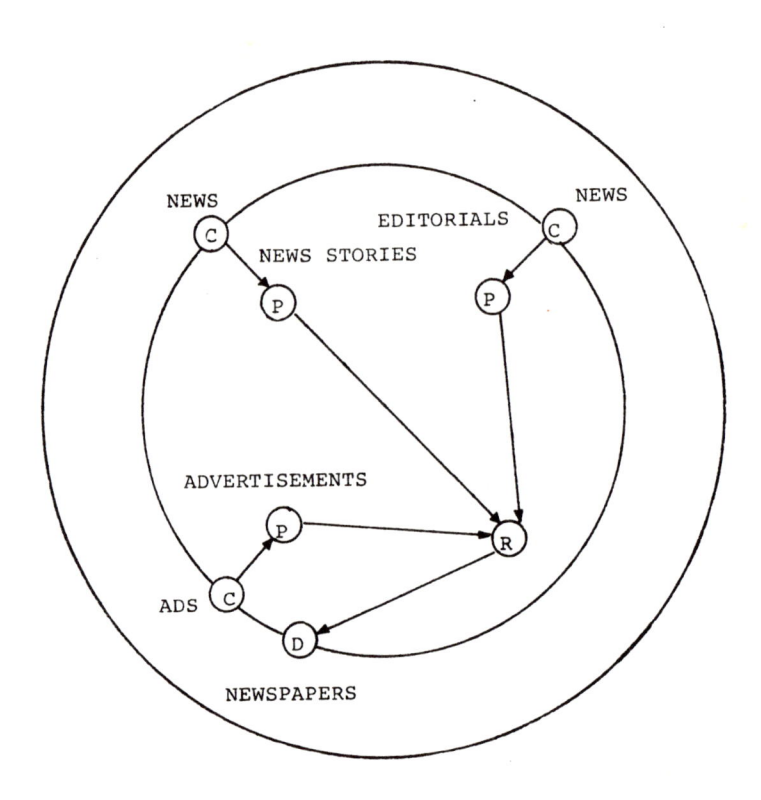

Figure 3:3. The Technology of Newspapers.
Explanations: C = Collection Phase
P = Processing Phase
R = Reproduction Phase
D = Distribution Phase

3.3 A Paradigm for Analysis

The analysis of technology below makes use of a paradigm suggested by Hickson et al. (1969), who distinguish between three facets of technology, viz.

Operations Technology: "the equipping and sequencing activities in the work flow"

Materials Technology: "the materials used in the workflow"

Knowledge Technology: "the knowledge used in the workflow"

In all three cases the authors refer to workflow as "the producing and distributing of output" (op.cit., p. 380).

Of these three concepts of technology, the first, operations technology, would seem to be most closely related to the variations in technologies ("long-linked", "mediating" and "intensive") mentioned by Thompson (1967), whereas the two other concepts, materials technology and knowledge technology, are more closely related to work by Perrow (1967).

The only technology concept Hickson et al. (1969) use in their empirical studies is operations technology, which they define in terms of three subconcepts, viz.

- "the equipment used in terms of automation of equipment"
- "the sequence of operations in terms of work flow rigidity"
- "the specificity of evaluation of operations" (op.cit., p. 380 f.).[1]

---

[1] In later studies the Aston-group extended the classification to include five scales of technology: workflow rigidity, automaticity mode, automaticity range, interdependence of work flow segments and specificity of criteria of quality evaluation (cf. e.g. Pugh et al., 1969). For our purposes, however, the three sub-concepts will do.

Perrow (1967) defines <u>materials technology</u> in terms of two characteristics of raw materials: (1) the understandability of its nature and (2) the variability of the material. This dichotomy enables Perrow to construct a four-by-four matrix housing the pairs: (1) uniform -- non-uniform (variability) and (2) not well understood -- well understood (understandability).

Perrow uses a similar approach with respect to <u>knowledge technology</u>, which is defined by (1) "the number of exceptional cases encountered in the work" (<u>op.cit</u>., p.195) and (2) "the nature of the search process that is undertaken by the individual when exceptions occur" (<u>Ibid</u>., p.196). The four-by-four matrix is here built on the dichotomies: (1) few exceptions -- many exceptions and (2) unanalyzable problems -- analyzable problems.

In applying the described paradigm in the present chapter we shall use neither the scales used by Hickson et al. (1969), nor the dichotomies of Perrow. Instead, a compromise will be applied: a rough scale (low, medium and high) will be used for all sub-concepts in the three types of technology. This should yield sufficient distinctions for our present purposes.[1] These scales will be applied to the four phases. Graphically expressed, we are going to investigate the matrix shown in Table 3:1.

---

[1] Of course, the classifications are open to criticism, since they are based on subjective judgements. The main purpose of the analysis, however, is to illustrate the mixed character of newspaper technology.

Technology Aspects		Phase in the Production Process			
		Collection	Processing	Reproduction	Distribution
Operations Technology	Automation				
	Workflow Rigidity				
	Specificity of Evaluation				
Materials Technology	Understandability				
	Variability				
Knowledge Technology	Number of Exceptional Cases				
	Analyzability				

Table 3:1. <u>A Summary of the Aspects to Be Investigated in the Present Chapter</u>.

3.4 The Collection Phase

The two types of information handled in the work flow of a newspaper, then, are news and advertisements. The information collection acitivites with respect to these two types of material constitute a linkage between the newspaper and the environment. In the case of news the number of competing news items is screened, whereas most ads ordered are published (the exception being ads which do not meet legal or moral standards). In both cases material is both offered to the paper and sought out by newspaper employees.

News is obtained from several principal sources in the environment. The wire services are the basic sources of national and international news, particularly for provincial papers. As regards local news, news tips from private citizens as well as routine checking of local government dockets and agendae generate a corresponding flow.[1] Press releases from organizations and private persons seeking coverage constitute another abundant source.[2] News tips are filed and consulted in "The Book". But, news gathering is not necessarily a question of selection among incoming tips or telegrams. Particularly in recent years many journalists have argued for a more active journalism, i.e. in which newspaper reporters "dig" for stories and engage in more in-depth reporting.[3] This would make it possible to plan the contents of the paper better than is the case following the usual, more or less haphazard "selection strategy". Newspapers would also be less dependent on information-makers and gatekeepers in other news organizations such as the wire service news agencies.

In other words, information gathering activities generally contain quite a bit of screening, a circumstance which has led several authors to point to the "gatekeeping" activities in newspapers.[4]

---

[1] The possibilities to check dockets and official diaries of local government are great in Sweden, where all incoming and outgoing letters of public servants are open to public scrutiny. Some few exceptions to this rule do exist.

[2] In interviewing Phil I mentioned the word "flow". He immediately commented on this by: "You talk about flow. There's a flood of written material into my room. Today, for instance, my mail contained a foot-and-a half stack of stuff about the Trade Union Congress."

[3] For further discussion of this topic, cf. Chapter Nine.

[4] The gatekeeper model was first formulated by Lewin (1947). Several studies have been performed to investigate the model, the most famous being White (1950). Efforts to simulate the screening process have been made by Carendi et al. (1970) and Berg & Kinell (1971).

The basic and most important of these gatekeepers is the
news editor, the "boss" of the news-room, who makes the initial
selection among potential stories. As was shown in Chapter One,
this selection is at The Record first manifested at the morning
news conference, where reporters are given their assignments for
the day. Later in the day the news editor's selection is summarized
in a memo to the night editor and the copy editors.

The means to acquire news information include different communication devices such as telephones, teleprinters, etc., as well
as personal visits to presumptive news sources (cf. e.g. Chapter
One, Section 1A3: "In the Field").

Telephone and personal visits are also the means used to gather
advertisements for a newspaper. Although, some ads are simply
ordered, others require considerable effort on the part of advertising consultants. Active efforts to sell space in the paper
are particularly frequent when special pages, supplements or
special issues are published. On such occasions advertising
consultants contact presumptive advertisers and solicit advertisements. Another primary strategy is long-term contracts with
advertisers guaranteeing their purchase of a certain volume of
advertising space.

Applying the paradigm suggested in Section 3.3 to the collection
phase of the newspaper production, we may now draw some conclusions concerning the technology of this phase of production.

As far as operations technology is concerned, we may note that
the degree of _automation_ of news and advertisement collection is
fairly low. The automatic components in news-gathering are the
wire services, whereas no such components are used in the
collection of advertisements.[1] With respect to _work flow rigidity_
and _specificity of evaluation_, too, news-gathering scores low:
there is often no specific time sequence and the size and hetero-
geneity of the audience make it hard to determine whether infor-

---

[1] Although the wire services constitute highly automatized equipment, the
classification "low" nevertheless seems appropriate, since there are extremely
selective elements in the collection phase. In addition, some papers only use
the wire services to a limited extent.

mation collection has been performed well or not. Advertisements, on the other hand, exhibit somewhat higher work flow rigidity and specificity. More clearly defined procedures are used in the ordering of advertisements (the filling out of forms, negotiations on design and format, payment, etc.), and it therefore seems appropriate to classify this activity as "medium" with respect to work flow rigidity. As for specificity of evaluation, the score is even higher; it is quite clear whether or not solicitation has been successful: Either the contact has produced an ad (success) or it has not (failure).

In terms of understandability of the material processed, news material appears to score medium, since news is occasionally quite ambiguous and difficult to interpret. Advertising information, on the other hand, is generally quite straightforward, and the appropriate score therefore seems to be "high".

There are also differences between news and advertisements as regards variability, news exhibiting somewhat higher variability than advertisements. In terms of the scales, news appears to qualify for the rating "high" and advertisements "medium".

Turning to the number of exceptional cases, the earthquake coverage described in Chapter One, "Suddenly the Ground Started to Shake ...." (Section 1A1), may give the impression that exceptions are frequent in news-gathering. But, fortunately, events like the earthquake are not everyday situations. Instead, "editorial production seems to [be] an example of 'constrained variability': while the words on paper and their substance may vary considerably from day to day, the process by which information is acquired [is] mainly rather routine [...] picking up press releases, recording and summarizing press briefings or speeches, verifying a few bits of information by telephone".[1] The classification "medium" therefore seems more appropriate than "high" on the scale indicating number of exceptional cases. The corresponding score for advertisements is "low",

---

[1] Leon V. Sigal in a private communication to the author.

Finally, newspaper personnel would seem to be quite able to analyze the problems encountered in news-gathering as well as the selling of ad space. Thus, in both cases analyzability would seem to be "high".

The above characterization of the collection phase can now be summarized in the technology profiles shown in Figure 3:4, which point out the differences between the collection of news and advertisements.

```
                                  Low       Medium      High
Automation
Workflow Rigidity
Specificity of Evaluation
Understandability
Variability
Number of Exceptional Cases
Analyzability
```

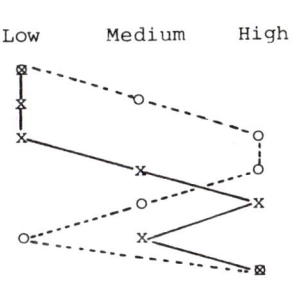

Figure 3:4.   Technology Profiles of the Collection Phase.[a]

Note:
[a] x———x = News
o-----o = Advertisements

3.5 The Processing Phase

The distinction between the collection phase and the processing phase is not always quite clear. Now and then these two phases are intertwined, information collection being followed by processing, which is followed by still further information collection. This is particularly true of the processing of news information. It may happen that the reporter starts writing, finds he needs further information and therefore goes through several cycles of information collection and processing. In other instances the development of the story itself may motivate turning from information processing to renewed information collection.

In addition to writing up the story, the processing phase may also include the development and selection of relevant pictures.

The pictures and the story are then handed over to copy-
editors, who make space estimates and put the story on to a
dummy of a page. In addition they edit and code the story.[1]

Advertisements are handled by the advertising order office, where
the requested location of the ad is booked, space estimates are
made, and the ad is drawn into page dummies.[2] In addition, the
ad may be designed in the lay-out office, if it has not been
prepared outside the newspaper.

In terms of the paradigm of Section 3.3 the processing of news
is characterized by low degree of <u>automation</u> of equipment. The
equipment used involves typewriters, paper, pen and different
slide rules for size computations, all handled manually. The
processing of advertisements, on the other hand, is somewhat more
automatized. In this work different photographic equipment can
be used (cf. Section 1A4: "The Neartown Car Dealer"), and, furthermore, computers nowadays are sometimes used for ad space estimates
as well as accounting. The appropriate scores therefore seem to be
"medium" for advertisements and "low" for news.

The <u>work flow rigidity</u> of the news processing is quite high: the
writing of the story has to precede the editing of the story.
This is in contrast to the processing of advertisements, which
does not require such distinct sequencing: some of the administrative work may very well be done parallel with the design work.

The opposite is true for the <u>specificity of evaluation</u>. As was
the case in news-gathering, the criteria for evaluating the processing of news are rather unclear. The only clear criteria are
certain rules of behaviour: if these are exceeded, reactions are
communicated, otherwise not.[3] With respect to advertisements, on
the other hand, there is only one judge, the advertiser. If he

---

[1] The description refers to The Record. There are, of course, variations
in procedure.
Coding refers to specification of type-set.

[2] Most advertisers specify the ad's location in the paper. The last page and
page 3 are very popular, as are all outer columns on right hand pages.

[3] For a further discussion of this topic, cf. Chapter Nine.

considers the advertisement good, it is good, and vice versa.
The specificity of evaluation for news and advertisements
therefore seems to be "low" and "high", respectively.

The <u>understandability</u> of the material seems to be medium for news
items and high for advertisements. The lower rating for news has
to do with the uncertainty of incoming news information.

The <u>variability</u> of news items is high, and the same reporter may
thus be working on many different stories. An excellent example
in this context is Nick's situation in Section 1A1, when he
had to switch from the Italian earthquake to a local Red Cross
meeting. Some variability can also be observed with respect to
advertisements as a result of differences in the desires of
different advertisers. But, on the whole, variability in the
material is low. The same can also be said with respect to the
<u>number of exceptional cases</u> in advertising, whereas they are more
frequent in news processing, i.e., in terms of the scales, on a
"medium" level.

The <u>analyzability</u> of arising problems seems the same for the two
types of material. With respect to news and advertisements alike
there seems to be ample opportunity to analyze arising problems.

Summarizing the technology of news and advertising processing, we
obtain the profiles shown in Figure 3:5.

	Low	Medium	High
Automation	x	o	
Workflow Rigidity	o		x
Specificity of Evaluation	x		o
Understandability		x	o
Variability	o		x
Number of Exceptional Cases	o	x	
Analyzability			x,o

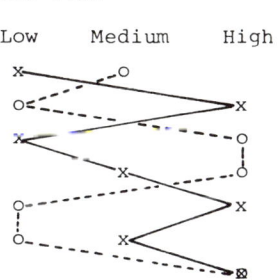

Figure 3:5. <u>Technology Profiles of the Processing Phase.</u>[a]

Note:
[a] x———x = News
o——––o = Advertisements

3.6 The Reproduction Phase

The reproduction phase contains two sub-phases: composing and printing. In neither of these two sub-phases do news and advertisements differ very much. One possible difference is variation in the work requirement, depending on the availability of ready-made material.

Composing is the process by which manuscripts of stories and advertisements are transferred to printable form. As was shown in Figures 3:1 and 3:2, this process involves a consecutive series of activities. Irrespective of the composing technique applied (hot-type or cold-type), this process culminates in the production of plates of the respective pages, which are then delivered to the press room.

The steps on the way to the press room are different, however. In the case of hot-type composing the information in stories and advertisements is transferred to lead type (the letters are in relief). When stories and ads for a certain page have been composed, they are put together (finished), and a galley-proof can be made. After proof-reading corrections have been made (make-up), the type and plates are put into a page frame, from which an impression of the page is transferred to a cardboard matrix, which, in turn, is used for the molding of the printing plates (stereotyping).[1]

In cold-type composing, on the other hand, the written information is transferred to magnetic tape by keypunching. The magnetic tapes can then be plugged into video screens on which proofreading takes place. On the video screen, the proofreader can go back and forth in the text, making the necessary corrections.[2] These corrections having been made, the contents

---

[1] Time permitting, the corrections are also proof-read.

[2] An alternative procedure involves proofreading from a composed text. This approach requires the recomposition of lines containing errors.

of the magnetic tape are fed into a computer, which processes
the information, performing syllabification, evening ends of
lines and responding to the codes indicating different type-
faces. A photo-composition machine then emits the text on
photographic paper.[1] The stories and ads are subsequently waxed
and put onto a full-size dummy of the page they are intended
for. As the pages are filled, they are delivered to engraving,
a process in which a full-size photo of each page is taken.
Negatives of the photographic "art" on each page are added to
these photos and, after retouch, plates are made from them.

With respect to printing, the main difference between the two
approaches is that hot-type composing is followed by letter-
press printing, whereby print is obtained from a raised inked
surface. Cold-type composing, on the other hand, is often
combined with offset printing, whereby the print and non-print
parts of the plate are on the same level. Offset-printing
involves greasing the print areas. The greased areas attract ink
from rubber blankets and this ink is then transferred to newsprint.

If we look at the reproduction process by means of the suggested
paradigm we find a relatively high degree of _automation_ in the
work flow. And, this automation is even more pronounced by the
introduction of cold-type composing and offset printing, which
implies the utilization of computers and photographic equipment.

Work flow rigidity is quite high in the reproduction process. The
different steps in the process have to be undertaken in a certain
order, which cannot be changed. Proofreading, for instance,
has to precede platemaking, otherwise the process must be started
over again.

---

[1] In cold-type composing there is thus no height difference between the text and the background.

$\underline{Specificity}$ $\underline{of}$ $\underline{evaluation}$ is quite high in both composing and printing. Printing errors and errors in make-up are the criteria with respect to composing while in printing the corresponding criterion is delivery of the paper to distribution people at or before a fixed deadline. In addition, printing may be evaluated in terms of the distinctness of the printed letters.

The $\underline{understandability}$ of the materials employed seems to be "medium", although it is declining as new technology enters the composing room.[1] $\underline{Variability}$, on the other hand, is low: the same type of material enters the composing room and the press room every day. This circumstance does not exclude, however, that a "medium" $\underline{number}$ $\underline{of}$ $\underline{exceptional}$ $\underline{cases}$ occur. Now and then the normal routine must be broken in order to handle exceptional cases. The case "Suddenly the Ground Started to Shake..." in Chapter One, Section 1A1, offered one example of this.[2]

The $\underline{analyzability}$ of arising problems was quite good in hot-type composing, but as new equipment has entered the composing room, the possibilities for analysis seem to have declined. In the words of a compositor: "Earlier you could fix the problem yourself, but now you can't. The machines are too complicated. We give it a few tries and then we call the serviceman."

In summary, this means the technology profile of the reproduction process will be that shown in Figure 3:6.

---

[1] "Understandability" does not refer to the contents of the articles, since that is not necessary for the tasks to be performed in the composing room. Instead, it refers to the reproduction material.

[2] Other deviations from routine may be caused by mechanical malfunctions or breakdowns.

```
                              Low      Medium    High
Automation                                        ⊠
                                                  |
Workflow Rigidity                                 ⊠
                                                 /
Specificity of Evaluation                       ⊠
                                            ,-'
Understandability                       ⊠-'
                                      ,'
Variability                        ⊠
                                    `.
Number of Exceptional Cases           `⊠
                                       |
Analyzability                          ⊠
```

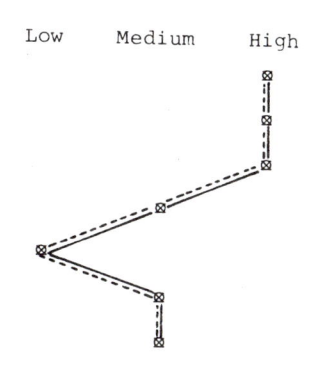

Figure 3:6. <u>Technology Profile of the Reproduction Phase</u>.[a]

Note: [a] The reproduction process for news and advertisements is the same.

3.7 The Distribution Phase

Upon leaving the presses, copies of the newspaper are delivered to the distribution staff, who see to it that the newspaper reaches the reader. The physical distribution of the paper, which is based on updating of the list of subscribers during the day, starts with the packing of finished copies into piles of various sizes. These are then given destinations and are transported away from the press building. Papers sold mainly by the single copy are delivered to different news-stands, tobacconists, etc., whereas subscribed papers have elaborate delivery systems which carry the product directly to the home of the final consumer.

In terms of our paradigm for classifying technology, we find the distribution phase to have a low degree of <u>automation</u>. Automation is largely limited to the packing of piles of newspapers, whereas in other parts of the process human labour dominates. Like the printing phase, <u>workflow rigidity</u> and <u>specificity of evaluation</u> for the distribution phase is high. A certain sequence of tasks must be performed and there is a very clear criterion of evaluation: either the newspaper reaches the reader or it does not.

On the scale of <u>understandability</u> of the material, too, the score is "high" in the distribution phase, whereas <u>variability</u> is medium. Differences in inflow of news and advertisements will have certain implications for the size and weight of the newspapers to be distributed.[1] In addition, especially "hot stories" may stimulate the sales of copies. Therefore, different news days will make different demands on the distribution system.

It also seems appropriate to classify the number of <u>exceptional cases</u> in the distribution phase as "medium". In most cases the handling of the printed newspapers will follow a routine procedure, but depending on how certain stories develop, special demands may be made on the distribution system in the form of special deliveries to certain areas, the printing of extra news-bills, etc.

The <u>analyzability</u> of arising problems seems to be rather high. Exceptions are occasions with late-breaking stories, when the distribution staff may have problems predicting the actions taken in the news-room.[2]

A summary of the technology of the distribution phase would thus look like the profile shown in Figure 3:7.

	Low	Medium	High
Automation	◨		
Workflow Rigidity			◨
Specificity of Evaluation			◨
Understandability			◨
Variability		◨	
Number of Exceptional Cases		◨	
Analyzability			◨

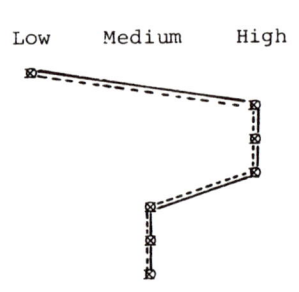

Figure 3:7. <u>Technology Profile of the Distribution Phase.</u>

---

[1] For a further discussion of this topic, see Chapter Six.

[2] This is not to imply that people in the news-room and in the dispatch room do not cooperate. Rather, it reflects the problems the news-room has on determining whether a given story will develop or not.

3.8 Concluding Remarks

A convenient way to summarize the reasoning of the previous sections is to fill out the matrix shown in Table 3:1, with the following result:

Technology Aspects		Phase in the Production Process			
		Collection[a]	Processing	Reproduction	Distribution
Operations Technology	Automation	Low/Low	Low/Medium	High	Low
	Workflow Rigidity	Low/Medium	High/Low	High	High
	Specificity of Evaluation	Low/High	Low/High	High	High
Materials Technology	Understandability	Medium/High	Medium/High	Medium	High
	Variability	High/Medium	High/Low	Low	Medium
Knowledge Technology	Number of Exceptional Cases	Medium/Low	Medium/Low	Medium	Medium
	Analyzability	High/High	High/High	Medium	Medium

Table 3:2. <u>A Summary of the Technology of Newspaper Production</u>.

Note: [a] The dual scores refer to the collection of news and advertising, respectively. The same principle is used for the processing phase.

Table 3:2, then, indicates that the technology of newspaper production is characterized by

- low degree of <u>automation</u>, the exception being the reproduction phase

- high degree of <u>work flow rigidity</u> in the processing of news, and the reproduction and distribution phases, but lower degree of work flow rigidity in the collection of news and the processing of advertisements

- high <u>specificity of evaluation</u> in processes other than the collection and processing of news

- high or medium degree of <u>understandability</u> of the material

- a mixed picture with respect to _variability_ of material, variability being high for the collection and processing of news, medium for the collection of advertisements and distribution, low for the processing of advertisements and reproduction

- medium or low _numbers of exceptional cases_ in all processes, and

- high or medium degrees of _analyzability_.

Or, in short: the technology of newspaper production is characterized by a mix of characteristics on the scales used. In this context it seems that a basic difference exists between the creative parts of the process and the more technical parts. This has been mentioned by Ellis and Child (1973) in conjunction with their investigation of organizations using a paradigm built on the criteria: (1) the "manufacturing-service dichotomy" and (2) "variability in product and technological environments" (_op.cit_. p. 235). Ellis and Child concluded that newspapers "contain an important service element (editorial) as well as a manufacturing one (production). The parameters of the editorial work content are subject to a high degree of variability, while those of production are not." (_loc.cit_.) Their reasoning is expressed graphically in Figure 3:8.

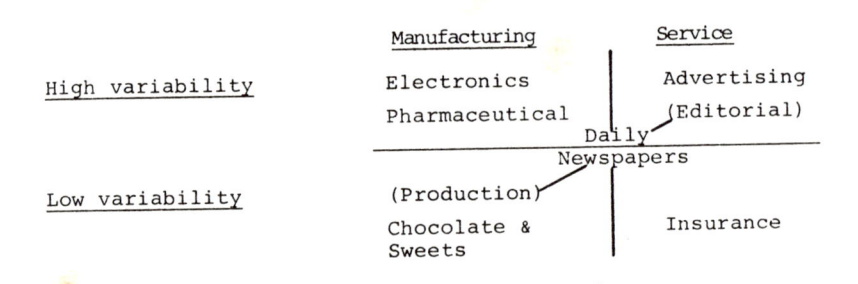

	Manufacturing	Service
High variability	Electronics	Advertising
	Pharmaceutical	(Editorial)
	Daily Newspapers	
Low variability	(Production)	
	Chocolate & Sweets	Insurance

Figure 3:8. _Manufacturing-Service Paradigm_
Source: Ellis & Child (1973, p.236)

That newspaper constitute a kind of hybrid in terms of traditional classifications of technology is further underlined when we apply the three varieties of technology suggested by Thompson (1967) to newspapers. Thompson's typology includes:

- long-linked technology: "involving serial interdependence in the sense that act Z can be performed only after successful completion of act Y, which in turn rests on act X, and so on." (op.cit. p. 15 f.)

- mediating technology: a primary function of this technology is "the linking of clients and customers who are and wish to be independent." (Ibid. p. 16). And, complexity in this type of technology comes from the necessity of operating "in standardized ways, and extensively; e.g. with multiple clients or customers distributed in time and space." (Ibid. p. 16)

- intensive technology: "a variety of techniques is drawn upon in order to achieve a change in some specific object; but the selection, combination,and order to application are determined by feedback from the object itself." (Ibid. p. 17)

As a matter of fact, newspapers seem to fit into all three of Thompson's classes: the high work flow rigidity points to serial interdependencies and the existence of a long-linked technology, the linking of advertisers and readers as well as the linking of opinion-makers and readers point to a mediating technology, and the mix of techniques and the public opinion-making function (changing and interacting with society) point to an intensive technology.

With respect to the existence of a long-linked technology, it may be recalled that although a newspaper in a sense produces a new product every day, i.e. a product with varying contents and size, the process is rather routine. This is particularly true in the non-creative parts of the process, but as was mentioned above, routines are developed in the creative parts as well.[1]

There are, of course, subjective elements in the classifications made in the present chapter. Some readers might argue that the various ratings in the profiles ought to be shifted somewhat. And, no doubt some ratings may be detatable. The main purpose of the present chapter, however, has been to point out the mixed character of newspaper technology, and this conclusion will not be altered even if some of

---

[1] Cf. Section 3.4 above. The point is discussed further in Chapter Six.

the scores are changed. This conclusion looks like it will hold for the future, too, as changes in technology bring about changes in the different profiles.

Two further conclusions may be drawn from the analysis in the present chapter. First, the existence of a number of different tasks tends to produce differentiation among newspaper personnel. Second, interdependencies between different tasks are likely to create a need for integration. This is particularly important, since the ultimate aim of the different tasks is the production of a joint product.

CHAPTER FOUR.   NEWSPAPERS' ENVIRONMENT

4.1   Introduction

In describing the technology of newspapers, the previous chapter pointed to three types of interaction between newspaper personnel and newspaper environment (cf. Figure 3:3): contacts with readers, news sources and advertisers. In terms of the organization model discussed in Chapter One, readers may be classified as a group of customers, whereas news sources are a group of suppliers. Advertisers, finally, play a mixed role as both customers and suppliers (whereby they must pay for the privilege of providing input into the newspaper!)

Figure 3:3 thus stressed relations to customers and suppliers. In addition to these connections, the organization model described in Chapter One includes relations to financiers and governments. Finally, newspapers are influenced by the actions of competitors.

The purpose of the present chapter is to demonstrate how these environmental groups influence the working conditions and activities of newspaper personnel.

4.2   Customers

As far as their customers are concerned, newspapers differ from other organizations in that they have one group of customers who buy the end product (readers) and another who buy space in the product (advertisers).

Starting with the readers, there are a number of important characteristics worth noting in relation to the consumption of daily newspapers. For one thing, readers require that the product appear at quite short intervals, at specific times and at certain locations. This makes certain demands on the production process. Secondly, an individual will not buy more than one copy of a particular newspaper a day, irrespective of the price. Either he buys a copy or he does not; he almost never buys two, three or more.

A third characteristic of newspaper consumption is that the same copy can be consumed by a number of persons. As a result, newspapers reach a much larger group of readers than that indicated by circulation figures. Members of one household consume only one copy of a paper, and, similarly, colleagues at a given place of work may share a subscription. The one limit to this cooperation is, of course, time: during the course of the day the newspaper gradually becomes obsolete.[1]

A fourth characteristic of newspaper consumption seems to be considerable brand loyalty, particularly for subscribed morning papers.[2] According to one interviewee, it seems to be the rule that people go on subscribing to the newspaper their parents used to take.[3] Having started with one paper, "it is as difficult to change as it is to change a **wife**".

The latter three characteristics imply important restrictions on the strategies whereby newspapers in general, and minor newspapers in particular, can seek to increase circulation. These restrictions are further reinforced by the fact that radical product developments, i.e. radical changes in the contents of a paper, are difficult (cf. Chapter One, Section 1A5: "The Policy Discussion"), the reason being that old subscribers may be repelled by the new image, while would-be subscribers are unaware of the change.[4] Consequently, radical product developments require considerable financial strength.[5]

---

[1] Note the stark contrast to books, for example, which may be circulated long periods of time.

[2] Subscriptions also have the advantageous function of providing financing through prepayment. Moreover, subscriptions yield more stable income than advertising, the latter being very sensitive to the business cycle (cf. below Chapter Six, Section 6.1).

[3] In the words of a printer at The Record: "Everybody says: 'We had The Chronicle at home when I was young, so we stick to it.'"

[4] A recent example of such problems is Göteborgs Handels- och Sjöfartstidning (cf. Nyström et al., 1976), which was in a poor financial condition when it undertook changes. The paper ceased publication in 1973.
Another Swedish example concerns readers' reactions to the removal of a vignette. These were so strong as to force the editors to reinstate it. The vignette, which included a number of flying birds, was then removed gradually by removing one bird at a time!

[5] It should also be mentioned that a change in ownership may cause problems. Examples are Stockholms-Tidningen and Aftonbladet, which experienced great difficulties after The Confederation of Trade Unions (LO) had bought them. (Cf. Sörmark, 1971, p.132: "Newspapers can be bought, but not readers." (My translation from Swedish.)

Turning, then, to <u>advertisers</u>, it is important to stress that their demand for space in newspapers creates important revenues for subscribed newspapers (Cf. Chapter One, Section 1A5: "The Policy Discussion"). As a matter of fact, in most newspapers advertising revenues exceed the revenues from readers (cf. Hadenius & Weibull, 1972, p. 164 ff. <u>i.a.</u>).[1] This is also the basis of the so-called "circulation spiral theory", which predicts that concentration of advertising money to the major paper in an area will kill its minor competitors.[2]

Advertisers are also a fairly heterogeneous group, ranging from the ten-year-old who places a classified ad to find his parrot to the large corporation that buys full pages. The difference is not only limited to space, however: there is also a difference in the communication links between advertiser and the paper: the ten-year-old (or his parent) turns directly to the newspaper, whereas the corporation in most cases goes through a wholesaler, the advertising agency, which provides advertisers with various services.[3] Gustafsson & Wickström (1972) mention as many as nineteen different tasks accomplished in "the advertising system", e.g. different types of planning and media research, lay-out, ordering, etc. (<u>op.cit.</u>, p. 35 ff.). In return for these services agencies are remunerated by different systems of commission.

Sometimes the ads also pass through an advertising consultant before they reach the advertising agency. Thus, there are three alternative paths from the advertiser to the newspaper: (1) direct advertising, (2) direct ordering through an advertising agency, and (3) ordering by an advertising consultant through an advertising agency.

One very important consequence of the work of advertising agencies is that permanent relations can be created between them and advertising staffs in newspaper organizations. Such relations no doubt benefit their mutual cooperation.

---

[1] Hadenius & Weibull report that on average advertising revenues accounted for 55 percent of total revenues for Swedish newspapers in 1967, (<u>op.cit.</u> p. 165).

Concerning the importance of advertising revenues, Reddaway (1963, p.205) offers a slightly modified view: "At the risk of a slight digression, I wish to emphasize that a large part of what the advertiser pays is absorbed by costs attributable to advertising, rather than serving as a straightforward subsidy to the dissemination of news [...] For a popular dialy newspaper only about one-third of what the advertiser pays is available as a 'subsidy'."

[2] For a further discussion, see Section 4.6 below.

[3] For a discussion of advertising in the Swedish context, cf. Gustafsson (1970, 1974 and 1975) and Gustafsson & Wickström (1972).

Concluding the discussion of the customers of a newspaper, it is relevant to point out that newspapers frequently also have a third group of customers: buyers of other printed products.[1] Non-newspaper printing permits more intensive utilization of equipment, and for papers moving from old to new technology this type of activity also offers a good alternative in relocating employees (cf. Chapter Seven, Section 7.4).[2] It seems, however, as though a number of newspapers have had bad experiences in their extra printing operations, since they lacked sufficient knowledge of the market as well as the necessary network of customers to succeed in this market segment.[3]

The characteristics of customers described here put certain restrictions on the performance of the different tasks. Readers, for example, require that the four phases of the production process be completed at a certain time, since the readers expect the newspaper to appear at certain locations at the same time every day. This condition creates a need for integration of the tasks involved in production.

It is also important that the collection and processing phases produce stories in accordance with the expectations of the readers, i.e. that there is a certain mix of news and advertisements and that the paper prints (as well as does not print) certain types of stories.

Regarding advertisers, it is necessary to create such relations with this group that advertisement orders are obtained and manuscripts for ordered ads are delivered at the right time.

---

[1] Still another approach is vertical integration. Dagens Nyheter, for example, holds a part-ownership in a papermill, and The New York Times Co. includes a papermill. In the latter case it is even said that the owners earn more money on other newsprint than on that they use for printing The New York Times (Stangerup, 1975).

[2] But, in this context, too, the major paper is a difficult competitor for a minor paper: "We have the extra capacity in the presses, but The Chronicle got there first. They skimmed the market for offset printing."

[3] The importance of such networks has been demonstrated in Engwall (1976).

The need for good external relations are extremely important vis-à-vis buyers of printed products.

4.3 External Providers I: Suppliers

One group of suppliers, advertisers, has already been mentioned in the previous section. Another group of suppliers mentioned in the beginning of this chapter was news sources. Newspapers receive much of their supply of news free of charge, since a number of persons or groups generally furnish local newspapers with news items in order to communicate certain ideas or to make events known. An illustration of this circumstance is the inflow of material one Swedish provincial newspaper reported: more than 15 pounds of volunteered information was received during a single month (cf. Petersson, 1966, p. 94 f.).

Besides the news information volunteered, a great deal of information either is obtained through wire services or has to be sought out by reporters. Subscription to the wire services provides a newspaper with a continuous flow of telegrams on national and international events. These telegrams are not only offered in written form but also as punched tape, which can be fed directly to the composer. This is a particular advantage with respect to radio and TV program schedules as well as lists of results of sports events.[1]

In addition to a continuous input of news and advertisements, newspapers require an inflow of a great deal of other types of input. Newsprint deliveries are particularly worth mentioning in this context. Even for a small provincial newspaper like The Record the requirements are considerable: the printing of a 20-page issue requires about 100 kilo (220 pounds) of newsprint per thousand copies and day.[2] Thus, issues printed in 20, 40 and 60 thousand copies require about two, four and six tons of newsprint, respectively, each day. Considering, then, large metropolitan newspapers with circulation figures expressed in hundreds of thousands

---

[1] Provincial papers, which generally do not stress national and international news, do not use the wire services to any great extent. They are used "just in case" (cf. Chapter One: "Suddenly the Ground Started to Shake ...") and for sports results and radio-TV program schedules, etc.

[2] In addition, the equivalent of one-third of a roll becomes waste paper nightly.

and issues containing far more and larger pages than small provincial papers, it is not surprising that the delivery of newsprint constitutes a difficult logistical problem for those located in the central parts of a city. This used to be the case for The New York Times and the Stockholm dailies, for example, before they moved out of their respective cities.

Other types of input required in newspaper production include ink and composing materials. With regard to the latter, an important change has occurred as new technology has been introduced. Earlier, lead was the basic material used, and it could be re-used, whereas most of the material used in the new technology has to be thrown away.[1] As a result price hikes seem to strike harder in the new technology.[2]

The introduction of new technology has not only changed supplier relationships with respect to composing material, however. It has also implied that producers of computer equipment have become important suppliers to newspapers, a development which no doubt has involved quite a bit of uncertainty as to the choice of suppliers

In conclusion, it should be noted that the ability of suppliers to present their goods and services on time provides important prerequisites of the work of newspaper personnel. In addition, it is clear that the prices charged by different suppliers influence the economic situation of the newspaper.

---

[1] The exception is the liquid for developing the plates: This liquid contains a precipitate of silver. Consequently, the used liquid claims a higher price than the unused.

[2] It is also worth noting that materials costs are rising fast in the new technology. In recent years the annual price hikes for photographic materials, for instance, have been 10 per cent. This price trend is to a large extent a result of price hikes for silver and oil emulsions. By far the most important price hikes, however, have been those for newsprint. (Stangerup, 1975, reports a rise of 60 per cent in 1974 for the Springer press.)

[3] Important issues in deciding on investments in new technology are: Should an investment be made today, despite the fact that the old equipment is still usuable? Should the decision be postponed in wait of another technological breakthrough? (Cf. Chapter Seven, Section 7.3: "The Procedure of Introduction".)

4.4 External Providers II: Financiers

A basic resource for newspaper enterprises, like all business organizations, is the funds provided by financiers. Different financial institutions play an important role, but regarding the control of operations, funding from owners is crucial. This has been stressed in traditional economic theory and may still be stressed, despite the appearance of alternative theories pointing to the transfer of influence in large corporations from owners to management (cf. e.g. Marris, 1964, and Galbraith, 1967). In small firms, which most newspaper firms are, the influence of owners has particularly important repucussions on the operations of the firm. In newspapers such influences are especially crucial since owners may put restrictions on the working conditions of journalists.

Tingsten (1947a) argued with regard to the press that different types of ownership would lead to different types of products. He identified three types of ownership: (1) political parties or organizations, (2) private groups or persons, and (3) special foundations.[1] The same philosophy found in most business organizations will be particularly common in newspapers owned by private groups or persons, whereas owners of the other two kinds might be less profit-oriented. In other words: the first and third groups of owners might be willing to accept minor profits or even losses for the privilege of publishing a newspaper. Therefore, Tingsten argued, one would expect privately owned, non-socialist papers, to be better managed than Social Democratic papers, since the former are more often operated as business firms. As an example of the effects of private ownership Tingsten mentions the improved economic situation of The London Daily Herald after it changed from being a party paper, to fifty-percent private ownership (Tingsten, 1947 b).[2] He also pointed to the dangers of limited freedom in opinion making when newspapers are owned by political parties or private persons. Regarding the latter form of ownership Tingsten exemplified his reasoning by pointing to the very detailed instructions given by British press lords to their editors (cf. Tingsten, 1947 a and 1971 b, p. 235 f.).

---

[1] For an international comparison of press ownership, se Nixon & Hahn (1971). The states of ownership in Scandinavian countries are treated in Almé (1974), Furhoff (1974a), Lund & Thomsen (1974) and Westman (1974).

[2] Tingsten's conclusions are, of course, open to discussion, since many other factors than ownership may influence the economic conditions of a newspaper.

Tingsten's discussion points to the advantages of ownership by
special foundations, and this conclusion is supported by a
Swedish study from a journalistic point of view (Journalistkåren i Sverige, 1971). This study indicates that the
board of directors is least constraining for journalists
in foundation-owned newspapers. It should be added, however,
that Furhoff (1974 $\underline{a}$, p. 97) has pointed to the fact that
such ownership may imply problems in the event the newspaper
faces economic difficulties.[1]

An additional type of ownership, which was not mentioned by
Tingsten, is employee ownership. Although this type of ownership is not very common, it seems relevant to elaborate somewhat on such ownership, since it is likely to be more common
in the future. A prime example of how such an organization
works is the French newspaper Le Monde.[2] This newspaper is
a "Société à Responsabilité Limitée" (S.A.R.L.), implying
that the company does not belong to any one individual or
institutional owner. Instead, five groups decide on the policy
of the paper as well as economic issues (investments, etc.).
The share of the votes and the employees belonging to these
groups are shown in Table 4:1.

---

[1] For a discussion of a newspapers' transition into foundation ownership, see Nielsen (1974).

[2] Another example of an employee owned newspaper was The Scottish Daily News, which was started by employees from Beaverbrook's The Scottish Daily Express when the latter discontinued printing in Glasgow. This paper was managed by a work council consisting of ten persons, of which six were elected among the employees. The Scottish Daily News was forced to discontinue publication, however. (Dagens Nyheter, October 29, 1975, p.19). Still another example of employee ownership and more successful than The Scottish Daily News, is the Danish newspaper, Information (cf. Krogh, 1974).

Group	Per Cent of Votes	Per Cent of Employees
Founding Shareholders and Successors ("The Partners")	40 %	-
Journalists	40 %	15 %
Non-Journalist employees	4 %	73 %
"Les cadres" (management)	5 %	12 %
Two directors:		
Managing Editor	7 %	-
General Manager	4 %	-
Total	100 %	100 %

Table 4:1 The Distribution of Votes in Le Monde
Source: Personal communication with Mr. Pierre Viansson-Ponté, Le Monde.

The stock belongs to the groups collectively -- with the exception of the partners -- and thus remain within the groups, irrespective of employee mobility. Thus, the stock of the two directors is not their personal property, but belongs to them ex-officio.

Representatives of the different groups meet at regular dates quarterly to discuss the economic situation of the paper, but they also meet at other times when various contingencies arise. Nine persons participate in these meetings: the two directors, a representative of the partners, representatives of the three employee groups, each bringing an assistant. The stands taken by the different representatives at these meetings are based on internal discussions within the different groups.

A basic rule regarding the deliberations of the company board is that major decisions have to be made with three-quarters majority, a rule which implies that the partners as well as the journalists must be agreed. But, the meetings rarely lead to taking a formal vote on issues.[1]

---

[1] This is not to say there are no differences of opinion: in the 1974 presidential election, for instance, Jacques Fauvet -- the Managing Editor -- wrote an article favouring one candidate, whereas the journalists decided on another.
For discussions of Le Monde, cf. Schwoebel (1968), Gaskell (1970) and Legris (1976).

At present there are no Swedish examples of employee ownership of newspapers. It would appear, however, that the impact of owners on the daily work in large newspapers such as Dagens Nyheter, is tending to decrease over time.[1] A journalist at this paper thus pointed to the possibility that the relationship between owners and the newspaper might in the future be more like that between a finance institution and a borrowing company. An indication that this is almost already the case, is the publication of critical stories in September 1976 on foreign business operations undertaken by the Chairman of the Board of Dagens Nyheter.[2] The Chairman, in a debate after the publication of the above-mentioned stories, also expressed the feeling that owners in newspapers have lost their importance.[3]

Summing up, financiers' demands put restrictions on newspaper operations: Creditors want their interest payments, and owners would like profits, provided the aim of their investment is to earn money. If the main purpose of their involvement in the firm is not to earn money, certain restrictions are likely to be put on the contents of the newspaper. The latter type of constraint may also occur when stories interfere with the business interests of profit-oriented owners.

---

[1] This does not preclude owners' exerting significant influence through allocation decisions.

[2] There seems to be clear historical reasons why the critical stories could be published. For one thing, Tingsten, when he acted as editor-in-chief for Dagens Nyheter, declared that as long as he held a contract with the paper, he was the one to decide on its contents. Second, it was made clear to the Chairman in 1972, after he had written a letter to the managing editor, that the Chairman of the Board "like the King, should be careful in expressing his opinions". (Fria Moderata Studentförbundet, 1974, p. 22, my translation from Swedish.)
It is worth noting, however, that the popular evening paper published by the Dagens Nyheter company, Expressen, did not carry any follow-up story of those in Dagens Nyheter, while the other Stockholm papers did have such stories.

[3] The debate took place at The National Press Club, September 8, 1976.

It should be mentioned that according to the diaries of the former foreign editor, Ulf Brandell, owner influence used to be of significance in Dagens Nyheter (Cf. Brandell, 1976, e.g. p. 135).

4.5 External Providers III: Governments

The basis for the relationship between newspapers and governments in any given country is the theory of the press prevailing there. Siebert et al. (1956) have suggested a classification of four such theories of the press, viz.

(1) the authoritarian
(2) the libertarian
(3) the social responsibility
(4) the Soviet Communist

The *authoritarian theory* looks upon the press as a "loudspeaker" of the state, i.e. the press faithfully disseminates what the government wants communicated. Different retaliatory measures on the part of government are common under this theory. An important symbol of the authoritarian theory of the press is thus censorship (cf. SOU 1975:79, p. 93). Other measures available to governments subscribing to this theory are legislation regulating the media as well as economic and physical retaliations (op. cit., p. 93 f.).

Libertarian theory, on the other hand, assumes the task of newspapers to be "to inform, entertain, sell, but chiefly to help to discover the truth and to check government". (Siebert et al., 1956, p. 7.) The theory is built on the assumptions of a competition of opinion and free entry into the newspaper market. A free press is expected to promote democracy and keep governments under scrutiny. (SOU 1975:79, p. 95)

The *social responsibility theory* was formulated in the United States just after World War II by the Commission on the Freedom of the Press (Leigh, 1947). This commission concluded that the press has to take a social responsibility in order to remain free. In addition, they expressed five demands on the media, viz.: (1) news should communicate truth and meaning, (2) media should be public carriers of ideas and opinions, (3) media should give a representative picture of society, (4) media should present and clarify the goals of society, and (5) media should give citizens full access to all relevant information.[1] Thus, according to Siebert et al. (1956),

---

[1] For discussions of the social responsibility theory, cf. e.g. Fjaestad & Nowak (1972, pp. 35-37) and Lyons (1947).

the chief purpose of newspaper according to the social responsibility theory, in addition to "inform, entertain, sell," is to "raise conflict to the plane of discussion" (op. cit., p. 7).

The chief purpose of the press according to Soviet Communist theory finally, is "to contribute to the success and continuance of the Soviet socialist system, and especially the dictatorship of the party" (loc. cit.). As Vallinder (1971, p. 9), among others, has pointed out, this theory constitutes a modern variation of the authoritarian theory.

The theories applied in the United States and Western Europe are primarily the libertarian and the social responsibility theories. A movement from the libertarian toward the social responsibility theory can also be observed. In Sweden this theoretical basis is underlined by the four main functions of media mentioned by the Parliamentary Commission on the Press. In terms of the reasoning of this committee, media should

(1) provide all-round information
(2) comment on the events of the day
(3) survey and scrutinize those in power
(4) facilitate the communication within and between organized groups (SOU 1975:79, p. 127f.)[1]

The Swedish Parliamentary Commission on the Press is but one manifestation of the interest shown by government in newspapers. It is not the only one, however. In Sweden, government has, in response to the declining number of newspapers (cf. below Section 4.6), undertaken a number of actions to support daily newspapers and to counteract the trend of newspaper deaths. These actions include several Government committees (cf. SOU 1965:22, SOU 1968:48 and SOU 1975:79) as well as various measures designed to support the press, viz. advantageous loans, subsidies, and distribution rebates

---

[1] A sub-project within the Commission was devoted to evaluating the fulfilment of these four tasks. The study focused on four areas of Sweden differing with respect to political majority as well as to competitive situations among newspapers (cf. SOU 1975:78 and SOU 1975:79, Ch. 7).

(cf. Gustafsson & Hadenius, 1976).[1]

Sweden is not an isolated example, however. In the United Kingdom, three Royal Commissions on the Press (1941, 1961 and 1974) have been appointed over the years. In an interim report (Royal Commission on the Press, 1976) the most recent Commission proposed certain beneficial loans for newspapers, a proposal which aroused considerable discussion due to fears that government might intervene in newspaper operations, thus impinging upon press freedom.[2] In 1976 some form of public support to the press existed in as many as nineteen countries (_Pressens Tidning_, October 1976, p. 17). This circumstance, in the context of the earlier discussion, may suggest that governments subscribing to the libertarian or the social responsibility theory of the press always hold a positive attitude toward newspapers, but doubtless many government have mixed feelings vis-à-vis the press: its role as auditors of government performance may result in disadvantageous stories being printed. Counter-strategies of governments have therefore been to suppress information or to provide newspapers with desired views. Important factors influencing the possibilities to apply the first strategy are press laws and the openness of the public administration in the country. These conditions vary considerably between different countries: in some countries, like the United States, there are numerous possibilities for contact with initiated information sources, whereas corresponding figures in other countries, like the United Kingdom, are less apt to speak. Thus, in Washington it is relatively easy to get a statement from a Congressman, while an M.P. is not likely to provide a journalist with such information. Instead, information seeps out through different types of leaks, which create the opening line: "It's said in Westminster".[3] Such leaks are also a

---

[1] It is also worth mentioning that newspapers are exempted from excise tax and that they benefit from favourable postal rates (cf. e.g. Furhoff, 1963, p. 61).

[2] The report proposed that the newspaper companies should lend money from the private financial institution, _Finance for Industry_, in order to invest their way out of overmanning and old technology. It also proposed that 4% of the interest would be paid by Government during the first two years. Finally, the report contained a proposal that those companies not meeting the standards required by _Finance for Industry_ would obtain loans on the same conditions from Government.

[3] The leaks may be obtained through different types of briefings off the record. Similar systems are sometimes also used in the United States: Thus Dr. Kissinger often used to be quoted as "a high official in the State Department" (cf. _Dagens Nyheter_, November 30, 1975, p. 18).

part of the second strategy mentioned above, i.e. to cultivate desired views. Other means of accomplishing this task are briefings, press conferences, press releases, etc. (cf. Chapter One, Section 1A3: "In the Field").[1] Different types of threats of retaliation should also be referred to this strategy.[2]

As a final note, it is relevant to point to the fact that governments obtain some revenues from newspapers in the form of taxes (corporate tax, advertising tax, etc.). These sums are relatively small, however.

To sum up, governments put a basic restriction on newspaper work by means of different external rules for publication expressed in press legislation. In addition, governments may be restrictive in allowing journalists access to different types of information. In many European countries governments, however, impose restrictions on newspaper work, while they also provide indirect or direct support to make free debate possible. This support may serve to counteract negative effects of competition as well as stimulate product development and the introduction of new technology.[3]

---

[1] Cf. also Rivers (1965, particularly Ch. 7 & 8) and Sigal (1973, Ch. 5).

[2] Woodward & Bernstein (1974) report the experience of The Post's veteran White House correspondent that "many of his old sources on the Nixon staff refused to talk to him after November 7, when it no longer served their purposes". (Op.cit. p. 220 note). They also write that "[......] the White House began excluding The Post from covering social events at the Executive Mansion." (loc.cit.) Cf. also one of my interviewees:"You become dependent on your sources. You're really in a bind when your employer wants you to do a job and your interviewee doesn't like you."

[3] Cf. e.g. Royal Commission on the Press (1976).

4.6 Competitors

Finally, the organization faces competition for its customers as well as its providers. Competitors for customers are mainly other newspapers, but other activities than newspaper reading also compete for people's time.[1] Similarly, the competition for providers involves all sorts of organizations.

In economic theory discussions of competition generally focus on the pricing of products, and, indeed, there are newspapers which have made successful breakthroughs by means of price competition (e.g. Aftonbladet, Dagens Nyheter and The New York Times.) But, today the market seems fairly standardized with respect to price: for some reason newspapers, in Sweden in any case, tend to need price hikes at the same time.[2] Thus, newspaper firms seem to be quite adaptive to their competitors with respect to pricing. The same appears to be true with respect to content, particularly in daily newspapers sold by the single copy. Thus, if one paper introduces a new feature, its competitor is quite prompt to follow suit.[3] In terms of the theory of oligopoly, then, product development in the newspaper industry seems to fit the model of the kinked demand curve.

Another mode of oligopolistic behaviour which can be observed in competition between newspapers is cooperation. One example of this is two Stockholm evening papers, which in 1966 created what Cyert and March (1963) would term "a negotiated environment" by agreeing to limit their publication of scandal stories. This was done in order to avoid "a kind of journalism which threatened to stop [their] joint growth on the newspaper market" (Sörmark, 1971, p. 244; my

---

[1] The competition from other media, particularly television, is a very important factor. In countries with commercial TV-stations there is also competition with respect to advertisers: much national advertising money goes to the TV-companies in those countries.

[2] Major papers seem to be price leaders, however.

[3] This is exemplified in the two Stockholm evening papers, Aftonbladet and Expressen. (Cf. e.g. Ågren, 1970, p.23, 31, 88, 107, 110 and Sörmark 1971, p. 173, 232 and 240 f.) The game of "follow-the-leader" is also played with respect to news: editorial offices frequently respond to news carried by competitors by publishing follow-ups. (For an example cf. Hammenskog, 1969, p. 109.) Major papers are not necessarily leaders in the case of news. (Cf. e.g. Brandell, 1976, p. 168.)

translation from Swedish). It should also be mentioned that only very rarely do newspapers write unfavourable stories on their competitors: "Things we would feature as a front-page scandal if they happened in another corporation we keep to ourselves when they concern newspaper publishing houses." (Ekeflo, 1976, my translation from Swedish.) Criticism of other newspapers is thus limited to criticism of their political stands on the editorial pages.[1]

Other Swedish examples of cooperation are joint ownership of the news agency TT and cooperative purchase of newsprint.[2] In the last decade there has also been a trend toward cooperation in the distribution of newspapers in response to governement subsidies to jointly distributed papers. And, in recent years joint printing has even been considered.[3] So far the latter discussions in Sweden have not been very successful, but such arrangements do exist in the United Kingdom.[4]

An important stimulus for cooperation is the fact that strict competition among newspapers in most countries has led to a decline in the number of daily newspapers. In Sweden, for instance, the number of daily newspapers published more than twice a week has decreased by about 40 per cent, from 179 in 1946 to 108 in 1971 (Figure 4:1).[5]

---

[1] Similar remarks have been made by Rasmussen (1975), who pointed out that newspapers never discuss price hikes on their own product, their dependency on advertising or newspapers as an environmental problem.

[2] More limited cooperation occurs between newspapers having similar political orientation (cf. SOU 1975:11, pp. 15-18; and Torbacke, 1972, p. 308).

[3] Cf. e.g. SOU 1975:11, which elaborates on cooperation between newspapers. The main problems in joint printing are fears of news leakage and scheduling with respect to printing time. Examples showing that the first type of fear may have some ground is provided by Ågren (1970, pp. 132 and 189 ff.) who worked in a company publishing two newspapers. The scheduling problem is illustrated in two case studies presented in SOU 1975:11, Ch. 2.

[4] The Sunday People, which is published by The Daily Mirror Company, is printed in The Daily Mail building. Similarly, The Mirror, prints on Times presses in Manchester, The Guardian prints on Times presses in London, etc. The cooperation between companies with respect to printing is thus quite developed in the United Kingdom. One of my interviewees added, however: "I doubt that anybody would print the Communist paper The Morning Star!"

[5] For a more extensive analysis as well as a list of the newspapers involved see Engwall (1974 a).
The period studied covers the years up until direct production subsidies were introduced.

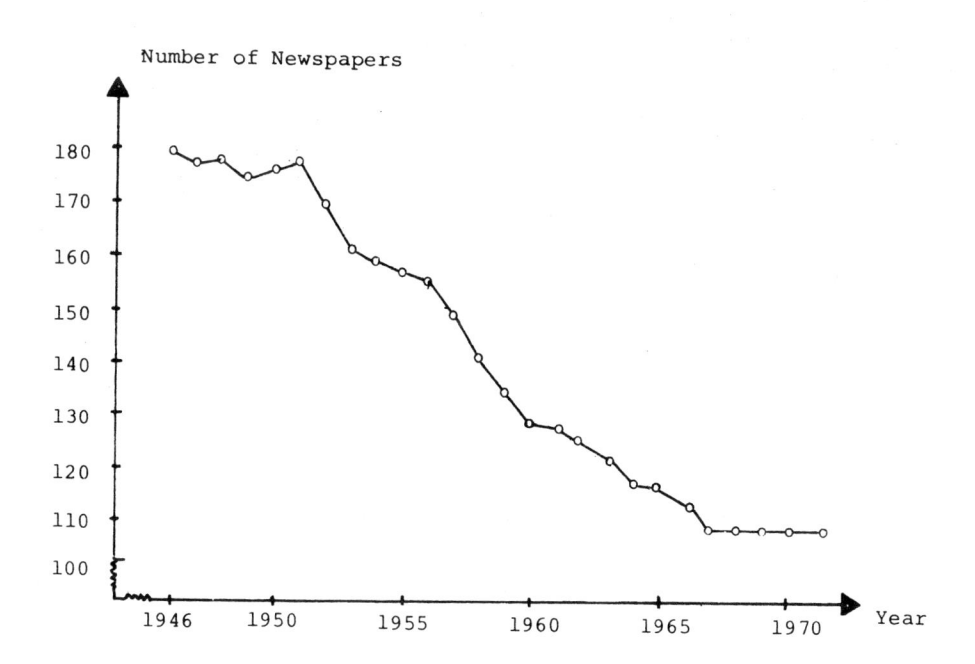

Figure 4:1. <u>Number of Newspapers in Sweden During the Period 1946-1971.</u>

The number of titles is only a part of the picture, however. In the same period the average weekly circulation has trebled (Figure 4:2)

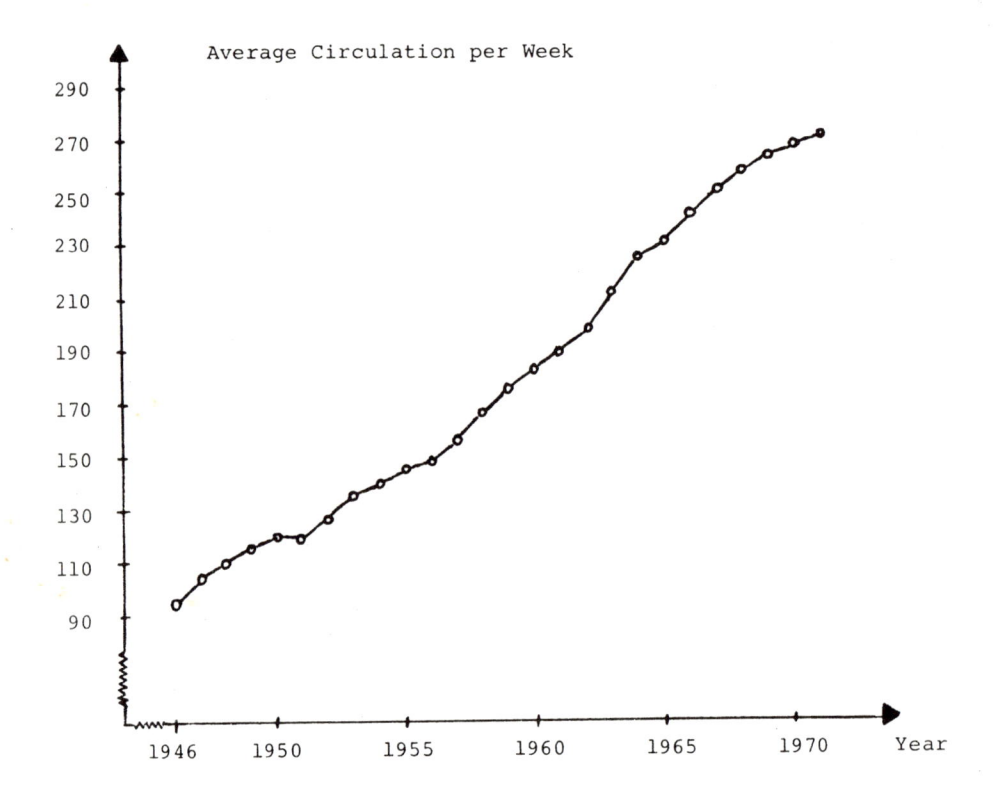

Figure 4:2. Average Weekly Circulation Among Swedish Newspapers During the Period 1946-1971.

The graphs in Figures 4:1 and 4:2 refer to the industry as
a whole, but as Reddaway (1963, p. 202 f.), among others has
pointed out, newspapers are locally differentiated as well as
differentiated with respect to the product. Distinctions can
therefore be made between nationally, regionally and locally
circulated newspapers, between morning and evening dailies
as well as between popular and quality dailies (loc.cit.).

As far as the Swedish scene is concerned, most newspapers are
local morning papers, whereas few have national circulation.
Among the latter the evening tabloids have been the most expansive segment of the market during the post-war period. The
national circulation of the Stockholm evening papers, Aftonbladet
and Expressen, has been particularly important in this context, as is shown in Figure 4:3.

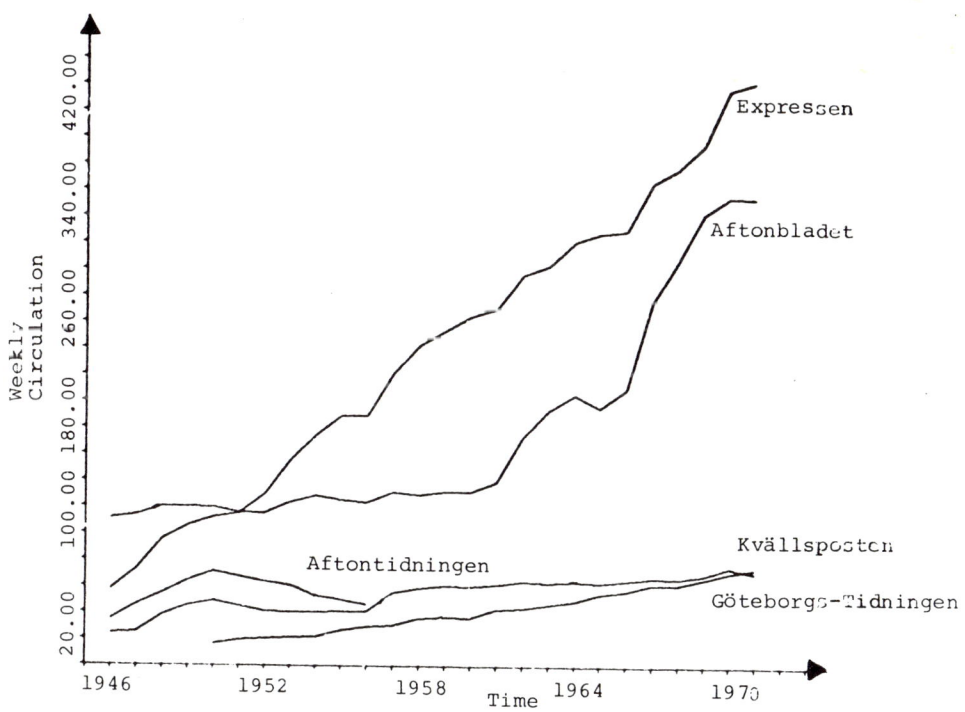

Figure 4:3 Trends of Weekly Circulation in the Tabloid Group 1946-1971.

The local differentiation of newspapers and the circumstance that newspapers sell two products, news and advertisements, in one package are the basic ingredients of <u>the circulation spiral model</u>.[1] According to this model the lesser paper(s) in terms of circulation (minor papers) in any given area will attract fewer advertisements than the major newspaper. As a result, the minor newspaper(s) will have less resources at their disposal than the major newspaper, a circumstance which will influence the quality of the minor newspaper(s), ultimately resulting in switches in consumer preferences from the minor newspaper to the major one. And as consumer preferences change, so do the preferences of advertisers, which means that the minor newspaper(s) will attract ever less advertising and resources, etc.[2] And, so the process will go on until the major newspaper has reached a monopoly position. Thus the model contains two spirals: a downward one for the minor newspapers and an upward one for the major newspaper. These two mechanisms are summarized in Figure 4:4.

---

[1] This model, which has been widely used to explain newspaper deaths in Sweden, seems to have a Norwegian origin and to have been first applied in Sweden by Hernelius (1961). However, it has become more widely known through the work of Furhoff (cf. e. g. Furhoff, 1967).

[2] A similar idea is presented by Springel (1965, p. 314). He writes: "[...] supposing that all newspapers have a similar journalistic contents and quality, we can say that many readers are inclined to prefer a 'thick' newspaper to a 'thin' one. More pages, therefore, lead to higher sales. This in turn makes the paper attractive to the advertiser. <u>And so the spiral continues</u> [.....]" (Italics added.)

Minor Paper / Major Paper

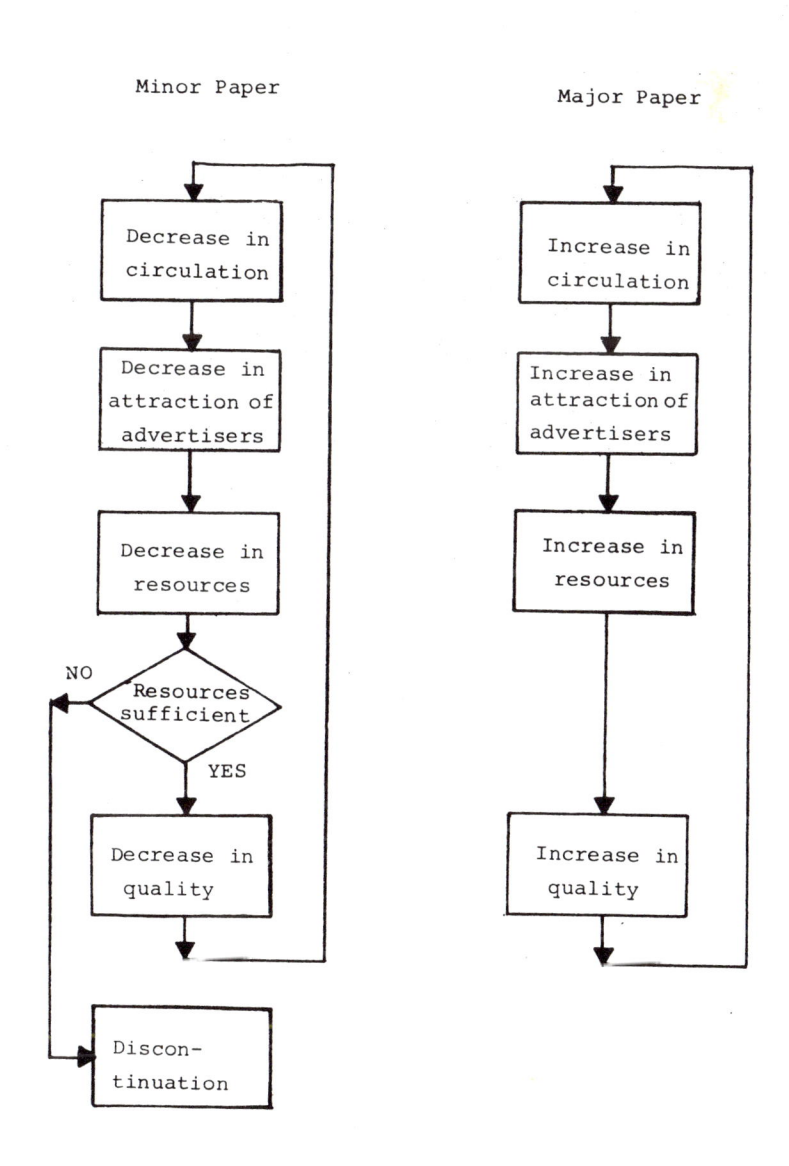

Figure 4:4 <u>A Summary of the Circulation Spiral Model</u>

A demonstration of circulation trends consistent with the spiral theory is given in Figure 4:5. This figure refers to the Örebro area, which contained four newspapers in 1946. Of these, two minor newspapers disappeared in 1956, and from 1950 onward the gap between the two remaining newspapers has progressively increased.[1]

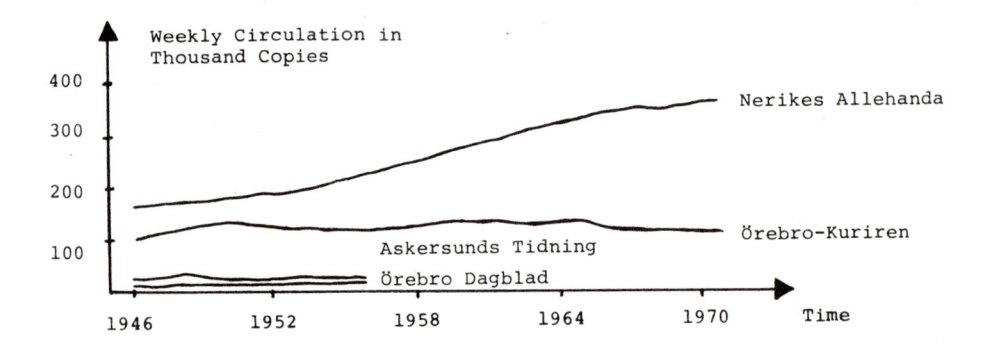

Figure 4:5 Trends of Weekly Circulation in the Örebro-area

A counter-example is to be found, however, in the Gävle/Sandviken area. One newspaper in this area folded in 1956, but there is no evidence of any tendency toward an increasing circulation gap between the two remaining newspapers. Instead, the minor newspaper of 1949, Gefle Dagblad, has closed the gap to its competitor Arbetarbladet, attaining a slightly larger circulation in 1971. (Figure 4:6).[2]

---

[1] For an analysis of the competition among newspapers in the Örebro-area cf. Blomé (1967) and Furhoff (1969, pp. 220-221).

[2] For an analysis of the competition among newspapers in Gävle, cf. Elfving (1967) and Furhoff (1969, pp. 214-215). - The conditions in this area have often been mentioned in the debate on production subsidies. In 1971 the circulation of Gefle Dagblad was twice as big as Arbetarbladet in the town of Gävle while Arbetarbladet was read more in the surrounding area.

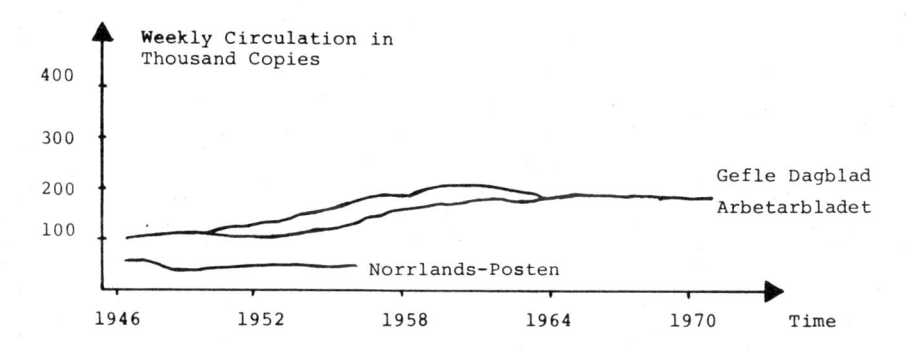

Figure 4:6 Trends of Weekly Circulation in the Gävle/Sandviken-area

A second counter-example is the Borlänge/Falun area, in which three newspapers have been able to compete during the entire period, with only slight increases in circulation.[1] Figure 4:7 shows the circulation trends within this area.

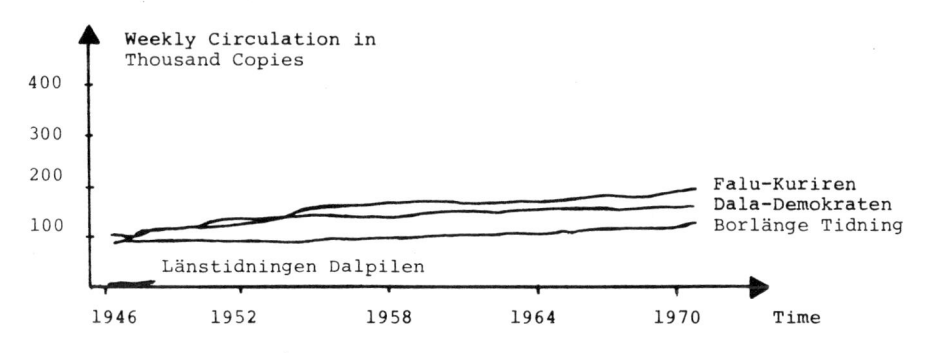

Figure 4:7. Trends of Weekly Circulation in the Borlänge/Falun-area.

---

[1] There are several circulation areas, however, in which the circulation trends seem to support the circulation spiral theory (e.g. Circulation Areas 10, 21, 28, 31, 36, 42 and 48).

The circumstance that the circulation spiral model has not been able to account for all changes in the newspaper market has raised some question as to its validity.[1] As a result, the model has been somewhat moderated in more recent works by Furhoff (cf. e.g. Furhoff, 1973 and 1974 b): the degree of coverage within the circulation area has been introduced as a variable (Furhoff, 1974 b, p. 161).

The main empirical support of the spiral model is the impressively high ratio of minor newspapers among discontinued newspapers (cf. SOU 1968:48, p. 48). However, this circumstance may as well be explained by the existence of <u>economies of scale</u>. As a matter of fact, in other industries, too, -- i.e. industries which do not sell "two products in one package" -- we find that discontinuing companies are seldom those with the largest market shares.[2] Companies with a small market share are more vulnerable and thus most likely to discontinue.

Thus, economies of scale are often mentioned in market analyses as sources of competitive advantages for large firms over small firms.[3] In this connection it is interesting to note that some students of cost curves have tended to reject the traditionally assumed U-shaped cost curves (cf. e.g. Bain, 1968, p. 173 ff.), since the originally assumed diseconomies of scale above a certain size -- through managerial problems, etc. -- have not been verified.

Several students of the economics of newspaper production have also verified that economies of scale do exist in the newspaper industry.[4] Among them Rosse (1967) reports that an econometric analysis of two samples of American newspapers revealed evidence for substantial economies of scale among smaller daily newspaper firms, [...] additional evidence that such economies extend to all scales of newspaper production, and [...] some evidence that such economies have not changed over time."(<u>Op. cit.</u>, p. 522).

---

[1] Cf. e.g. Swartz (1965), Hadenius (1968) and Thomsen (1968).

[2] Cf. Engwall (1973 a, pp. 121-122) for evidence on exits of firms in the automobile and shoe manufacturing industries. For similar results from other industries, cf. Carstedt & Isaksson Pérez (1974, Part II, pp. 59-61).

[3] It has been argued that there are also advantages of smallness (cf. Robinson, 1931, pp. 48-51 and Ramström, 1971, p. 179). Robinson, for instance, points out that in a small firm "with fewer persons to consult and pursuade, decisions can be reached much more quickly and easily". (<u>Op.cit.</u>, p. 48.) The small firm, it is argued, has particular advantages in industries where important decisions are frequent and quick decisions are urgent (<u>ibid.</u>, p. 49).

[4] Cf. Rosse (1967), Thomsen (1968) and Nussberger (1971).

Not only are cost advantages important in competition among existing firms, they also serve as a barrier to entry.[1] When economies of scale exist in a market, to be able to compete with already existing firms, an entrant is almost forced to start at a size above that where economies of scale begin to function. In the case of newspaper production, this means that the investments necessary to start a new newspaper will be considerable. However, even if these investments are made, the chances of attaining a sufficiently large circulation to break even may be small in the short perspective.

Irrespective of the theory used for analysis - the spiral model, or economies of scale - the competitive disadvantages of minor newspapers are crucial. These disadvantages are well illustrated in the case "Suddenly the Ground Started to Shake ..."(Chapter One, Section 1A1): The Record, a minor paper within its distribution area, was at a disadvantage with respect to the input of news; its main competitor, The Chronicle, had access to an Associated Press (AP) printer, whereas The Record had only teleprinters from the Swedish News Agency (TT). The nature of this disadvantage is further illustrated in Figure 4:8, which shows the cumulated number of cable lines at given points of time.[2]

The figure shows that the international news agency AP was able to issue information on the event much earlier than Swedish TT.[3] They were also able to give much more extensive information. It is not until three-and-one-half hours (210 minutes) after the event that TT is able to top the international agency. But, by this time most provincial papers were bound to have their presses rolling in order to be able to distribute the paper on time.

---

[1] Barriers to entry as a general problem are discussed, for instance by Bain (1956) and Scherer (1970). Barriers to entry in the newspaper industry have been treated by Ray (1952) and Smythe (1960).

[2] The figures have been obtained by visiting the Swedish News Agency and the Associated Press, where I went through the telegrams they sent out to the newspapers. The figures in the diagram refer to the time, when the cable first left the news agencies. For the provincial papers the receiving time may be somewhat later, since telegrams are proofread before they are issued to provincial papers. (This is done in order to facilitate the direct use of the punched tape.)

[3] This is not intended as criticism of TT. It only shows how an international news agency is better equipped to gather information from a large number of correspondents throughout the world.

The table does not, of course, say anything about eventual qualitative differences between the two news agencies, but it seems that subscribers to the Associated Press printers also got earlier warnings of the seriousness of the earthquake. Thus, a telegram at 10.40 p.m. (100 minutes after the event) was given "FLASH" status, whereas none of the telegrams from the Swedish TT were so classified.[1]

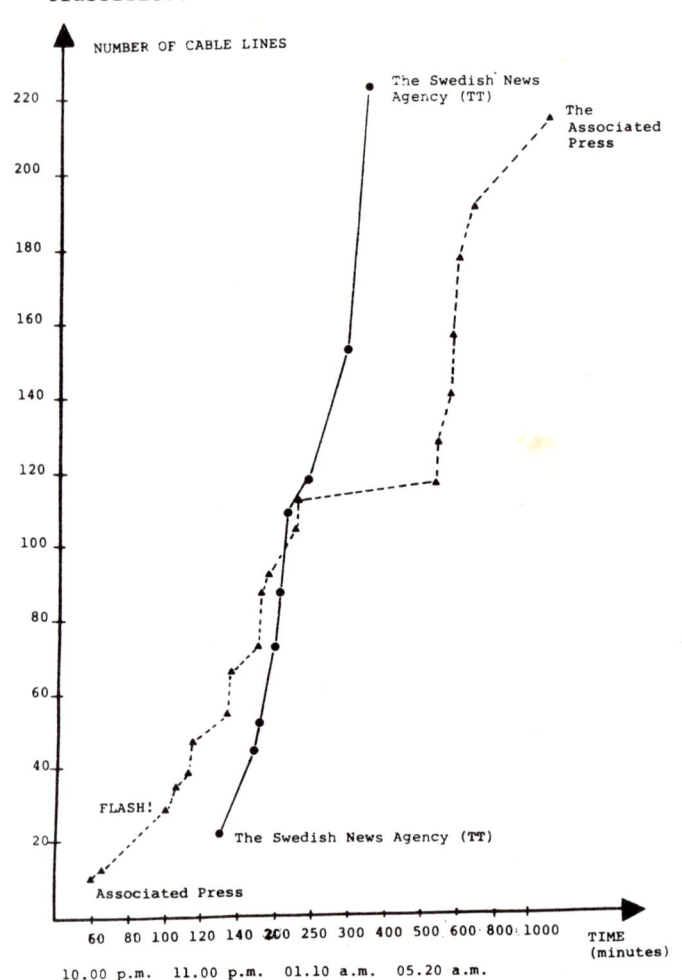

Figure 4:8 The Development of Cable Lines During the Earthquake. (Semi-logarithmic scale)

---

[1] In relation to this circumstance I had an informal conversation with one of the journalists employed at TT at the time of the earthquake. He remarked on the vagueness of the incoming telegrams. For instance, a very long time passed before any victims were mentioned.
A "FLASH" is an urgent telegram. It breaks other telegrams and is announced by a a ringing bell.

Summing up the discussion on competitors, great differences exist among newspapers. Some are monopolies or dominate an area, whereas some work hard to stay in business. These differences in competitive conditions, of course, greatly influence the working conditions of newspaper personnel, those in small and economically weak newspapers have few degrees of freedom in their work, while those in large, wealthy newspapers may be less restricted. The competition is thus important for the relations between a newspaper and its customers. For one thing, it may have an important impact on the mix and the contents of the product. And, second, it influences the possibilities to govern the behaviour of advertisers.

4.7 Concluding Remarks

This chapter has discussed five components of the environment of newspapers: customers, suppliers, financiers, governments and competitors. These have been discussed in general terms in order to identify different environmental characteristics of newspapers. In all cases the discussion has been rounded off with a discussion of the restrictions placed on the work of newspaper personnel by the different components, with particular emphasis on environmental requirements with respect to delivery time, economic performance as well as product mix.

CHAPTER FIVE.   NEWSPAPER PERSONNEL

5.1 Introduction

The previous two chapters have pointed to a need for differentiation in newspapers, i.e. a need to employ different personnel groups in order to accomplish different tasks. This differentiation was also demonstrated in Chapter One, where we met various actors on The Record: Larry, the night editor; Chris, the copy-editor; Jack and Dick, the engravers; Joan in the advertising order office, to mention but a few. (Cf. Sections 1A1 to 1A5)

The present chapter shall look further into the different groups of personnel in newspapers.[1] We shall first look at differentiation within newspapers and then at different types of integration.

5.2 Differentiation

Etzioni (1961) characterizes newspaper organizations as "typically [having] a dual organizational structure, with a highly utilitarian wing in which the newspaper is actually produced and a normative editorial wing in which it is written and edited." (Ibid., p. 52) [2] Looking at these two wings, we find that they differ in their orientation, as the following comment of an administrative employee indicates: "Some people argue that one characteristic of an organization is that its members strive toward a joint goal. If so, this is not an organization!"[3] He went on to draw a diagram like the one shown in Figure 5:1, indicating that the joint goal in a newspaper is only a small part of the goals pursued; in many newspapers the different groups share no more than the idea that a newspaper should be published.[4]

---

[1] An earlier study elaborating on personnel relations in newspapers is Rühl(1969). Chapters 4 and 6 are particularly worth mentioning in this context.

[2] See also Ellis & Child (1973), who were quoted above in Section 3.8.

[3] Note, however, Weick's (1969) remark: "Organizing is not necessarily an attempt to attain some specific goal. The absence of a goal in the Grook makes it more, rather than less, like an organization." (op.cit., p. 7)

[4] In the opinion of this interviewee the tendency is accentuated by the "influx of young journalists who do not sympathize with business operations".

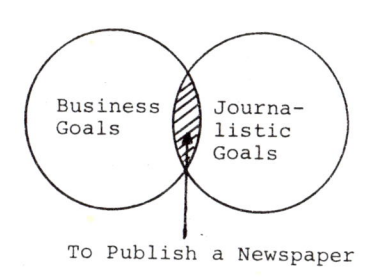

```
      _____
     /    /\     \
    ( Business  Journa- )
    (  Goals  / listic  )
    (        /  Goals   )
     _____/_____/
          |
   To Publish a Newspaper
```

Figure 5:1. An Interviewee's Perception of the Relation Between Business and Journalistic Goals.

More specifically, we may note at least three dimensions in which the two organizational wings differ. *First*, their criteria of success differ in clarity, the utilitarian wing having relatively clear and easily measureable criteria such as profit, turnover, production efficiency, etc., and the normative editorial wing having less clear criteria of success such as excellence in journalism. *Second*, the two wings are likely to exhibit differences in time orientation, journalists having relatively short-term time orientation, and some others having a somewhat longer time orientation.[1] *Third*, we may expect that persons belonging to the normative editorial wing to have more of an outward orientation relative to personnel belonging to the utilitarian wing.

---

[1] A good characterization of the short time horizon of journalists was offered by an editorial writer who previously worked in research: "This is quite different from research, where you work and work without seeing the result. Here you write your editorial, and the job is done!" The same person also pointed to the short life time of an editorial: "It's a flash which fades away."

It is also worth noting that journalists and people occupied in the printing process produce a visible product every day. The administrators, on the other hand, "do the unglorious job behind the scenes, but can't see the result of their labour to the same extent". (An administrative employee.)

The model of the two organizational wings does not seem to
provide the complete picture, however. Using Figure 3:3 from
Chapter Three, in Figure 5:2 we identify two groups in the
normative editorial wing: a news oriented as well as a politically
oriented group. Similarly, it is possible to identify two groups
in the utilitarian wing: a business oriented and a technically
oriented group.

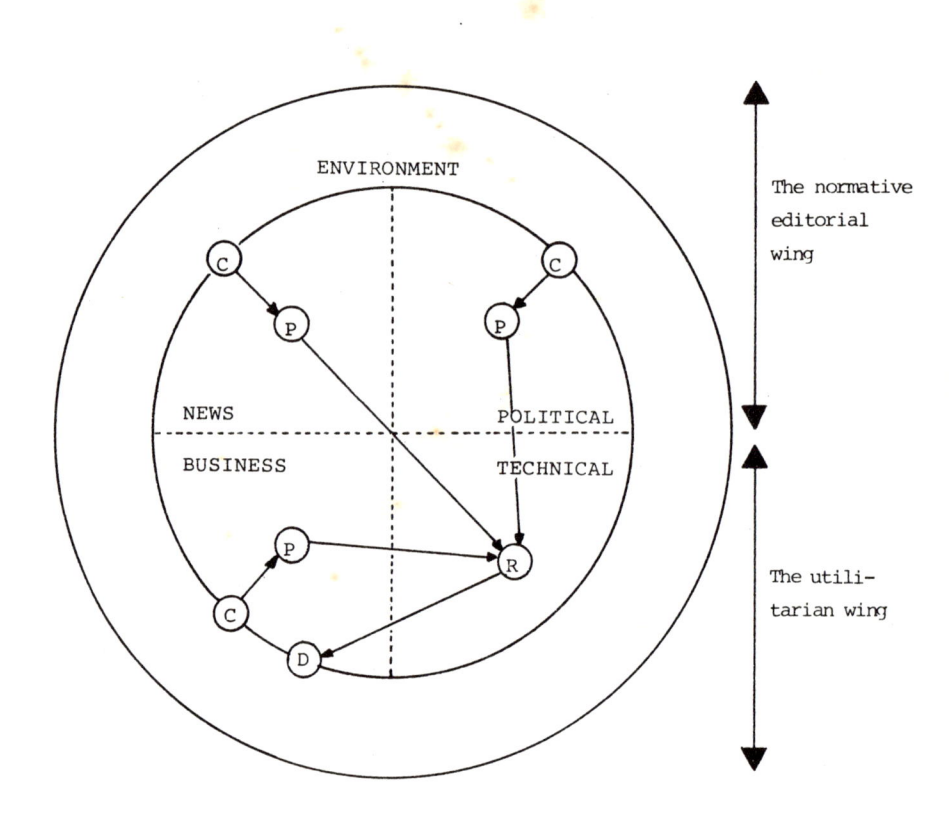

Figure 5:2.   Four Groups of Personnel

The <u>news oriented</u> group is devoted to collecting and processing news information and they are typically eager to acquire news of high topicality. The members of the <u>politically oriented</u> group take part in the same type of activities in the production cycle, but they differ from the news oriented group in that they are devoted to communicating certain political ideas. In both these groups the freedom of the press and the role of the press as a "fourth branch of government" are basic values.

The members of the <u>business oriented</u> group are occupied with the collection and processing of advertisements as well as the distribution of the printed newspapers. In addition, they take part in the administrative operations of the newspaper. They tend to stress the economic consequences of various activities.

The members of the <u>technically oriented</u> group, finally, are involved in the reproduction phase, and they tend to value a technically rational production. This in turn implies that they strive for an even load on the production facilities and to avoid interruptions in the reproduction phase.

The described differentiation is formally manifested through the creation of different departments in the organization. An illustration of this (or how newspaper managements look upon their organizations) is provided by the organization charts of six foreign newspapers interviewed. They are shown in Figures 5:A1-5:A6 in the Appendix to this chapter.

The organization charts are all taken from large newspapers, i.e. newspapers in which <u>horizontal differentiation</u> is particularly manifested.[1] It should be noted, however, that similar tendencies of differentiation can also be observed in small newspapers, a circumstance which made a researcher specializing in small businesses to conclude: "For small firms, newspapers are enormously differentiated and immensely filled with barriers."

---

[1] As is pointed out in ANPA (1970, p. 7) small dailies often have only an office (handling the information processing and the business operations) and a shop (setting the type and printing the newspaper). Medium sized and large daily newspapers, on the other hand, usually "have five major departments: editorial/news, business, mechanical or production, administrative, and promotion."

The main difference between large and small firms with respect to horizontal differentiation is the degree of specialization within groups and departments. In the <u>news oriented</u> group of large newspapers barriers thus easily arise between journalists working at the foreign news desk, the local news desk and other specialized departments such as business and medicine. These departments may even have an internal differentiation so that different journalists specialize in specific areas. To take an example: at <u>The London Times</u> the Business News journalists work in three sections: Finance (analysis of company records), Industrial Section (activities of major industries) and Economic Section (commenting on different economic issues). In each of these sections there is then further specialization. In the Industrial Section, for instance, each person has three or four industries to cover as his primary task.[1]

One type of differentiation, however, which is found in almost all newspapers, be they small or large, is the sports deparment's special status within the news oriented group. As one sports journalist expressed it: "I suppose you realise that we are a State within the State." Contributing factors to this circumstance are (1) the special knowledge required to cover sports, (2) the condescending attitude of some journalists vis-à-vis sports journalism, and (3) the fact that sports journalists often work at other hours than most of the rest of the people in the news-room, since the events they cover often happen late at night, on Sundays and holidays.[2]

The horizontal differentiation between journalists is likely to create a number of problems. For <u>one</u> thing, it may lead to difficulties with respect to reserve capacity. Thus, as the editorial

---

[1] In addition to their primary task each journalist has another three to four industries, where they are "second string", i.e. where they could jump in when the first man is sick or if the demand for commentaries is too high for "No. 1".

[2] It is worth noting that the "sports department [is] normally situated in a corner of the news-room." (ANPA, 1970, p. 5.)
As for working hours, one sport journalist exclaimed: "Being a sports journalist you have awful working hours. I have been free only five Sundays in nine years." Photographers have similar problems.

office is very much differentiated, the members of certain desks are not likely to be able to give other temporarily overloaded desks assistance. Second, horizontal differentiation may have the effect that the transportation of cables and other messages between different news departments is delayed.[1]

It is not only within the news oriented group that a horizontal differentiation can be observed, however. Similar tendencies are also present within the <u>business oriented</u> group, which embraces those engaged in marketing activities as well as those engaged in management. These two groups, although they share basic values, seem to differ in the way they work. This circumstance is particularly stressed by the external orientation of the marketing people. Or, in the words of an interviewee in a management position: "The advertising department is quite different from our department. They put a little zing into it. It's more like an advertising agency."

Within the <u>politically oriented</u> group horizontal differentiation is developed in large papers. Interviews have thus verified that specialization arises over time: "Certain 'preserves' are staked out, which means that certain topics are covered by certain writers." This specialization is not always without problems since many an issue nowadays touches upon several of the traditional fields. Therefore, the horizontal differentiation within the politically oriented group may require extensive deliberations between different specialists before the editorial is written.[2]

Finally, with respect to the <u>technically oriented</u> group horizontal differentiation has emerged with the introduction of new technology.

---

[1] In a small paper a great deal of improvisation is possible, even if special departments exist: "At special events, the high-jacking for instance," a journalist told me, "we gathered all our people in the news-room." The same person also reported floating borders between the national and international news desks of his paper.

[2] In small newspapers the editor-in-chief is often the only editorial writer who has to cover everything ("It's no easy task as editorial writer to jump between different subjects"). In some instances he is supported in his job by syndicated editorials, however.

This change in production facilities has produced a division between hot type and cold type compositors.[1] This is particularly apparent when the new printing technology is installed gradually. Age seems to play an important role here, younger employees finding it easier to adapt to the new technology.

The differentiation discussed so far is an effect of functional specialization in order to accomplish different types of tasks in newspaper firms. A second type of differentiation, also a result of newspaper technology, is _temporal differentiation_, i.e. differentiation as regards working hours. This differentiation arises since the production process requires activity almost round the clock. This was illustrated in Chapter One, particularly by the cases "Suddenly the Ground Started to Shake ....." (Section 1A1) and "The Pankab Bankruptcy" (Section 1A2), both of which point to the use of shifts in the production process. This type of differentiation is present in the news oriented and the technically oriented groups, whereas the other two groups have more regular working hours. The main consequence of this arrangement is that the contact between the administrative staff, on the one hand, and journalists, compositors and printers is limited: "Now and then you see them in the canteen."

Shift work has other effects, too, however. For one thing, communication between day and night shifts becomes a crucial factor, since it is important that the night shift be well informed about the work of their predecessors. Otherwise, duplication of work or omissions of certain material may well occur.[2]

A second effect of the 24-hour schedule is difficulty in gathering labour union members for meetings and in arranging informal discussions of union matters among employees working different hours. The time available for meetings of blue-collar unions is thus fairly limited, the alternatives being "the overlapping hour" or Saturdays.[3]

---

[1] A still further differentiation in the technically oriented group is that between compositors and printers.

[2] It may happen, for example, that two work crews publish the same story.

[3] On _The Record_ "the overlapping hour" may be used for union activities.

A third effect of the shift work schedule concerns physiological complaints, insomnia and digestive disorders, among individuals who must change working hours frequently: e.g. compositors, who change from day to night shift once a week, and night shift printers on their days off.[1]

Temporal differentiation is in many cases also a question of differentiation with respect to age: the younger members of the staff are more likely to be assigned to the night shift, and as they grow older they may be transferred to the day shift: "When I used to work in the news-room, my contacts were best developed with people on the night shift. Nobody was older than 35, and very few had a family. I think maybe one out of ten had a family. Thirty-five was the age to marry and settle down." (A former journalist.)

Finally, it may be relevant to point out that the 24-hour operations imply an extra economic burden on newspapers, since work during "inconvenient hours" is more expensive than other work. The problem is particularly acute in newspapers with a small staff, since they are more hurt by sickness or absence due to training, etc., as compensation for overtime, whatever the reason, is quite expensive.

5.3 Integration I: Hierarchy

"With all these types of differentiation, how do newspaper organizations go about integrating the various activities?" Apparently they do manage, since newspapers appear with a high degree of predictability.[2] But, how do they go about it? Or, in the words of an Army officer visiting The London Times: "How can you do all this without having somebody shouting orders?"

---

[1] In words of a printer: "Normally I walk home early in the morning, and sleep until one or two in the afternoon. Then, I have eight hours before I start working. The problem is my days off, when I have to get up earlier in order to be able to sleep at night." (The regularly occurring "days off" are a consequence of the five-day week.)

[2] There are, of course, exceptions to the rule, which some examples in Chapters Seven and Nine will show.

As in most other organizations <u>hierarchy</u> constitutes an important answer. This means of coordination, in fact, adds another type of differentiation: <u>vertical differentiation</u>, i. e. differentiation between persons with different formal authority. The news oriented group thus contains reporters as well as editors, the politically oriented group editorial writers as well as an editor-in-chief, the technically oriented group compositors and printers as well as foremen and executives, and the business oriented group salesmen as well as executives.[1]

The hierarchies are created through the promotion of individuals "who can be trusted" to supervisory positions.[2] This may involve taking journalists from outside as well as inside the organization. In both cases, however, it is important to have the support of the journalists: "Such a job is impossible without the support of the employees." (A journalist)

Internal recruitment seems to be more common in the technically and business oriented groups. In the former group particularly it is very common that managers are internally recruited. One interviewee, who used to work in a technical department, estimated that almost 90 per cent of the heads of mechanical departments are recruited internally.[3] According to the same source, it is not unusual that "troublesome" union leaders are promoted to managerial positions.

---

[1] Vertical differentiation among journalists is not only limited to that between reporters and editors; there are also "star systems", i.e. certain journalists are given special privileges or special status (cf. Argyris, 1974, p. 60). The development of such systems seems to be an effect of TV-journalism. As a result it is not unusual nowadays that by-lines include a photo of the journalist. (This system is not appreciated by everybody, however: "I don't like the photos. I think it's nice to be able to sit on the train and watch somebody reading my story without him knowing that I wrote it."

[2] It is worth noting that vertical differentiation in many newspapers also is a differentiation by sex: both men and women are journalists, but most editors are men.

[3] A result of the recruitment system is that managers in the technically oriented group identify themselves closely with the technical system. It is thus not unusual that technical managers act as general trouble-shooters. As one such person said: "My work is supposed to be a nine-to-five job, but I step in at other times if necessary. If there are problems, they phone me."

The promotion of employees nowadays seems to occur mainly within the respective functional groups, due to increasing professionalization and growth in newspaper size. Earlier, mobility between groups was more common. In the United Kingdom, for instance, it was, according to one interviewee, not unusual that British journalists "went the long way" i.e. that office boys advanced through the journalistic hierarchy, perhaps not to become editor-in-chief, but to reach other high positions in the editorial office.[1]

Various types of meetings are important for the coordination of work within the different hierarchies. The central importance of meetings was illustrated in the case studies from The Record (Chapter One) where news conferences were held mornings (9.30 a.m.) and evenings (4.30 p.m.) in addition to policy discussions.[2] Similar procedures are also followed in larger newspapers, the main difference probably being that more meetings are required. At Dagens Nyheter, for instance, the procedure has been to gather news editors at noon meetings to discuss the paper of the following day. A second meeting is then held at 3.00 p.m., when some of the night editors have arrived. At 5.00 p.m. a final meeting is held, where space is allocated to the different news desks.[3] In addition, a number of meetings on policy issues are called by the head of the news-room.[4]

---
[1] The social status of journalists is quite low in the United Kingdom, according to my informant.
A factor counteracting the lack of mobility between groups is the introduction of new technology. Such innovation has rendered some jobs in the mechanical department superfluous, and since many newspapers observe a no-firing policy in such cases, new jobs in other departments have to be found.

[2] Furthermore, weekly meetings are held with department heads, where the situation of The Record is discussed and joint problems are solved.

[3] Another example can be taken from The London Times: The first two conferences take place at noon and 4.15 p.m., respectively. At the second conference, it was said: "A lot of events that we expected to happen have happened, and we have a rough idea of the next day's paper." The last conference takes place at 6.00 p.m. at which time it is decided what shall be the lead story, the second story, etc.

[4] In the words of a managing editor: "A big problem in large newspapers is that there are very few spontaneous meetings. Moreover, you cannot stop working for a couple of days in order to plan. Planning becomes occasional. You have to use temporary 'foot-bridges'."

It should also be stressed that unions play an increasingly important role the cooperation between low level employees and management in the different groups. One newspaper manager thus reported that "employees are tending to increase their union activity, which means time-comsuming meetings for management."[1] The issues raised at such meetings are particularly issues of recruiting, personnel management, wages and the introduction of new technology.[2]

This approach whereby management negotiates with employees through representatives has several advantages, of course, but it is not always without problems. Agreements reached between management and union leaders may not be approved by union members. This is said to be particularly the case with Journalists's Unions, which are said to be quite heterogenous with respect to opinions.

Meetings and memoranda do not seem to be enough with respect to personal interaction, however. My interviews thus indicate that the uncertainty and informality of their work make journalists apt to wish for daily personal interaction with their bosses. Thus, one editorial writer expressed his great admiration for his editor-in-chief because of his daily interest in what the staff is doing: "He gives himself the time to do it. And, I think that's very important for the atmosphere." The complaints of a provincial journalist about his boss are in the same spirit: "He is not the captain of the team. He his sitting in his room writing editorials. Now and then he rushes out, but that's only for a short time. It was much better earlier, when we had Mr. B. walking around the newsroom talking to people."

---

[1] It is also mentioned that union issues are particularly accentuated in newspapers, since they host so many different unions. Moreover, journalists were characterized as having split wills as well as an ability to express themselves, both being complicating factors.

The opinion that the meetings are time-consuming is not only held by managers but by union officials as well. As a result it is sometimes difficult to find candidates for office in local chapters of labour unions. A President of a local chapter thus told me: "The last President got another job. There was nobody else who wanted to have it, so I had to take it. When I have had my two years we have to find a new one."

[2] In some large newspapers there are meetings every week between union officials and management ("But, that system is very unwieldy.")

In their relations with their bosses journalists thus seem eager for feedback, positive as well as negative. In most cases, however, the latter predominates, and positive feedback is very rare.[1] This seems to be a deficiency in most papers, since journalists' work involves quite a lot of frustration, particularly in large newspapers. This emerges as a result of doubtfulness about the outcome, the intensity of the job, etc.

Hierarchical arrangements in newspapers cause frustrations not only among low level employees, however. Some editors, too, are frustrated because they miss the external contacts and the writing.[2] Bill, the news editor of The Record, thus stated: "I never go out on jobs. If I do any story, I do it on the phone. But, once in a while I wish I could get out and do some reporting." A journalist on another paper remarked: "In that job you have to learn to get your contact with the environment through agents."

A contributing factor to such difficulties in transition is the fact that promotion to editorships is seldom based on a demonstrated ability to direct the work of other people.[3] Rather, it is based either on demonstrated ability-or incapability-as a journalist.[4] Most editors thus have a journalistic background, a circumstance which often facilitates cooperation between editors and reporters.[5]

---

[1] "Members of the staff don't hear about the good things they do, only the bad things. As a matter of fact, the management of the news-room has been one of repressive tolerance." (An editor.)
Cf. also Chapter One, Sections 1A1 and 1A4: "Suddenly the Earth Started to Shake . . ." and "The Neartown Car Dealer".

[2] In addition, they face problems of "switching sides". This seems to be the case, even when journalists participate in the selection of editors: "Moving to editorships, they become part of management, and we have to negotiate" (Board member of a local chapter of journalists). Cf. also Brandell (1976, p. 153) for similar remarks regarding when Börje Dahlquist, former Chairman of the local union chapter, became Managing Editor of Dagens Nyheter.

[3] This is the same system as the one in -- at least Swedish -- universities, where good researchers become full professors with heavy administrative duties. This system may not always be successful, since it is indeed questionable whether good performance in one role is a good predictor of performance in another role. (Cf. Peter & Hull, 1969.)

[4] Incapability may be a matter of "bad" news judgement or difficulties in meeting deadlines. Other reasons for moving into administrative work are desires for status recognition as well as the desire for more regular working hours.

[5] But, there is of course the risk that even a good journalist becomes a generalist under the pressure of administrative duties, which in turn may "limit his credibility to his subordinates". (Hall, 1972, p. 279).

But, it is not only the transition from journalist to editor which is troublesome; transition in the other direction is even more difficult. One interviewee pointed to the difficulty in maintaining a well developed external communication network in the role as editor. Therefore, a system of job rotation and possibilities for retraining prior to transitions was recommended. Such a system would seem quite important since nowadays very few persons in managing positions go back to reporting. Consequently, some papers have introduced time limits on the term as news editor. According to an acting news editor, the time limits are to be preferred since otherwise it is very difficult to back out: "If there is a time limit you're not forced to choose."[1]

Hierarchy is basically a means to integrate the work within the four groups. On a high level in the organization, however, it can also contribute to integration between departments, as different conflicts are transferred upwards through the hierarchies for solution (cf. Argyris, 1974, p. 26). At the top there are then different approaches handling the conflicts. In some cases the organization design implies that one person fills the role of both as managing director and editor-in-chief.[2] In others a more collective leadership is employed.[3] In the latter cases the different leaders often represent different parts of the newspaper system, and conflicts are supposed to be solved through bargaining between them.

---

[1] Another problem is often finding a new job for the former Managing Editor. Just as it is not always wise to have the former President as Chairman neither is it advisable with respect to managing editors: "When you change the Managing Editors, it's not good to have the old one still in the house. - Another solution is to give him different consultancy jobs. But that's not good either. You should not make directors of journalists." (A former managing editor)

[2] Swedish examples are Dagens Nyheter under Dehlgren, Svenska Dagbladet under Gerentz, and Sydsvenska Dagbladet under Wahlgren.

[3] The two Stockholm evening papers are example of such collective leadership. Since Nycop left Expressen in 1962 the troika Wrigstad-Ågren-Hallerby run the paper (Ågren, 1970, p. 29). Aftonbladet had two editors-in-chief (Fredriksson and Arvidson) in 1970 (Sörmark, 1971, p. 282).

5.4 Integration II: Lateral Contacts

Hierarchy is not the only means of integrating the different groups, however. Another basic means to achieve this type of integration is the creation of formal and informal contacts between different groups of personnel. Figure 5:2 (cf. Section 5.2 above) gave some indication of the need for such contacts: communication is needed between the processing units (the news oriented, the politically oriented and the business oriented groups) and the reproducing unit (the technically oriented group). Furthermore, there is a need for communication between the reproducing unit (the technically oriented group) and the distributing unit (the business oriented group).

The first type of interaction (that between processing and reproducing units) is particularly pronounced between the news oriented and technically oriented groups, since the former delivers a large amount of material to the composing room and delivers it continuously almost until the final deadline for printing. The politically oriented group, on the other hand, needs less cooperation with the technically oriented group, since their material in most cases is not delivered late in the production process and has a lesser volume than that of the news oriented group. The business oriented group, finally, delivers a large amount of material, but only insignificant parts of their material make claims on the capacity in the composing room during the final hours before printing. Ranking the contacts between the technically oriented group and the other three groups, then, the news oriented group seems to place first, followed by the business oriented group, with the politically oriented group in third place.

Among the news oriented personnel, contact with the technical group is particularly pronounced for news desks with late news, such as the sports department, where continuous revisions of and additions to stories are made as different matches develop. This situation leads to close cooperation between the sports department and the composing room: "We work together almost every night. So, we know each other's problems." (A sports journalist.)[1]

---

[1] There are also other views on this cooperation. A technical manager thus exclaimed in an interview: "Don't mention the sports department. They're our special problem. They are often late. Especially all their pictures are a problem."

The opportunities for interaction between the news oriented and the technically oriented groups seem to have increased as newspapers have changed from hot type to cold type composing. This has been accomplished through educational efforts before the change as well as through locating the news-room and the composing room closer to each other. At The Record, for example, the two departments are now situated in adjoining rooms.[1] This arrangement facilitates communication between the two groups, but it is interesting to note that the interaction between journalists and compositors mainly takes place in the composing room. Thus, among the compositors the foreman was practically alone in entering the news-room (asking for editorial copy), while the traffic in the other direction was much more intensive, particularly during the last hour of the night shift when copy-editors and the night editor cooperated with compositors to finish the different pages.[2]

The interaction of the business oriented group with the technically oriented group mainly consists of the delivery of advertising manuscripts (cf. Chapter One, Section 1A4: "The Neartown Car Dealer").[3] This interaction may involve discussions on the design of advertisements. Due to their earlier delivery schedule, the advertisning

---

[1] At The Record's main competitor, The Chronicle, a more integrated approach is used: the news-room, the composing room and the advertising department are all located in the same large room.

[2] Note here, too, Gaye Tuchman's comments on interactions between departments: "First, only four editors (situated in the news-room) interacted with technical staff, the compositors who set their pages. These were the assistant managing editor who was responsible for page 1; the wire services editor, responsible for page 2; the local editor, page 3; and the assistant managing editor's subordinate, responsible for all other general news pages. This last editor also got the mock-up sheets from the advertising department. And, the assistant managing editor would clear late changes with the compositors' and printers' technical supervisors. This last relationship was somewhat close, for the technical supervisor would come up to chat after the first edition had hit the street at midnight. He was more prone to visit the news-room for these chats on nights when problems were anticipated -- snowy nights or the night Martin Luther King died." (Personal communication to the author.)

[3] In recent years deliberations concerning the introduction of new technology have given rise to greater need for cooperation between the two groups (cf. Chapter Seven, Section 7.3).

personnel do not have the same intensive contacts with technical personnel as those working in the news-room. The opposite is true, however, of circulation personnel, who have intensive interaction with printers in order to be able to get the printed newspapers to readers on time.

The contact patterns outlined here arise from the production flow described in Figure 5:2. It might also be appropriate, however, to look at other lateral relations between the different groups. Starting then with the interaction between news oriented and politically oriented groups, we may conclude that the need for cooperation between these two groups is rather limited. Thus, one editorial writer described the news and the editorial departments as "two watertight bulkheads" (cf. also Argyris, 1974, Ch. 8.)[1]

Exceptions to the poor cooperation between departments may occur in the case of special events (such as a convention of a political party), when news journalists, editorial writers, cartoonists and photographers work as a team. But, as soon as the team returns to the main office it dissolves, and the old pattern of work resumes.[2]

---

[1] He therefore stressed the need for increased communication between them in order to decrease the rigidity of the system.

Another editorial writer said that: "contacts are taken on upper levels of the organization, if such contacts are taken at all," whereas a former journalist told me: "Two guys were writing editorials. We had no contact with them whatsoever."

In larger papers there is sometimes an exception to the rule, whereby editorial writers have some contacts with the Foreign news desk. Gaye Tuchman's experience is the following: "Also, although beat reporters who also wrote columns interacted with the editorial department, interactions between editorial writers and reporters were limited. The reporter-columnists would be called upon to give their views of events. The head editorial writer struck up a friendship with the local editor, with whom he shared liberal views (The paper's policy was moderate to conservative)." (Personal communication to the author)

[2] The interviewee was quite convinced that the stratification described here is largely a function of size: In small papers some integration between the groups can thus be observed. This integration is particularly pronounced where the editor-in-chief writes the editorials as well as participates in the work in the news-room. (A Swedish example is Christer Wahlgren, former editor-in-chief of Sydsvenska Dagbladet, who for a long time covered the budgetary debate in Parliament. Cf. Wahlgren, 1970, p. 136.)

There are also indications that the limited communication between journalists and editorial writers may contribute to conflicts between members of the two groups. This is particularly the case when news journalists express political comment on the news page.[1] In recent years it has become increasingly common that specialists like business and sports editors run their own columns. Their comments are restricted to their speciality, however, "trespassing" being likely to attract comments from editorial writers: "You have no business commenting on that!"

The insulation of editorial writers is also stressed by their limited contacts with the business oriented group, the exceptions being situations when the business community respond to editorial stands taken by the paper (cf. Chapter Nine).

A somewhat larger degree of interaction can be observed between the news oriented and the business oriented groups. One such interaction is constituted by decisions on space allocation, while another is cooperation in relation to promotional activities of the paper.[2] As for the latter, journalists take part in their planning as well as discussions on how to handle them on the front page and the newsbill (cf. Chapter Nine for results).[3]

Summing up the employment of lateral contacts as integrating devices, we are able to draw Figure 5:3.

---

[1] It may be noted that in one editorial writer's view the decreasing number of newspapers may push politically oriented people into the news pages: "On our paper we have, as you know, several persons who apply the principle,'each his own editorial writer'."

[2] A third exception, based on man-to-man contacts, is the pay-office.

[3] Representatives of the two groups naturally look differently upon promotion. As an advertising man expressed it: "We see it more commercially than they do. We would prefer more coordination. When there is a commercial event, they should do something news-wise in order to complement the ads. But, we never ask them to write. Then they only say no. On the other hand, when we haven't said anything they sometimes publish pure 'puffery'."

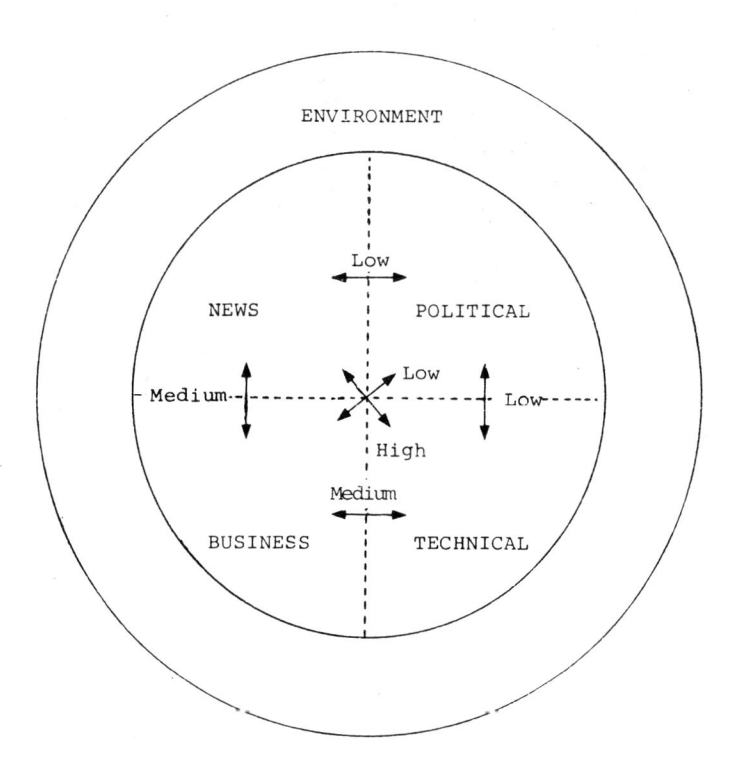

Figure 5:3. Lateral Contacts in Newspapers.

Here we note a high degree of interaction between the news oriented and technically oriented groups, whereas the communication between the news oriented and business oriented groups as well as between the business oriented and technically oriented groups on a medium level. The intensity of communication between the politically oriented group and the other three groups is low.

5.5 Integration III: Environmental Communication Links

Figure 5:2 not only points to a need for integration between different personnel groups, it also points to the need for the creation of relations between personnel groups and the environment.

Starting with the news oriented and the politically oriented groups we can see that they play an important gatekeeping role. Persons in those two groups have an opportunity to screen the inflowing material, deciding what events should be covered and to what extent these events should be covered.[1]

As was demonstrated in Chapter One (Section 1A3: "In the Field"), the external contacts of the news oriented and politically oriented groups involve permanent relations with colleagues as well as with news sources.[2] As for contacts with colleagues, Sigal (1973, pp. 37-39) shows how journalists from different newspapers cooperate on the beat, exchanging information and checking each other's interpretations.[3]

The creation of a network of external contacts was stressed by many of those interviewed. One put it like this: "As a matter of fact, the reporter knows very little; it's the network of contacts that counts." And, another said: "The thing is to know who knows."[4]

---

[1] Cf. e.g. Carter (1958), Gieber (1964) and Donohew (1967).

[2] Judd (1961) indicates that reporters who spend much time outside the editorial office are likely to pick up the values of their sources. This problem is similar to the one foreign offices face with their ambassadors: After a while they become assimilated in the foreign country, which circumstance makes most countries shuffle their ambassadorships once in a while.
In newspapers permanent relationships may lead to "corruption of friendship" implying too nice treatment of certain persons or organizations (cf. e.g. Hellmark et al., 1969 and Petersson, 1966, p. 86 f.).
Finally, it is worth noting that Lawrence and Kanter found in a study of mayors that newspapermen even are centres of complicated networks of communication (Paul R. Lawrence in personal communication to the author).

[3] "... reaching some agreement with colleagues on what is news and how to write a story about it helps to authenticate the news ..", op.cit., p. 39). In some sense the method has similarities with the technique used when employing the Delphi method (cf. e.g. Dalkey & Helmer, 1963). But, it may also be noted that group pressure may lead to absurd results (cf. Asch, 1953).

[4] In addition to personal contacts the same interviewee stressed personal files as the most valuable asset of a journalist. (These files, it appears, are personal in the sense that a journalist brings them with him as he moves from one paper to another.)

At The Record the use and maintenance of a network of contacts was demonstrated by Jim, a sports reporter, at a track and field event. During this event he concentrated on meeting the different leaders and active athletes in order to gather information. He did this very informally, taking no notes: "It's just for orientation. If there is something I want to dig deeper into, I'll call later on. - I have frequent contacts with the leaders. They even comment on my writing. They keep a lot of clippings, you know."[1]

A factor favourable to the construction of networks between journalists and corporations, government agencies, etc., is the fact that journalists generally have former colleagues now in public relations jobs. According to one interviewee, it is quite common that journalists step down from the hectic day-to-day news gathering on a daily newspaper, switching over to handle the information activities of a corporation or a government agency. Their earlier contacts in the newspaper world no doubt constitute an asset in their new job.

The mobility of journalists also leads them to cooperate between different geographic locations: "Professional contacts between different journalists often result in an exchange of services. If something happens in the other end of the country, you just call a colleague of yours who happens to work there and he does a story as 'our special correspondent'." Such extra jobs, which provide additional money for the journalists, are not always appreciated by newspaper managements.[2] In some newspapers it is even stipulated in journalists' contracts that they may not write stories for other papers without the permission of the managing editor.[3]

---

[1] This way of working is based on a specialization. As the same reporter pointed out, "The only way to build up and maintain contacts is to specialize in a couple of areas." One drawback of this system is that sources in the field have a tendency to remain silent when they do not get in touch with their contact person on the paper.

[2] For photographers the general rule implies that photos taken by a photographer are the property of the newspaper. If they are sold, they are thus sold by the paper (cf. Chapter One, Section 1A1: "Suddenly the Earth Started to Shake ....")
For a description of possible effects of this system, cf. Rifbjerg (1974).

[3] It happens, however, that such rules are evaded by the use of pseudonyms.

A particularly important group of personnel with respect to communication with the environment is regular employees of the newspaper, who do their job outside the main production site, i.e. local and foreign correspondents (the latter particularly in metropolitan newspapers).[1] Some of these persons are quite loosely linked to the paper, and in fact more closely related to their local society than to their newspaper. Their "outside" location sometimes leads to differences in values between correspondents and the home office. They therefore also run a higher risk of being rejected.[2] There are two reasons for this: First, they do not participate in all the discussions going on in the editorial office and are therefore less able to express their way of thinking than journalists in the home plant. Second, their location away from the editorial office makes it easier to reject them: They won't come arguing the next morning.

On the other hand, local correspondents are very important for the circulation of local newspapers. Hiring competent local correspondents may improve circulation considerably outside the main circulation area. Therefore, local correspondents can exercise some influence on news editors.

Yet another communication link to the environment is the group of outside experts and freelance writers, who are called upon for particular stories or who offer their services. Such freelance arrangements are particularly common with respect to cultural matters, i.e. book reviews, debate articles, etc. A common feature of freelance writers is their low degree of interaction with people in the newspaper building. They can bring certain expertise or certain

---

[1] For discussions on the working conditions of foreign correspondents, see Adler (1971, pp. 21-22) and Windahl (1975, pp. 74-76).

[2] "Now and then we hear from our local correspondents, complaining that we favour news from the town where we publish." (A manager.)
Another problem for the outside correspondent may be more severe time constraints in comparison to journalists in the editorial office.

values into the newspaper, which do not exist there otherwise.
The London Times, for example, in addition to maintain a large
group of inhouse specialists, also has specialists outside the
paper with competence in areas like archeology, astronomy, etc.
The Times uses these specialists for guidance as well as for
comment. For instance, when the night editor is suddenly presented with a story which he finds difficult to evaluate, he goes to
the list of experts ("The news editor's Bible"), picking up the
relevant expert for advice.

Freelance writers seldom have problems with publication when called upon by the paper.[1] They have the expertise, and the paper wants
it. In addition, inhouse persons may find it difficult to challenge
their expertise.

The reasoning on freelance writers particularly applies to the
news oriented group, but the practice of bringing in persons from
the outside may sometimes also occur in the politically oriented
group. This is particularly the case for newspapers affiliated with
a political party: in such papers it is not unusual that outsiders
are used during election campaigns in order to "sharpen the arguments".

So far the discussion on external relations has been limited to
the contacts with suppliers of news. We shall now turn to consider a second type of external relations: relations to customers.
Contacts between readers and newsmen are mainly of the negative
type, i.e. people express their dissatisfaction with the paper. In
the case of The Record, for instance, the deletion of a story on
Ingmar Bergman's emigration caused a lot of complaints. Similarly,
a sports reporter told me about the vociferous reaction when some
event has not been covered by the paper: "It happened a few times
that we missed an event, and we hear no end to it."[2]

---

[1] Such stories cannot always be highly topical, since most freelance writers have to mail in their stories. This, in contrast to correspondents, who are able to use telecommunication devices.

[2] For the same reason, Bill, the news editor at The Record, checks the TV-program obtained from the wire services with the evening papers in order to be able to handle eventual changes: "If we had a wrong TV-program, we'd get a lot of phone calls the following morning."

All in all, the feed-back from readers is limited, and discussions in the news-room are often based on guesses and hypotheses. Nevertheless, readers are frequently cited as the group that determines the contents of the paper.[1]

An important channel of information between readers and newspapers is the section, "Letters to the Editor".[2] In The Record this section has a large audience of readers, and the inflow of letters is great, particularly around elections.[3] "Letters to the Editor" is therefore considered an important feature of The Record (cf. Chapter One, Section 1A5: "The Policy Discussion"). The same was also stressed in The London Times, where it was even believed that some people buy the paper only in order to read this section. Moreover, the letters now and then give rise to stories in The Times and other newspapers.[4]

Moving, then, to contacts between the business oriented group and the environment, we may note that this group has a need for contacts with customers (readers and advertisers) as well as with financiers and suppliers. Contacts with the latter two groups are less frequent than those with customers, who interact with the newspaper daily through the circulation department and the advertisement order office, respectively. Orders are made, and complaints are voiced

---

[1] Here it may be relevant to quote Ekeflo (1976) in reviewing Ehnmark's (1976) satirical novel on Swedish evening papers: "When journalists make public statements, they say that they write for their readers. They seldom admit, not even to themselves, that they are actually writing for their bosses [......] News editors claim that the problem is that reporters are no good nowadays. Reporters put the blame on news editors' ignorance. The editor-in-chief blames the management, who blames the employees. 'Most of all, we blame the readers: they want to have the product'." (My translation from Swedish.)

[2] Some writers of letters seem to be more or less permanent contributors. (A portrait of such a person, who even stimulates the debate by writing counter-letters, is given in Lo-Johansson, 1954, "Hos byråkraterna", XI. Another example is Engström, 1966.)

[3] Just before the election 1973, The Record had a pile of 40 letters awaiting publication. The problem was solved by publishing all the letters printed in fine print.

[4] An indication of public interest in the section "Letters to the Editor" of The Times is the four hundred letters which arrive each day. All are answered, but on average only 18 are published. Published letters are never edited, except when the writer agrees to make suggested changes.

when papers are not delivered or there are problems with an ad. An example of such negative feed-back was given earlier in the case entitled "The Neartown Car Dealer" (Chapter One, Section 1A4), in which an advertiser was dissatisfied and lodged a complaint.[1]

With respect to distribution it may be relevant to point to the fact that it is, in Thompson's (1967) terminology, a "boundary spanning" job. We would thus, according to the same author, expect newspapers, assuming rationality, to seek to integrate these activities into the company. Exceptions to this proposition are to be found, however. The Washington Post, for instance, has chosen to sell by bulk to independent newspaper distributors, who run their own organization of newsboys. This arrangement has one obvious disadvantage in that The Post loses control over its distribution. On the other hand, however, it realizes two advantages: First, the arrangement affords a simple, decentralized system for the solicitation of subscriptions. Second, the distribution of the paper will not be disturbed by strikes, since most of those engaged in the distributing organization, young school boys, are not eligible for union membership.

A similar example is the situation among Swedish newspapers jointly distributed by an outside company within a given area. The motive here is the cost savings realized by avoiding the use of parallel distribution forces.[2]

The technically oriented group, finally, has no need for interaction with the environment in relation to the daily production flow. They do need contacts, however, with suppliers of materials. This need has increased during periods of technological change.[3]

---

[1] Advertisers sometimes also communicate their opinions on news coverage. This issue will be further discussed in Chapter Nine.

[2] It should be noted that government subsidies were required in order to bring about this joint distribution. It should also be noted that, quite in accordance with the reasoning of Thompson, minor papers are sometimes discontented with the system: "The distributing company pays more attention to the major papers, since it is easier to distribute the minor paper separately."

[3] Technological change has also generated a need for contacts between labour unions in different newspapers.

The discussion on the external communication links can now be
brought together in Figure 5:4, which indicates the news oriented
group's need for contacts with news sources as well as readers.
A similar need exists on the part of the politically oriented
group, whereas the business oriented group requires contact
with readers, advertisers, financiers as well as suppliers. The
external contact of the technically oriented group is mainly
restricted to relations with suppliers of reproduction material.

```
Readers                    ENVIRONMENT              Readers
News Sources                                        News Sources
(Govern-                                            (Governments, i. a.)
ments, i.a.)

                    NEWS      |    POLITICAL
                    BUSINESS  |    TECHNICAL

Readers
Advertisers
Financiers
Suppliers                                   Suppliers of
                                            Reproduction
                                            Material
```

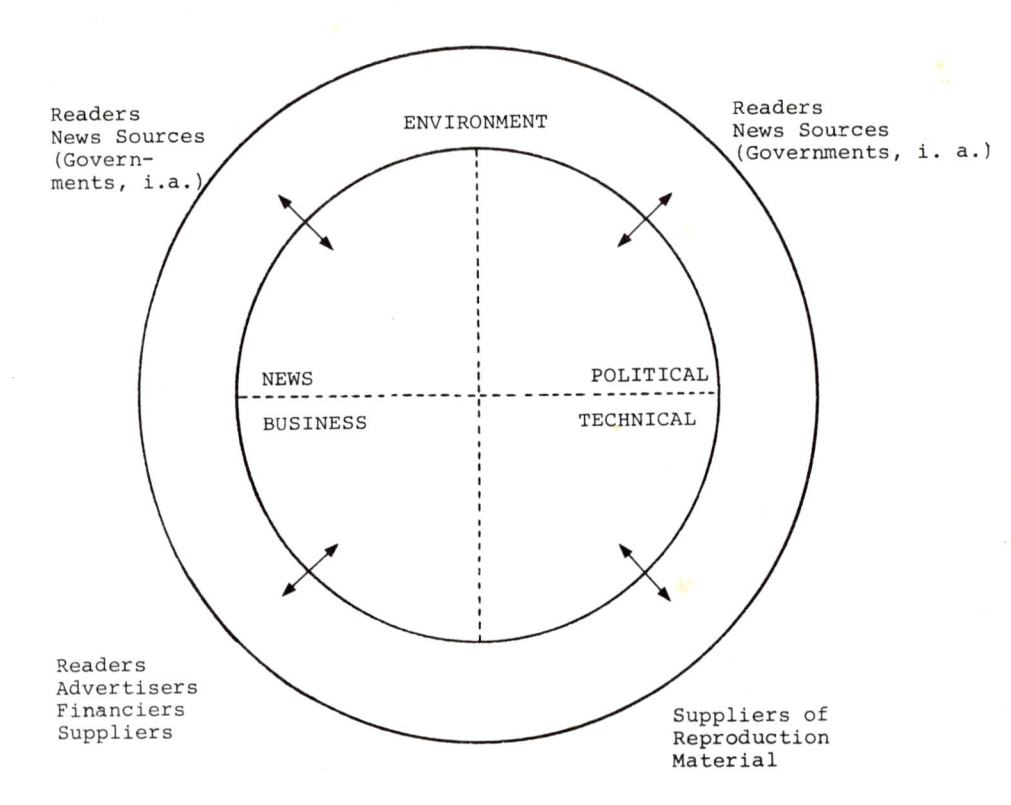

Figure 5:4.   External Communication Links

5.6 Concluding Remarks

This chapter has elaborated on the personnel of a newspaper, which one interviewee termed the most valuable asset of a newspaper: "If the plant disappeared, it would take us only four days to start up again, but if our personnel disappeared, the paper would die."

The chapter has pointed to differentiation of personnel in newspapers as well as different means of integration. It has been shown how specialization, combined with the demands of a nearly 24-hour schedule, creates differentiation, which in turn creates a need for integration. The latter is achieved through hierarchical as well as lateral relations. Moreover, integration to the environment is accomplished through the establishment of external communication links.

In addition to the integrating mechanisms discussed here, different rules and stardard operating procedures which have been developed within newspapers over the years are communicated through the hierarchy. Their importance as integrating devices between the different actors in newspaper organizations will be further investigated in the following four chapters, in which four central issues in newspapers are discussed.

APPENDIX TO CHAPTER FIVE.   ORGANIZATION STRUCTURES IN SIX NEWSPAPERS.

5A1. Introduction

This appendix provides some brief information on formal organization structures (or how top management looks upon their organization). The data refer to four American newspapers (The Boston Globe, The New York Post, The New York Times and The Washington Post) and two British newspapers (The Daily Mirror and The Times). The information was collected in late 1973 and during the Spring of 1976.

5A2. The Boston Globe[1]

The Globe has been a quite unstructured company for some time. But, growth of about 40 per cent in the past 20 years has produced a demand for a more structured organization.[2] Thus, new departments were created in the 1960's, among them a production department in 1967. The resulting organizational design is shown in Figure 5:A1.

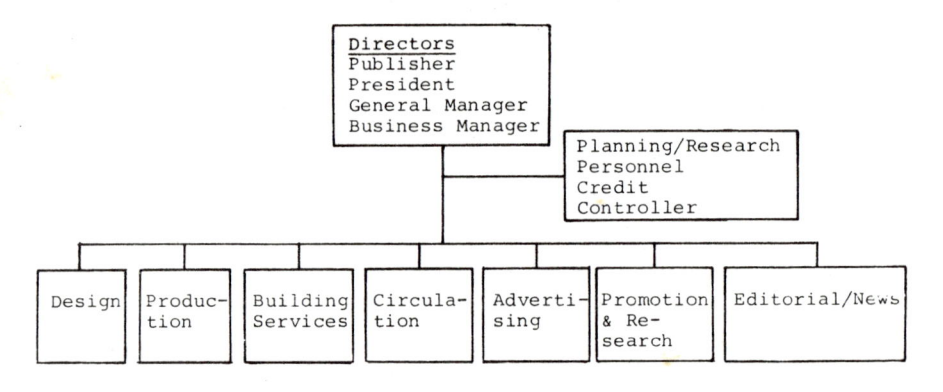

```
                    ┌─────────────────┐
                    │ Directors       │
                    │ Publisher       │
                    │ President       │
                    │ General Manager │
                    │ Business Manager│
                    └────────┬────────┘
                             │       ┌──────────────────┐
                             ├───────│ Planning/Research│
                             │       │ Personnel        │
                             │       │ Credit           │
                             │       │ Controller       │
                             │       └──────────────────┘
    ┌────┬────┬────┬─────────┼──────┬────┬────┐
┌───┴──┐┌┴───┐┌┴─────┐┌──────┴┐┌────┴─┐┌─┴────────┐┌┴──────────┐
│Design││Pro-││Build-││Circu- ││Adver-││Promotion ││Editorial/ │
│      ││duc-││ing   ││lation ││tising││& Re-     ││News       │
│      ││tion││Serv- ││       ││      ││search    ││           │
│      ││    ││ices  ││       ││      ││          ││           │
└──────┘└────┘└──────┘└───────┘└──────┘└──────────┘└───────────┘
```

Figure 5:A1. Organization Chart of The Boston Globe

---

[1] In addition to interviews, information was obtained from the prospectus issued when the parent company went public (Affiliated Publications Inc., 1973).
For a history of The Globe, cf. Lyons (1971).

[2] As the general manager expressed it: "With more than 2000 employees it is hardly possible to hold the payroll in my pocket as my grandfather used to do."

As can be seen from the figure, the organization has functional departments and a fairly large top organization. Among the functional departments the production department plays an important role for decisions on overtime, allocation, deadlines, etc. Moreover, all departments are under top management control. Management thus steps in when different departments get out of line in any respect (overtime, costs, etc.). It should be stressed, however, that the editorial department works relatively independent of top management intervention. Nevertheless, although they are "running their own show", it was conceded that "too liberal editorials would lead to a meeting".

5A3. The New York Post

At the time of the interview, The New York Post was owned by Mrs. Dorothy Schiff, who served as president, publisher and editor-in-chief.[1] Next in command was the general manager, who handled the administration of all departments. His jurisdiction did not, however, include editorial and advertising policies.

The organization of the paper could be summarized as in Figure 5:A2.

```
                    Publisher
                    President
                    Editor-in-chief
                           |
                       General
                       Manager
                           |
  ┌──────────┬──────────┬──────────┬──────────┬──────────┬──────────┬──────────┐
Editorial/  Adverti-  Personnel  Business  Circu-    Produc-   Accounting
News        sing      & Indus-   Office    lation    tion
                      trial
                      Relations
```

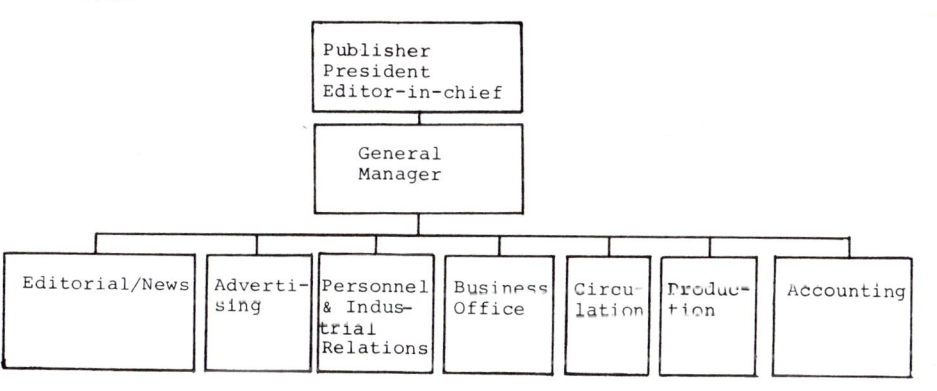

Figure 5:A2. Organization Chart of The New York Post

---

[1] In November 1976 The New York Post was sold to Rupert Murdoch. (Dagens Nyheter, November 21, 1976, p. 12.)

It should be noted that the owner took an active part in the editorial work. Most of the work in the editorial department was done by the executive editor, assisted by a managing editor and a number of assistant editors. The editorial page editor worked independent of the news-room.

The relations between the editorial and administrative staffs of the newspaper were said to be quite good. In the event of problems the executive editor could go to the publisher, but conflicts were reported to have been solved informally in discussions between the general manager and the executive editor.[1]

5A4. The New York Times[2]

The New York Times is published by the New York Times Co., which in addition to The Times, comprises a magazine group (publishing 5 magazines), a broadcasting group (one TV-station and one radio station), a group of 10 newspapers in Florida, and a number of subsidiary activities (news service, indexing, newsprint manufacturers, The International Herald Tribune, etc.). The lion's share of revenues and income still derives from The Times, but the contribution from other businesses is increasing. In 1972 The Times produced 71.1 per cent of all revenues, compared to 80.2 per cent in 1968.[3]

The New York Times Co. was reorganized according to new principles in 1973. The resulting organization structure is shown in Figure 5:A3.

---

[1] "If there are any problems, I tell him: 'Let's have lunch together.'"

[2] For description of the work at The Times, cf. Talese (1970), Adler (1971) and Sigal (1973).

[3] The corresponding figures for income before taxes are 50.6 per cent and 83.6 per cent, respectively. The figures for all computations have been obtained from The New York Times Co. (1973, p. 19).

```
                    ┌─────────────┐
                    │  Publisher  │
                    │  President  │
                    └──────┬──────┘
      ┌──────────┬─────────┼─────────┬──────────────┬──────────────┐
┌───────────┐ ┌─────────┐ ┌────┐ ┌────────┐ ┌────────────┐ ┌──────────────┐
│ Business  │ │Editorial│ │News│ │ Sunday │ │Subsidiaries│ │ Headquarters │
│Operations │ │         │ │    │ │ Edition│ │            │ │              │
│    of     │ │         │ │    │ │        │ │            │ │              │
│ The Times │ │         │ │    │ │        │ │            │ │              │
└───────────┘ └─────────┘ └────┘ └────────┘ └────────────┘ └──────────────┘
```

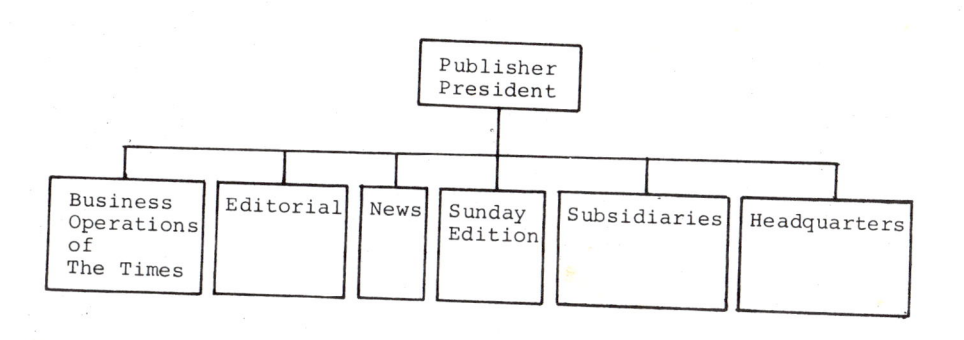

Figure 5:A3. <u>Organization Chart of The New York Times Co.</u>

The top structure of <u>The Times</u> is quite small, and on the whole, the administrative style of the paper seems quite informal. Accordingly, efforts have been made to remove barriers between the different departments.[1] As for owner intervention, the publisher takes part in the editorial work of <u>The Times</u>, but not that of the Florida newspapers.[2]

---

[1] In the words of the interviewee: "I make it clear that they have to work together".

[2] An example of the independence of the Florida group is that they supported Nixon in the 1972 election, whereas <u>The Times</u> supported McGovern. "But, we may interfere, if they go too far to the right."

5A5. The Washington Post[1]

The Washington Post is published by a corporation which also publishes the weekly magazine Newsweek and broadcasts over four TV-stations.[2] The principal owner of the company, Mrs. Katharine Graham, is chairman of the company board and publisher of The Post. The organization of The Post is summarized in Figure 5:A4.

An important feature of The Post organization is that three fairly independent parts function under the publisher, i.e. the news-room, the editorial group and the administrative department In other words: It contains not only a double structure but also a threefold hierarchy.

---

[1] For a description of the work at The Post, cf. Sigal (1973).

[2] A fifth TV-station was under way at the time of the interview.

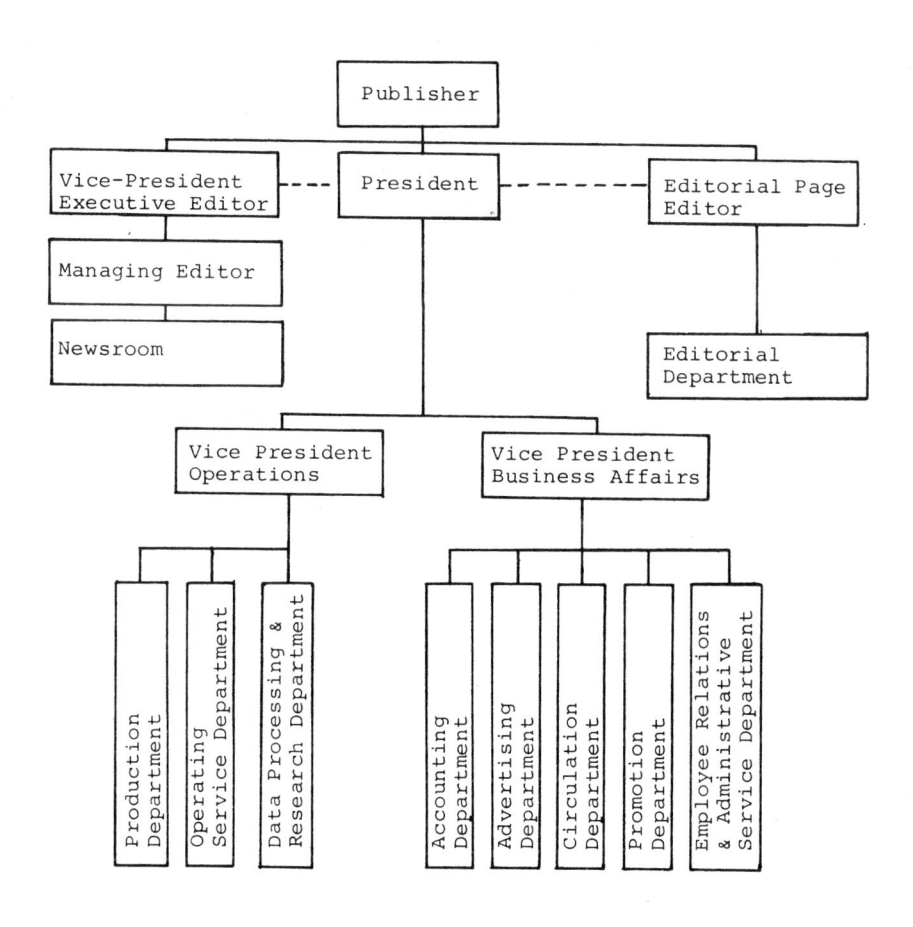

Figure 5:A4.   Organization Chart of The Washington Post.

5A6. The Daily Mirror

The Daily Mirror is a morning paper published by the Mirror Group, a 100-per cent subsidiary of the multinational Reed International Limited. The Mirror Group publishes a number of dailies and weeklies with a combined circulation of 40 million copies. These publications are managed by means of the organization structure shown in Figure 5:A5.

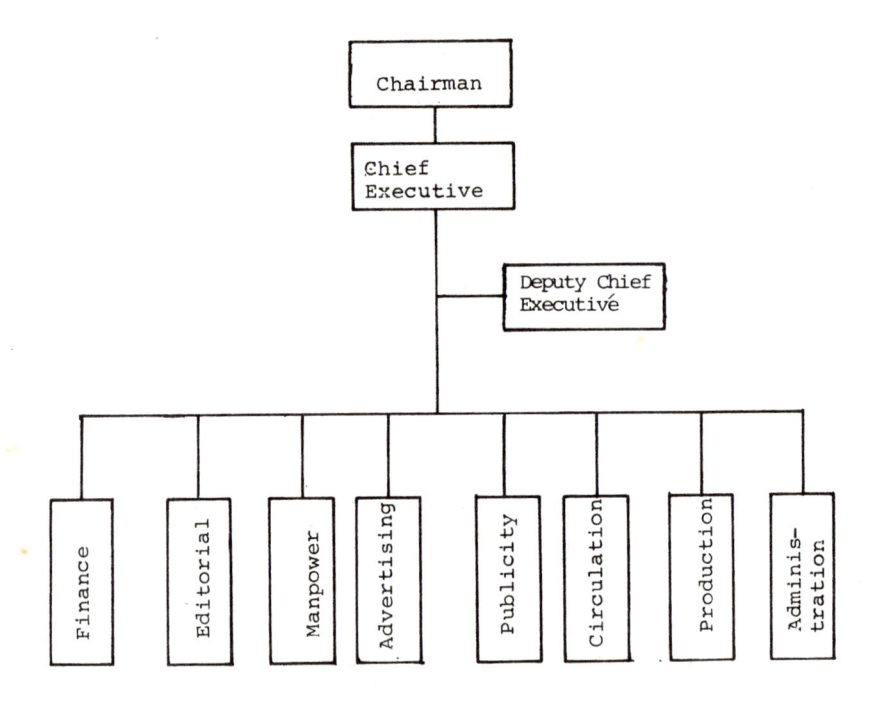

Figure 5:A5 Organization Chart of The Mirror Group

Thus, at the top of the organization is the chairman, who is not involved in business operations. Under him are the chief executive and the deputy chief executive, who work together as an interchangeable pair. Of the two, the deputy chief executive is responsible for planning. His duties include detailed plans for the coming year and an outline for the next three years. They are presented to the parent company in three-day discussions, and once they have been approved, there is no intervention from the top management of Reed International, provided the subsidiaries achieve what they promised, or have reasonable explanations for eventual deviations.

The activities of the different papers within the different departments are integrated to a greater or lesser extent. Finance is totally integrated, while circulation is very nearly totally integrated (to 90 per cent). Production is integrated to 50 per cent, whereas the editorial departments are not at all integrated. As far as production is concerned, processing is integrated, and there are plans to integrate the composing room in the near future.

5A7. The London Times

Times Newspapers Ltd. publishes five publications, of which The Times is published six days a week, The Sunday Times once a week, and three supplements -- devoted to Education, Higher Education and Literary, respectively -- once a week. These activities are coordinated via the organization structure shown in Figure 5:A6.

```
                                ┌─────────────────────┬──────────────────────┐
                                │ Editor, The Times   │ Senior Editors       │
                                │                     │ The Times            │
                ┌───────────────┤                     ├──────────────────────┤
                │ Chairman &    │ Editor, The Sunday  │ Senior Editors       │
                │ editor-in-chief│ Times              │ The Sunday Times     │
                └───────┬───────┤                     ├──────────────────────┤
                        │       │                     │ Editors, the         │
                        │       │                     │ Supplements          │
        ┌───────────────┴────┐  └─────────────────────┴──────────────────────┘
        │ Managing Director &│
        │ Chief Executive    │
        └─────────┬──────────┘
```

General Manager	Advertisement/ Marketing Director	Financial Director	Publishing Director
Ass. General Manager	Display Advert. Manager, The Times	Chief Accountant	Adv. Managers Supplements
Senior Industrial Relations Officer	Display Advert. Controller, The Sunday Times	Company Secretary	Circulation/ Marketing Manager Supplements
Production Manager	Classified Adv. Manager, The Times	Purchasing Controller	Directors of Companies within the publishing division
Administration Manager	Classified Adv. Manager, The Sunday Times		
Senior Projects Coordinator	Circulation Manager The Times		
	Circulation Manager The Sunday Times		
	European Adv. Manager		
	International Adv. Manager		
	Financial Adv. Manager		
	Marketing Manager The Times		
	Marketing Manager The Sunday Times		

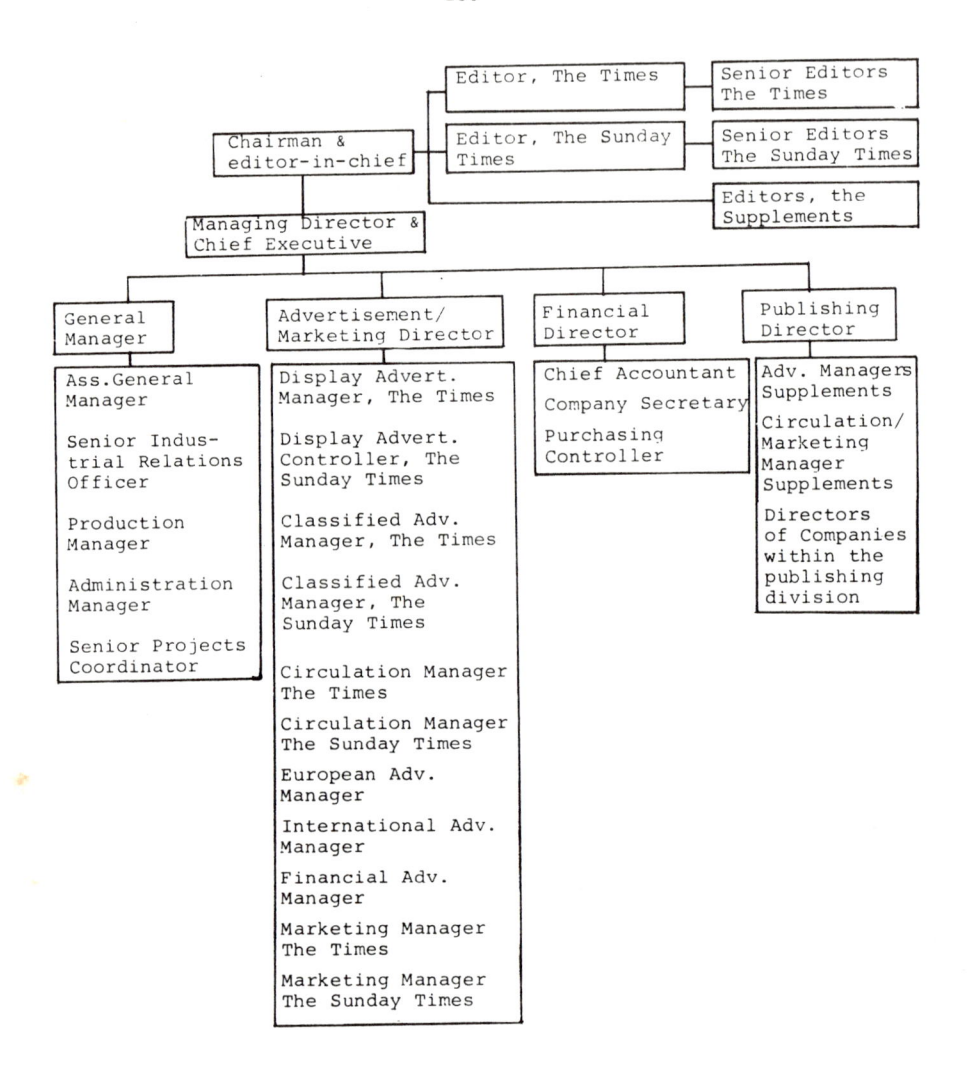

Figure 5:A6. <u>Organization Chart of Times Newspapers Ltd</u>.

Directly under the chairman/editor-in-chief are (1) the managing director and chief executive, (2) the editor of *The Times*, (3) the editor of *The Sunday Times* and (4) editors of the supplements.

The chairman/editor-in-chief is supported by an executive committee, colloquially referred to as "the Executive Board". This committee contains the Managing Director and Chief Executive, the General Manager, the Financial Director, the Advertising Marketing Director, the Publishing Director, the Editors of *The Times* and *The Sunday Times*. Of these, the General Manager is responsible for production, administration, new projects, building management and industrial relations. The Financial Director, as his title indicates, handles finances and is administrative head of the accounting staff. The Advertising Market Director, heading one of the largest clerical departments of the company (about 300-400 people), bears responsibility for the revenue sources of the company, i.e. for circulation as well as advertisement. This responsibility does not extend to the supplements, however, which are under the authority of the publishing director. The latter, a purely commercial branch, also heads the Readers' Offers, marketing wall charts, books, cassettes, etc.

PART III: FOUR ISSUES IN NEWSPAPER COUNTRY

FREEDOM

"Freedom means
you'are free to do
just whatever
pleases you;
- if, of course
that is to say,
what you please
is what you may."

(Hein, 1968, p. 25)

CHAPTER SIX. FLOW

6.1 Introduction

Chapter Three, dealing with newspaper technology, pointed to the dependencies between different steps in the work flow in the sense that one activity has to be completed before another can start. As a result, different work crews in the production flow are quite dependent on the performance of their predecessors, a circumstance which may give rise to conflicts.[1] These conflicts are further enhanced by the perishability of the product: the product has to be produced in time in order to catch the distribution system. If the newspaper misses the extremely important distribution deadline, the economic consequences of non-delivery or extra costs for special delivery systems may be considerable. In the case of papers sold by the copy such an error may even mean that competitors take over some readers who are unable to obtain "their ordinary paper".

In terms of the four groups of newspaper employees identified in the preceding chapter (Section 5.2), the flow issue arises mainly between the technically oriented group and the other three groups. The first mentioned group strives to obtain an even load on the production facilities, whereas the other groups are apt to postpone deliveries to the composing room. Journalists strive for a high degree of topicality and they want as much time as possible to write their stories. A statement by a manager of a technical department illustrates the conflict: "It might sound like a generalization, but it seems to me as though journalists have to wait for inspiration before they are able to write. And, in most cases inspiration turns up late."[2]

---

[1] Note here Ron's remark: "Whenever there are problems, the compositors put the blame on us." (Chapter One, Section 1A4: "The Neartown Car Dealer")

[2] Cf. here the remark of a sports reporter when a team captain pointed out that the reporter had plenty of time to write, since there wouldn't be any paper the following day: "It's much better when you feel stress like Hell. You just write. You don't have as much time to work on formulations."

Particular problems in the flow of editorial copy occur in evening papers, since, they, in contrast to morning papers, produce their late editions just as most news events occur. Moreover, they sell most of their copies by street sales, which means (1) that they have to be on the news-stands when people leave work, and (2) that late stories may stimulate circulation (cf. Nycop, 1971, p.108 f.). As a result, the technical group in such papers is "squeezed" between journalists and the distribution apparatus. An illustration of this "squeeze" is the situation faced by the two American papers interviewed, which publish evening editions (The Boston Globe and The New York Post): both want to include the closing stock prices on Wall Street, but since these prices are not delivered until 3.30 p.m. the papers have certain difficulties with distribution due to heavy traffic.[1]

Turning to the business oriented group we may expect its members to be reluctant to refuse late deliveries of advertising manuscripts, the main reason being of course, the significance of advertising revenue for newspapers. Therefore, late advertisements are even less likely to be refused in minor papers, since these are more dependent on advertising revenues than their major competitors. This circumstance, in turn, often undermines advertisers' respect for the deadlines of minor papers: "They know we have to take it. But, I'm sure they met the deadline of The Chronicle" (Employee in the advertising order office of The Record.)[2] The flow issue thus involves

---

[1] Of course, stock market prices have the advantage in that their arrival can be prescheduled, so that their handling can be planned (cf. the discussion below in Section 6.4: "Forecasting").

[2] The same person, telling me about critical remarks from the composing room on late deliveries, concluded by: "But, where should we turn? We can't start scolding the advertisers!"

conflict between the business group and advertisers.

Figure 6:1 summarizes the conflicts involved in the flow issue.

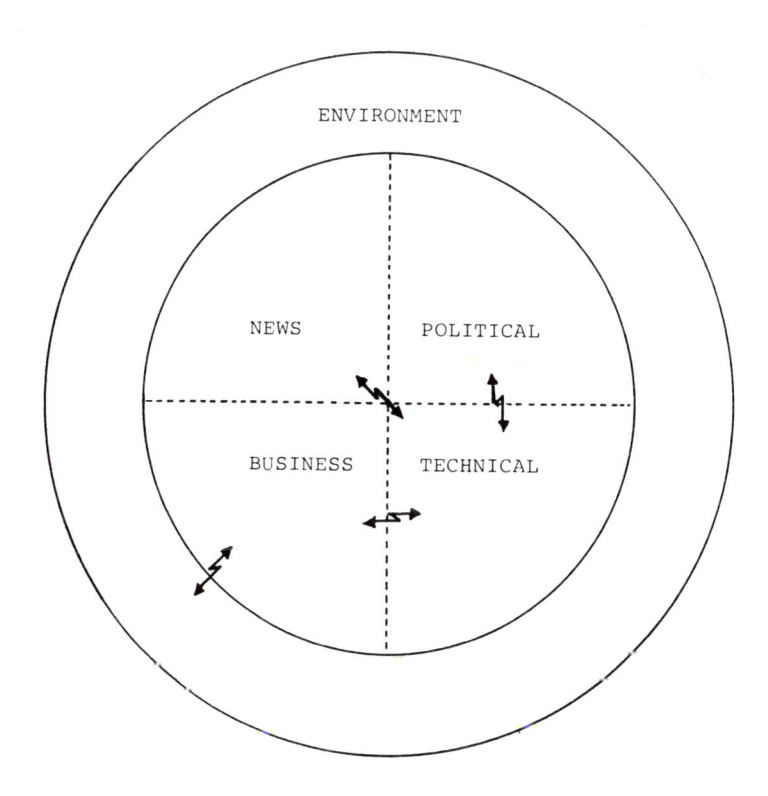

Figure 6:1. <u>Flow Conflicts Between Groups</u>.

A basic factor behind problems of flow is variations in input. The most important variations, of course, are those occurring within the scope of the day, since they tend to lead to "rush hours" as publication time approaches. In large newspapers these problems are complicated by problems of internal communication, which may imply that it takes hours before a cable received at the main editorial office reaches the relevant department (Cf. above Section 5.2: "Differentiation").[1]

In addition to daily variation, variations can be observed over the week, during the year and over the business cycle. As for day-to-day variations, Figure 6:2 shows page variations in a Swedish provinical newspaper.

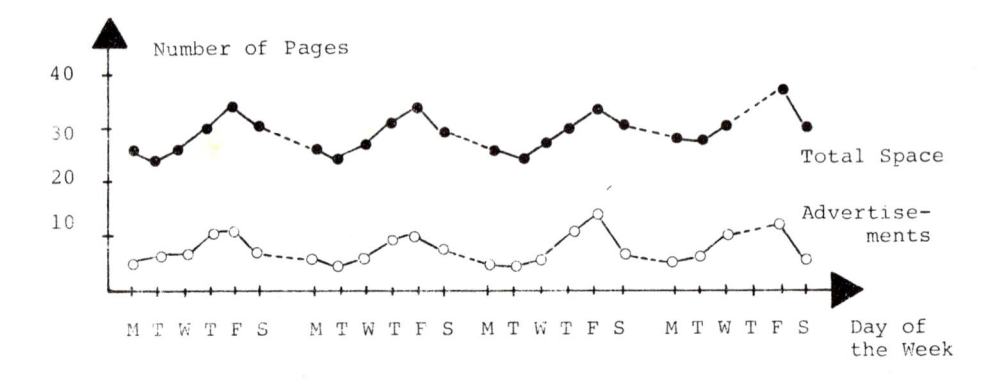

Figure 6:2. Day-to-Day Variation in Number of Pages in a Provincial Swedish Newspaper.
Source: Björk et al. (1974, p. 3, Figure 1)

---

[1] Business news, for instance, is often not communicated until after the Stock Exchange has closed. Further delays, therefore are very significant. It also happens that cables are delayed because they have required special handling: "[during] the evening the plane was shot down [in Congo], the story was delayed a couple of hours [!] since Wallin at the Foreign Desk put the cable aside and waiting for further information, he simply forgot it." (Brandell, 1976, p. 171, my translation from Swedish).

The diagram shows a gradual increase in the volume of the paper during the week, which peaks on Thursday-Friday and then subsides to a lower level. It is also worth noting that advertisements play a significant role with respect to total space. Daily variations are thus largely determined by the inflow of advertisements.[1] The interviews more or less confirmed the tendency shown in Figure 6:2. This was true of both metropolitan and provincial newspapers.[2]

Data from Le Monde show the cyclical variation in inflow of advertisments and news during a year. Figure 6:3 indicates the variations in news space, advertising space and total space. As the figure shows, the decline in inflow is particularly pronounced during the summer months.[3]

With respect to business cycle variations, finally, the variations are accounted for by the inflow of advertisements. An example of such variation is shown in Figure 6:4, which represents the advertising volume in Dagens Nyheter during the period 1965 to 1973, plotted on an index basis.

---

[1] The variations in advertising space have been discussed by Reddaway (1963, p. 202, i.a.).

[2] An interviewee on a metropolitan paper stated that: "Space varies over the week with the Thursday paper as the culmination. On Thursdays the flow of news has gathered speed, and the supermarkets put in their weekly advertisements." Similarly, a colleague of his in a provincial newspaper described the week like this: "Monday is a bad day for advertisements, since the advertising order office hasn't been open. The paper is dominated by the sports department. The flow hasn't really started on Tuesday, which can be characterized as a day of aftercrop. On Wednesday-Thursday the flow reaches a peak, to die down again. Saturday's paper is largely put together by routine. Permanent features dominate."

[3] In Sweden the search for news items is often quite intensive during the summer months: "There is no news in the summer. Local government closes between June 15 and August 15. Therefore, you usually look at the files of last year in order to get ideas." (A Swedish journalist.)
Cf. also Hammenskog (1969): "We haven't had one real story in two weeks, and today is worse than ever. Nothing on the way. Except this one. We can't have just dolls in bathing suits every day." (Op.cit., p. 32, my translation from Swedish.)

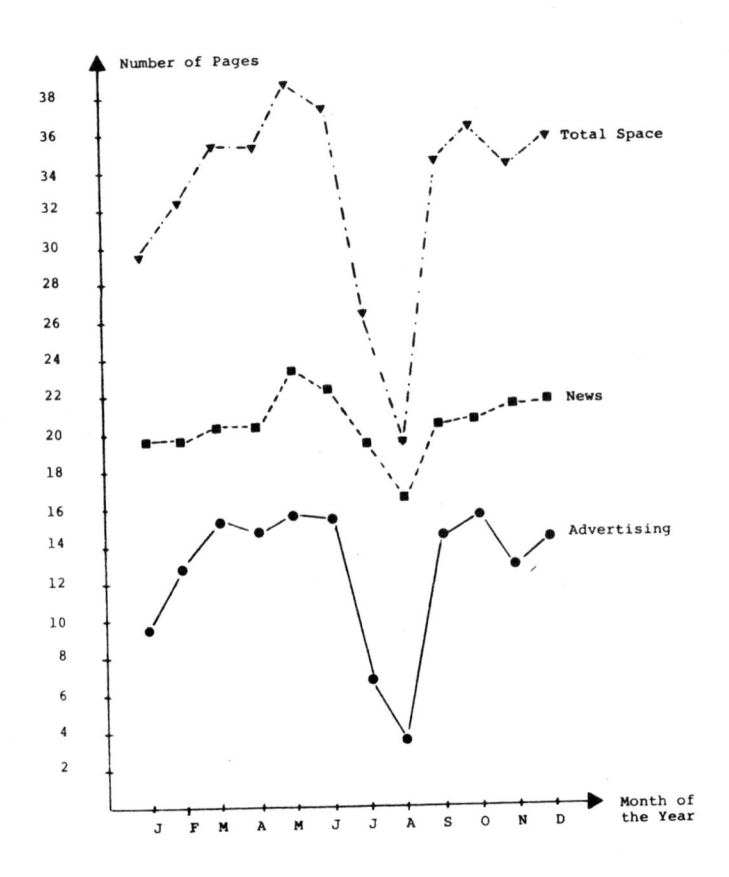

Figure 6:3, Le Monde: Average Number of Pages Allocated to Different Categories per Month, 1974.

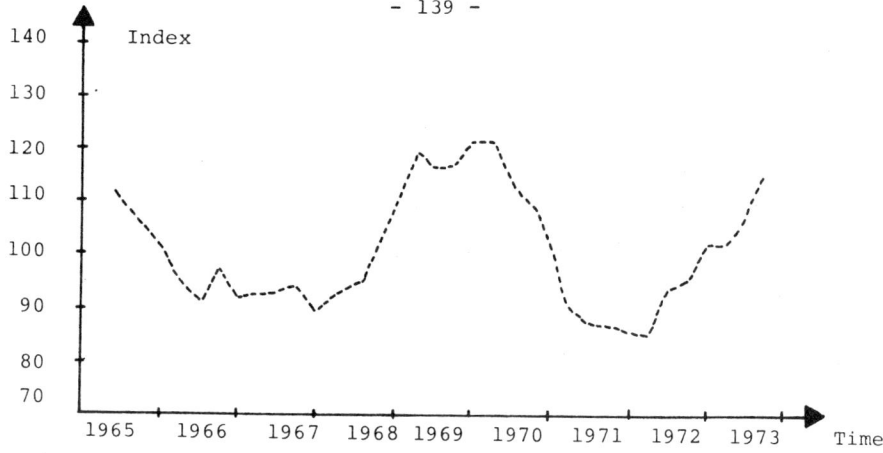

Figure 6:4   The Advertising Volume in Dagens Nyheter 1965-1973 Plotted on an Index Basis

Source: Gustafsson & Olsson (1975)

Given the described variations in input, it is interesting to note Thompson's (1967) observation that "organizations subject to rationality norms seek to seal off their core technologies from environmental influences." (Op.cit., p.20) In four propositions he points to the means used toward this end, viz.

- "Under norms of rationality, organizations seek to buffer environmental influences by surrounding their technical cores with input and output components."

- "Under norms of rationality, organizations seek to smooth out input and output transactions."

- "Under norms of rationality, organizations seek to anticipate and adapt to environmental changes which cannot be buffered or leveled."

- "When buffering, leveling and forecasting do not protect their technical cores from environmental fluctuations, organizations under norms of rationality resort to rationing." (Ibid., pp. 21-23)

These four means -- buffering, leveling, forecasting and rationing -- are also used in newspapers to a greater or lesser extent. How they are used will be discussed in the following four sections.

6.2 Buffering

At first glance it may seem as though the possibilities to employ buffering in newspapers are limited, since a great deal of the inflowing material will be out-of-date the day after to-morrow. This impression is not completely valid, however, as most newspapers have a system of stocking "timeless" material, e.g. human interest stories, features and editorials.[1] Such stocking appears to be particularly common weekends, since fewer employees are working than on weekdays. The latter condition is, of course, an effect of the extension of the five-day week to newspaper employees.[2] It should be noted, however, that news producers also observe weekends: not that much "happens" weekends.[3]

The stocking of material involves not only manuscripts for stories but composed material as well. Again, this is particularly the case on Sundays. There is no day-shift on Sundays at The Record, a circumstance which requires stocking of material as well as intensive work on the part of the night-shift.[4]

Newspapers are also able to stockpile on the output side to some extent, too. In recent years, for example, there has been an increasing tendency for Swedish newspapers to print special sections

---

[1] "Writing an editorial on the French atomic bomb to have ready when it detonates -- I think it will be in a couple of days, but Sven thought it might happen without any notice . . . I therefore roughed out an editorial to have on hand." (Brandell, 1976, p. 28, my translation from Swedish.)

[2] At The Record, only two reporters work on Sundays, whereas seven are working on weekdays. The number of news editors and copy editors is the same on all publication days. (These figures do not include the sports department, which has a very hectic time Sunday nights.)

[3] Of course, newspapers themselves play an important role in determining whether or not there is news.

[4] "The night-shift on Sundays is the worst -- mainly because there is no day shift, and there are a lot of sports events on Sundays." (A compositor). In order to produce material in advance the night shift on Fridays works one hour overtime.

in advance. Thus a differentiation is made between sections which must be printed close to distribution time and others containing relatively "timeless" material which can be printed earlier. This principle has long been used by American newspapers for Sunday editions, which contain a large number of sections.[1]

Stockpiling may also include the stocking of printed material within a twenty-four hour period. The need for such stockpiling has to do with the capacity of the composing and press rooms. In the Paris paper *Le Monde*, for instance, only twenty-one pages can be printed the morning of the day of publication. Therefore, some articles, all supplements and all advertisements must be printed the day before.

In newspapers working under such conditions afternoon news conferences fill a particularly important function in determining the load on composing coming from the different departments.[2] This coordination has become less necessary, however, as the more rapid cold-type composing and offset printing have entered the newspaper world.[3]

Another type of stockpiling is the stocking of previously composed material which can be used over again, e.g. headlines for different types of advertisements, vignettes and templates for ads. This type of stocking seems to be especially advantageous in cold type composing.[4]

---

[1] American newspapers also carry a "larger number of pre-printed advertising inserts, often for specific sections of the newspaper's distribution area" (Winsbury, 1975, p. 18)

[2] In the Stockholm daily *Svenska Dagbladet*, for instance, no more than forty columns can be left at the four o'clock meeting.

[3] Composing of advertisements, for instance, is estimated to require fifty per cent less time for composing using cold type technology. Thus, the new technology relieves some of the conflict between different desks and the composing room. The situation at *The Record* is illustrative in this context: "Earlier we fought for capacity in the composing room. The sports department and the general department had their battles. People came up with stories asking compositors to help them."

[4] As a matter of fact, clippings from earlier issues of the paper can be used.

6.3 Leveling

The leveling strategy in newspapers is manifested in the use of deadlines for the submission of editorial copy and advertisements. As far as manuscripts are concerned, deadlines may limit the usual postponement of writing, a behaviour quite well illustrated by Phil (cf. Chapter One, Section 1A2), who wanted to gather more information before writing his story on the bankrupt company until he finally was forced to produce the story in haste.[1] Similarly, deadlines for ads serve to control the behaviour of advertisers to the advantage of the newspaper.

This leveling strategy often implies that deadlines are differentiated so that certain types of material are scheduled to arrive earlier than other types of material. For example: The Boston Globe requires the delivery of ads (except classified) at noon-time, whereas classified ads are due at 4 p.m. In addition The Globe offers different kinds of discounts to encourage earlier deliveries.

It is not only for advertising material that deadlines are differentiated, however. A similar technique is used for editorial copy in that different pages are "closed" at different times. In this way the flow of manuscripts may be smoothed out, avoiding the kind of situation wherein copy "flows to the composing room in a sporadic manner during most of the period before the final news deadline [and then] as the deadline approaches, the dam breaks and a flood of copy reaches the copy-cutter's desk in the composing room." (ANPA, 1970, p.7).

The procedure for handling manuscripts used in a Swedish provincial newspaper offers an illustration. Here the material is split into five groups, the material for the first group being

---

[1] Recall Phil's remark: "The advantage of postponing writing a story is that you then have to write it." In Phil's case external commitments also enforced a deadline.
It also happens that a reporter may negotiate for more time: "Is it possible to postpone my story a day? I've got some things I have to check." -- If it has been a "good newsday", such extra time may be granted.

delivered before the day of printing, and the last between 9 and 12 p.m. on the day of printing. In this way, the maximum number of pages to be made up should follow the diagram shown in Figure 6:5. Early deliveries contain feature material, letters to the editor, cartoons, radio programs, serial stories, etc. none of which have extreme topicality (cf. also Adler, 1971, p. 53).[1]

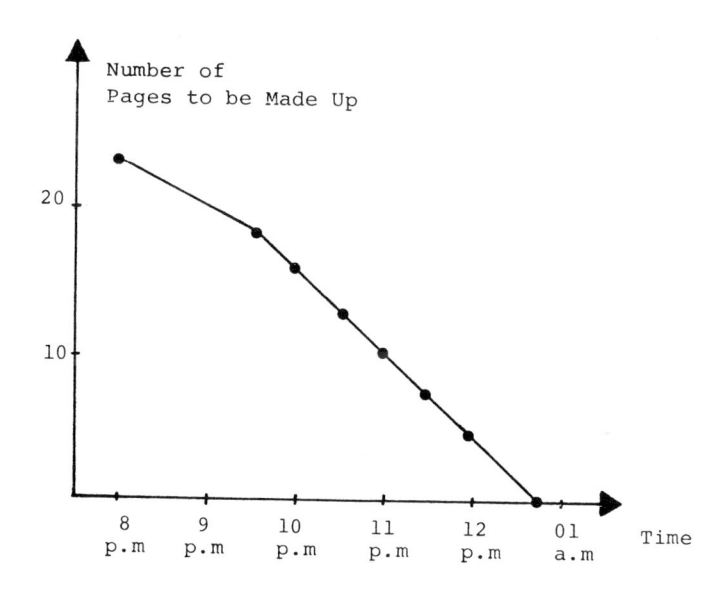

Figure 6:5. <u>Number of Pages to Be Made Up at Given Points in Time in a Swedish Provincial Newspaper</u>

Figure 6:6 illustrates the flow into and out of the composing room on a specific day at <u>The Record</u>.[2] The flow into the composing room is represented by the per cent of pages which are expected to be delivered from the news-room to the composing room according to the established deadlines.[3] The flow out of the composing room is represented by the per cent of pages delivered from the composing room to engraving at a given point in time.

---

[1] It is also interesting to note that international correspondents can exploit the difference in time zones (Adler, 1971, pp. 21-22).

[2] The number of pages in the issue considered were 16, i.e. a small paper. The curves are very similar for issues of all sizes, however.

[3] This is an approximation of actual deliveries, since deadlines are sometimes violated.

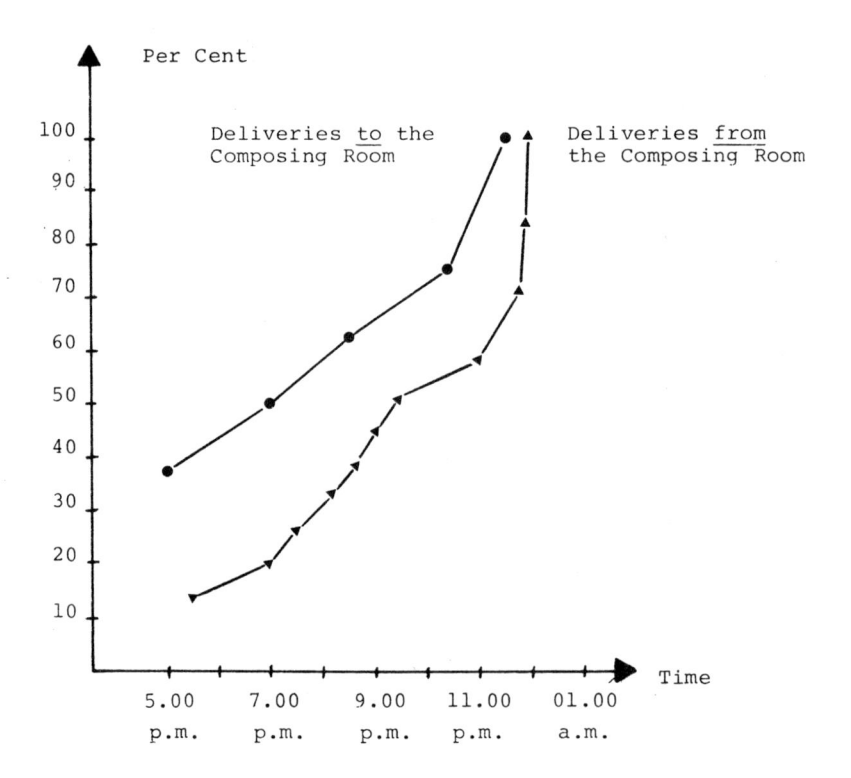

```
                    Per Cent
100                                          Deliveries from
        Deliveries to the                    the Composing Room
 90     Composing Room
 80
 70
 60
 50
 40
 30
 20
 10
        5.00    7.00    9.00    11.00   01.00              Time
        p.m.    p.m.    p.m.    p.m.    a.m.
```

Figure 6:6. Flow Into and Out of the Composing Room one Day at The Record

Both curves climb relatively smoothly and similarly until 11 o'clock, at which time both curves shoot up sharply. This increase corresponds to the work on "last minute stories". At The Record the material for these pages is supposed to be delivered to the composing room 30 minutes before mid-night. In this way late news can be included on the front and last pages, and late sports events can be covered by the sports journalists. It should also be noted that a certain basic inflow to the composing room has already taken place before the night shift starts work at 4.30 p.m.[1]

---

[1] At The Record deadlines are set by the managing editor, who draws up a page-key, showing the combination of pages, the planned contents on each page and the delivery time. The combination of pages is needed since the pages are printed in pairs.

In order to facilitate leveling, some papers have appointed a technical editor.[1] In terms of Likert's (1961) terminology the technical editor serves as a "linking pin" between the news oriented and technically oriented groups. He serves as "gatekeeper" for the latter group as well as a "manuscript-whip", urging the different desks to make their deadlines.

The leveling strategy is often combined with different systems for control. At <u>The Record</u>, for instance, daily reports on delivery times to the engraving room are filed, but they are only consulted in cases of trouble.[2]

More refined systems of control are likely to appear if and when computer technology, with video screens operated by journalists, is introduced into the news-room. Such technology makes it possible to plug in different rules for manuscript deliveries into the computer. This, in turn, permits continuous checks as to whether different desks keep their schedule, and the issue of warning messages when they are late. In addition, it will be possible to keep a continuous log showing deliveries of manuscripts into the system.[3]

---

[1] <u>The Record</u> used to have a technical editor. When he left <u>The Record</u> for another job, no successor was appointed. His tasks are now performed jointly by the night editor and the supervisor in the composing room. ("This works fine. It's an advantage being few. You have to work together.").

[2] Cf. here also the comment by Leon V. Sigal: "The Times tries to bring about compliance with its copy deadlines by a daily report on copy flow, noting the rates and calling attention to late copy and attendant costs."(Private communication to the author.)
An interesting question in relation to deadlines posed in a study by Arvedson (1974) is to what extent deadlines influence behaviour. The main conclusion of this experimental study, however, was as vague as, "Deadlines make a difference". (<u>op</u>. <u>cit</u>., p. 86)

[3] This will make it very easy to determine why the paper was late. At present, this is difficult due to the change of shifts. The new systems have, according to one informant brought stricter application of deadlines: "Earlier, deadlines were only paper tigers. People tended to deliver too much editorial copy in a lump at the final deadline for copy."

In addition to facilitating control of deadlines, computer technology will also make it possible to save time in the production process. Similarly, the use of electronic transferral for printing in remote plants will make it possible to delay deadlines, since transportation time can be saved.[1] In this way differentiation in printing time between different editions is cut down, which is an advantage, since the printing of successive editions implies problems of redesigning the paper.[2] A particular problem in this context is that some stories in the first edition must go to make room for late stories such as theatre and cinema reviews (Adler, 1971, p.196).[3] A rule facilitating the redesign of the paper is "the rule of the inversed pyramid", which implies that the contents of the article are presented in descending order of importance (cf. e.g. Sigal, 1973, p. 73). In this way, late changes can be accomplished by cutting articles printed in earlier editions.[4]

---

[1] Such arrangements are, for instance, used by the two Stockholm evening papers Aftonbladet and Expressen. Plans to print The Washington Post in satellite plants in Virginia and Maryland were also mentioned in interviews. (Cf. also Bagdikian, 1971, p. 246.)
Besides certain advantages, there are also, as will be shown in the following chapter, quite a few problems involved in the use of computer technology.

[2] There is, of course, the advantage that the product can be gradually improved from edition to edition. Misprints and bad formulations can be corrected.

[3] At The New York Times, for instance, the critics' reviews are usually cleared by the copy desk at 11.30 p.m. (Adler, 1971, p.208.)
The sports department works under similar conditions, since many sports events continue late into the night. The problem is solved through successive phone calls from the field to the paper, where sports journalists work with the material, editing, putting in headlines, etc. As the games are over, the results are added to the stories, each edition successively more complete. The most accurate stories are included in the so-called "cigarr-edition", i.e. the last edition, which is distributed to the tobacconist's shops.

[4] Note that "the rule of the inversed pyramid" cannot be used for editorials. The buffer here is constituted by quotations from editorials in other newspapers. In addition, editorials can be composed in different styles, requiring different amounts of space.

6.4 Forecasting

The strategy for handling environmental changes which cannot be buffered or leveled mentioned by Thompson, is to try to predict them and to plan according to those predictions. This strategy is used by newspapers for advertisements as well as news. The forecasting of advertising input is often considered particularly important since the inflow of advertisements fluctuates over the business cycle (cf. above, Section 6.1).[1] Such forecasting is of special importance for subscribed daily newspapers, since they obtain the major part of their revenue from advertisements.

Some forecasting can even be done with respect to news.[2] This has been stressed by Tuchman (1973), who shows how newspapers work by routinizing the unexpected through the typification of news.[3] The basic dichotomy in this typification is that between (1) soft (feature and human interest) stories, and (2) hard stories. These two types of stories differ in their urgency with respect to dissemination, the publication of the former type being possible to delay (cf. Section 6.2 "Buffering"), whereas hard news is mere information if it grows old (op.cit., p. 118). But, there are differences, too, with respect to the possibilities to schedule and predict various items of hard news. Tuchman therefore makes a distinction between three basic types of hard news: (1) continuing news, (2) spot news and (3) developing news. Of these, _continuing news_ is pre-scheduled, which circumstance facilitates prediction. Coverage can therefore be planned in advance.[4]

---

[1] According to one interviewee, forecasts of advertisement inflow are often very accurate.

[2] Nycop (1970) has pointed to an increase in the planning of newspaper production. He goes so far as to state that newspapers today are "to a large extent made ready already the day before publication." (Op.cit., p. 125, my translation from Swedish.)

[3] The study involved participant observation in a newspaper and a television station.

[4] As shown by Tuchman (1973, pp. 125-129), predictions may turn out wrong (the British election in 1970 and Lyndon Johnson's announcement that he would not run are given as examples) and this turns the continuing story into "what-a-story!" Coverage produced earlier has to be removed to make space for the unexpected news.

One example is a party congress or convention: everybody knows in advance that it will take place, and information is also delivered prior to the congress. Similarly, a British editor remarked: "A lot of what's going to happen we know about. For instance, we know that the United States will elect a new President, but not whether Ford will win. Taking another example, we know that the new Prime Minister will lead the front page next Tuesday."[1] Journalists specializing in a certain field are also able, through their expertise and "inside information" from different informants, to predict what is going to happen in their field: "Much of newspaper work consists of being two or three days ahead of the official news." (McDonald, 1975, quoted in Alsterdal, 1976).

More difficult to predict is spot news, e.g. a fire, violent crime or an accident. Such news is characterized as "the specifically unforeseen event-as-news" (Tuchman, 1973, p. 120). The techniques mentioned by Tuchman to handle such news involves keeping the city desk staffed around the clock. The people in this "spot news reserve" are not completely idle, however: they are kept busy processing non-urgent information.[2]

Similar problems of forecasting arise with respect to developing news, cases where "the story develops", i.e. further information on the event is obtained over time. This type of news presents a particular problem for the newspaper, since a story might require several redesigns of the front page as well as the following pages.[3]

---

[1] This statement was made in early April 1976, at a time when the election concerning a successor of Mr. Wilson as Prime Minister was going on.

[2] Tuchman (1973, p. 120) writes: "Usually, they covered minor stories by telephone, rewrote copy phoned to them by correspondents scattered in small towns around the state, and wrote obituaries."

[3] An example of this type of news given by Tuchman is the assassination of Martin Luther King (op.cit., p. 122).
Cf. here also Adler (1971) who discusses the problem of whether to "rush into print with an indecisive fragment, or wait for confirmation" (op.cit., p. 180). Both spot news and developing news requires consulting between news editors, technical people and dispatch personnel. (Cf. here Chapter One, Section 1A1: "Suddenly the Ground Started to Shake ....", another example of developing news.)

In certain cases the forecasting of input can be handled by adapting manning to the input fluctuations. Such an arrangement can be observed in French newspapers, where the technical staff is not employed by the newspaper, but by the graphical union. Thus, every day the papers order the number of persons needed for the printing of that day's newspaper.[1] But, in newspapers employing their compositors and printers, too, the technical corps can be adapted to variations. This can be done by scheduling working hours so that more employees are working during the most hectic phase of production.

Regarding the forecasting of demand for the output, subscribed newspapers are at a great advantage, since fluctuations in demand are relatively small. Newspapers selling by the single copy are in quite another situation. They face a problem, which in operations research literature has become classic under the name "the newsboy problem" (cf. Hanssmann, 1961, p. 79, *i.a.*). This problem addresses the question of determining the optimal number of copies to be distributed to different retailers in order to minimize the sum of costs for shortage and overage.[2]

6.5 Rationing

The fourth and final strategy mentioned by Thompson (1967) is rationing, a strategy to be applied when all other strategies fail. In the earlier three sections we have seen that newspapers use the strategies buffering, leveling and forecasting in combination. These three strategies are also combined with rationing to some extent.

---

[1] The technical personnel were invited to participate in the ownership arrangements in *Le Monde*, but they declined.

[2] An example of such a system is one developed by Brandes (1971) in response to a situation in 1970, when "about 23 per cent of total supply for casual sales was unsold and returned as spoilage." (*Op.cit.*, p. 14; the value of this quantity was estimated to about 30 million Sw. Crs.)

Rationing is applied to limit the amount of editorial copy included in any given issue. There are certain technical restrictions as well as some rules in the newspaper with respect to the number of pages to be printed.[1] Now and then, these require rationing by either cutting stories, postponing their publication or refusing them.[2] In other words: newspapers can be selective among incoming stories when they have a large enough inflow. An extreme example of institutionalized surplus is the case of Le Monde: This paper handles its variations in inflow by having its correspondents each file one story a day. This results in an inflow of about three times more stories than can be printed.[3]

A more common procedure in newspapers is to ration news agency material, which can be used as "filling" on "weak news days" or if any of the planned stories fail.[4] Rationing among wire stories has one obvious advantage in that since nobody in the paper has written them, nobody takes it to the heart if they are deleted.

One characteristic of rationing is that priority is given to certain items.[5] In newspapers the general rule is that advertisements have top priority unless technical constraints make their publication impossible. Another priority rule is that news occuring close to the town of publication is more likely to be published than news occurring far away.

---

[1] These rules will be further discussed in Chapter Eight.

[2] This is related to the discussion of the publication issue presented in Chapter Nine.

[3] This system is quite in contrast to that in Swedish newspapers, whose foreign correspondents have daily telephone conferences with the news-room. During these, correspondents offer certain stories or are given assignments from the news-room. These telephone conversations result in decisions as to what the correspondent should work on. In this way, he is relatively certain that his stories will be published.

[4] A weak newsday locally is likely to bring a large share of the wire service stories into the paper. Cf. Bill's remark: "It's a weak newsday to-day. We will feature the train accident in Holland on the front page."
Cf. also Hanson(1968, p. 19): "The wire service material is used for two purposes, one journalistic and one technical. Technical use implies that the material is used to fill the empty space which the papers happen to have between ads and local stories." (My translation from Swedish.)

[5] Thompson (1967) gives an example: "The post office may assign priority to first class mail, attending to lesser classes only when the priority task is completed." (Op. cit., p. 23).

Rationing of physical output occurs as a consequence of unexpected variations in demand or production delays. As has been mentioned above, forecasting is often successfully used to take care of variations in demand, but in cases when the forecasts fail, priority has to be given to certain customers. For subscribed papers the priority is clear: the permanent customers, subscribers, come first. As far as the newsstands are concerned, sales potential as well as customer relations have to be considered, something which is also true in cases of production delays. In the latter case the distance between the newspaper and the customers also plays an important role: if the paper "misses" its distribution system, it becomes technically difficult or impossible to reach customers located too far away from the site of production.[1]

6.6 Human Relations Aspects on the Flow Issue

The previous four sections have elaborated on different means used in newspaper organizations to handle variations in the volume of input as well as output demand. The four strategies described make it possible for the organization to achieve the paramount task for a newspaper: to appear at the time expected by readers. The regular achievement of this task seems to have certain effects on the people working in a newspaper, however, since the variations in flow cannot be completely smoothed out. Employees in newspapers must be prepared for variations in their work load. It thus happens that compositors find their work dull at times when the flow of material is small. But they also have to be prepared for sudden changes in tempo. This implies, in the words of a compositor, "a difference between typographers on newspapers and other typographers. Working on a newspaper, you have to be able to shift gears, to work at low speed and then suddenly work very hard. Other typographers work at a more even pace."[2]

---

[1] An example is the case of _Dagens Nyheter_, where in the Spring of 1976 compositors laid down their work a couple of hours in protest of a new agreement on manning. As a result, _Dagens Nyheter_ did not appear in many places outside Stockholm, and it became very thin in the Stockholm area.

[2] "On the other hand", another interviewee told me, "there is a difference in precision between typographical work in newspapers and other typographical work. In a newspaper you can be more careless. -- You do things which you were taught not to do. We call such things 'evening paper items'."

Similar opinions were expressed by a British newspaper executive, who pointed to the possibilities of expanding capacity "beyond all scientific boundaries" due to employees identification with and involvement in the product.[1] He particularly pointed to the events when a story breaks: "It's like an injection of adrenalin in the paper. And, sometimes the increase in production is as high as thirty-five per cent."

The variation in work load on the different employees doubtless has certain human relations aspects. The above-mentioned remarks by the compositor thus produced the question: "Can you work like that? Don't you get an ulcer?" -- "Yes, I've had one, and I don't want to have it again. Others have had the same experience," was his answer.

Time pressure is not a problem limited to the people in the technical departments, however; it is also a problem for the people in the news-room.[2] An informant thus described the nature of the job in this way: "You work extremely intensely during a period of time, just to deliver the story and then catch your breath."

The pressure of time is also evidenced in behaviour. Chris, for instance, pointed to the fact the people rush about quite a lot in the news-room: "Have you noticed how people in the news-room get a 'go' in their pace? It's impossible to walk at a normal pace in an editorial office." But, the time pressure also creates certain frustrations, as is the case with Phil, who now and then experiences frustration after having written an article, because of the uncertainty of the outcome. -- "Sometimes after writing a story I have trouble sleeping, and I have to wait for the paper to arrive."

---

[1] In addition to identification with the product, the short production cycle was also mentioned as important. This was particularly stressed by an executive with previous experience in a manufacturing industry with a long production cycle, eighteen months, a figure which should be compared to six hours for the newspaper where he is working at present: "The product comes out fast. This means that everybody knows what is to be achieved, and when."

[2] Some journalists point to the fact that they have got used to working under time pressure. A film critic, for instance, thus answered a question on book writing in the following way: "No, I'm too impatient. I'm a journalist, not an author. Put the manuscript pages into the typewriter, out into the composing room, into the paper of the following day, and a fresh start the next day." (På Stan, October 25-30, 1975, p. 5.)

Similarly, Chris mentions problems relaxing after leaving the paper some time after midnight: "You are absorbed by your job. And, afterwards you have to cool down with a couple of beers." He also points to his bad habit of thinking about formulations as he tries to sleep: "This is no easy job. As a matter of fact it's a job for fools. It happens now and then that you start thinking, what the Hell did I write?"[1]

Of course, variations in inflow and time pressure are not the only factors contributing to psychological and human relations problems in newspapers. Another factor seems to be the individualistic working conditions of most journalists. This, in turn, may lead to the effects described by Argyris (1974) who, in an action-research project in an American newspaper, characterized this type of "living system" as "competitive and low in trust, and operating with win-lose dynamics". (op.cit., p. 32).[2]

The tough work environment in the news-room was particularly stressed by two interviewees who had worked for some time on local newspapers, but decided to quit. One said: "I'd had enough. It's an industry full of problems. It's not possible to be social." And, the other, being somewhat more expressive: "The conflicts frightened me; there were continuous and potential conflicts among the staff in the news-room. People had very decided opinions on competence, what their colleagues could do or couldn't do. Positive feedback was very rare. If something turned out good, they got jealous, instead. So, I gave up my plans to become a journalist because it seemed really miserable." The same interviewee was also influenced by the stories of his colleagues concerning

---

[1] Of course, not everyone develop the habit of thinking back on the work he has done. A female colleague of Chris expressed her surprise that anybody could be thinking about a formulation after the editing was finished: "I just forget about it." She also declared: "I am not the type of person who sits and wishes for a big story breaking just as I sit visiting one of my friends." Another of Chris' colleagues responded to this, saying: "Well, you hardly even manage to mobilize the interest when you're at work." (These two remarks should be compared to news editors' assurance: "When something important happens, everybody wants to join. It's easy to summons them to the job." Or the statement by a Times journalists: "You will have gathered that journalists are in the main dedicated people who love their newspapers as a sailor loves his ship. He identifies with it and in time it becomes a way of life.")

[2] In relation to this statement the results of an experiment with 25 Swedish journalists are quite illustrative. The journalists participated in a psychological test (a T.A.T. test), and their interpretations of the pictures were analyzed as if they came from one individual. The results indicate among other things, that the "group-individual" is (1) inhibited with respect to aggressions, (2) mistrusting of authorities, and (3) touchy about criticism and not very self-confident. (Billström, 1974, p. 21).

the touchy climate in national papers, where journalists found
the situation nearly unbearable because they were frozen out,
their stories were not published or ended up "buried" in the paper. Other indications of tough working conditions were the frequency of different stress symptoms as well as consumption of alcoholic beverages, even in the news-room: "Gastric ulcer was
very frequent." -- "There was quite a bit of drinking at parties,
particularly on Fridays, paydays. But, it happened now and then
they they pulled out 'the second-drawer-from-the-bottom' and took
a nip in the news-room."[1]

Such conditions seem to be a result of frustration and lost
illusions: "Once, I was committed. But, now, after more than
ten years in the trade, the commitment is gone. It's just a job,
a way to earn a living. I think what killed my commitments was a
lack of stimulation."[2]

6.7 Concluding Remarks

In short, then, the flow issue concerns how to handle variations
in input volume and to manage the fuzzy technology of journalism
in order to ensure that the newspaper appears at certain predetermined points of time. The present chapter has shown that
newspapers use a number of techniques in order to achieve this
task. It has also been demonstrated that these techniques can be
characterized in terms of the four strategies mentioned by Thompson
(1967): buffering, leveling, forecasting and rationing.

---

[1] It might be argued that these are stories from persons who did'nt make it in
the newspaper world, but similar accounts have been given by active journalists
as well. An editorial writer thus described some of his colleagues: "He arrives
in the morning, goes directly to the restaurant, where he eats lunch with beer
and snaps. About two o'clock he goes down with a group of people to 'drink beer'
as they say. Usually they end up sharing some bottles of wine. It's really fantastic. A woman colleague of mine says she can't write without being a little
tight. -- They offer me drinks once in a while, but I manage to say no because
I have to drive my car home."

[2] Similarly, a sports reporter remarked: "It's hard to be innovative after ten years
on the job." And, an editorial writer pointed to the risk that editorial writers
become worn out from the point of view of the readers. Many editorial writers
end up in a dead-end, writing editorials on routine, since they do not want to
go back to the less well paid reporting jobs.
Finally, a remark from an evening paper journalist: "A colleague of mine said
to me that he feels like a used car-dealer, and he wouldn't buy a car from himself!"

Although, all four of these strategies are employed, they are used at different steps in the production process, a circumstance summarized in Figure 6:7.

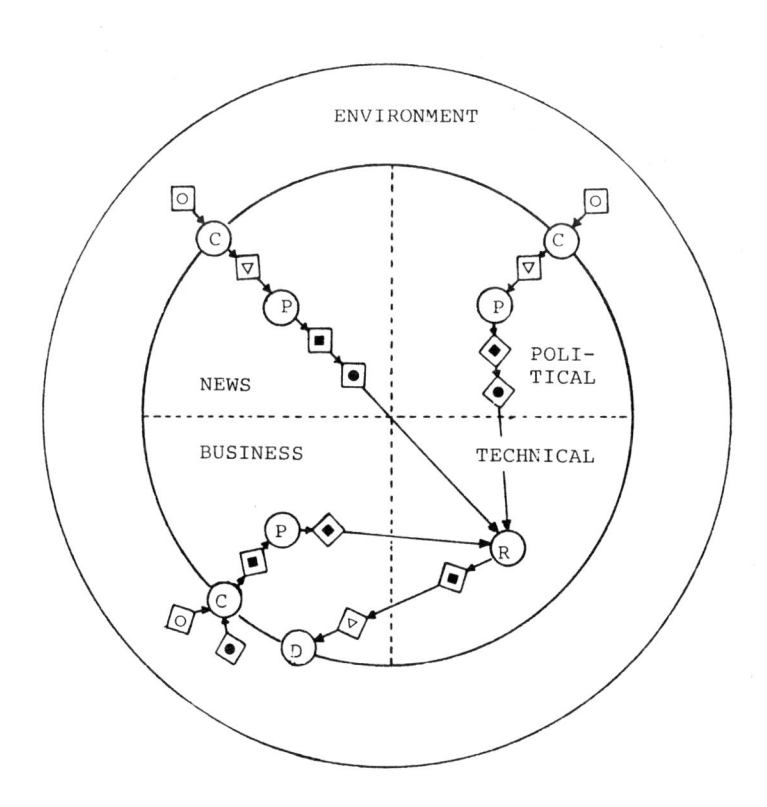

Figure 6:7. A Summary of the Strategies Used in Newspapers to Handle Variations.

    Key: C = Collection Phase
                P = Processing Phase
                R = Reproduction Phase
                D = Distribution Phase
                ■ = Buffering
                ● = Leveling
                ○ = Forecasting
                ▽ = Rationing

Starting with the link between advertisers and the advertising department, newspapers apply forecasting and leveling (deadlines), whereas the relations between "news producers" and the news-room are handled by forecasting and rationing. Inside the house the flow of advertisements and stories from the advertising department and the news-room to the composing room is managed by the use of stocks and leveling (deadlines). Stocks are also used between the composing room and the press room as well as between the press room and the dispatch room. In cases of short supply the dispatch room has to employ rationing among different groups of readers.

It should perhaps be stressed that there are no clear borders between the different strategies. They are used in combination, and may even be said to be used in interaction. Thus, buffering is facilitated through leveling as well as through forecasting. The stockpiling of editorial copy as well as advertisements is thus made possible by giving journalists and advertisers deadlines. Similarly, forecasting of certain events may make it possible to pre-produce material, which can be of use later on.[1]

Finally, as the chapter made clear, all variations cannot be eliminated from the processes involved in newspaper production. Therefore, time pressures give rise to psychological and human relations problems. These seem at least to some extent to be an effect of deadlines and routinization as well as the individualistic working conditions prevailing in the news-room.

---

[1] An extreme example of this sort is the advance writing of obituaries: all important men and women will die sooner or later, and the basic material can be prepared in advance. Cf. here Brandell (1976, p. 175), who in 1962 wrote in a diary:"[Wrote] an obituary on Brezjnev, who no doubt will live many more years." (My translation from Swedish). The described procedure involves some risks however: it once happened that a Swedish provincial newspaper accidentally published pre-prepared material on the life of Winston Churchill several years before he actually died!

Less extreme examples of forecasting are different stories initiated by the newspaper, particularly feature stories (cf. the discussion on more active journalism in Chapter Three (Section 3.4: "The Collection Phase"). Although, this type of journalism has the advantage that stories can be pre-scheduled, they have a drawback in that the required planning is time-consuming.

CHAPTER SEVEN. TECHNOLOGY.

7.1 Introduction

Newspapers have long been produced according to a technology which has remained more or less unchanged over the years: The art of printing in the early twentieth century resembled that of earlier centuries. The production of lead type and the manual handling of much of the material have been significant features of newspaper production. During the post-war period, however, this situation has radically changed as the computer and photo composition equipment have entered newspapers, particularly during the past 15-20 years. According to Winsbury (1975), in the United States in the early 1970's some 84 % of all daily newspapers were wholly or partly composed in cold type, some 63 % using the web offset technique (op. cit., p. 10). Similarly, we note a sharp increase in web offset printing among Scandinavian newspapers (Figure 7:1).

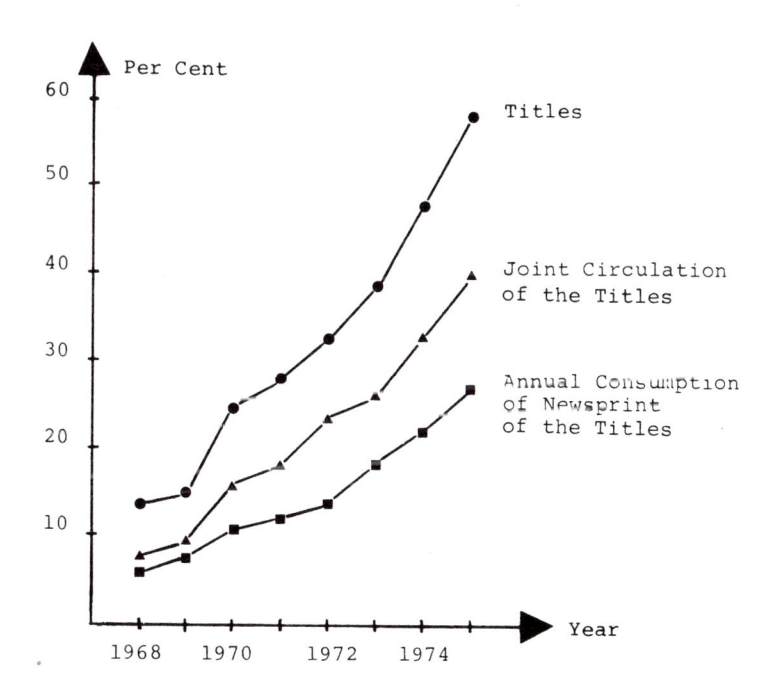

Figure 7:1. The Development of Web Offset Printing in Scandinavia.
            Source: Larsson (1976)

A further conclusion which can be drawn from Figure 7:1 is that the new technology has been introduced primarily in small newspapers: the per cent of newspapers using the new technology is larger than their shares of joint circulation and annual consumption of newsprint, a circumstance which is true both in Scandinavia and abroad. Winsbury (1975, p. 10) who points out that American papers employing photo composition and offset printing have lesser significance in terms of circulation than titles. Similarly, provincial newspapers in the United Kingdom have been quicker to adopt the new technology than Fleet Street papers.[1]

An important reason for many newspapers to adopt the new technology is that it is less labour intensive and therefore offers possibilities for cost savings. But such cost savings cannot gained without affecting a number of employees: some have to leave the company, others have to be trained for other jobs, etc. In addition, the new technology implies major changes in the traditional division of labour; it completely changes "the rules of the game", and new rules have yet to be drafted.

These problems will be referred to as _the technology issue_. In order to discuss this issue it seems appropriate first to consider somewhat further the pressures for new technology. This will be done in Section 7.2. Then, four subjects related to the technology issue will be discussed: _the procedure of introduction_, _the distribution of economic benefits_, _the demarcation problem_ and _human problems_.

---

[1] There are several explanations for the "hesitance" of larger papers. For one thing, introducing innovations is more complicated in large production systems. Second, earlier web offset printing was not a feasible printing alsternative for newspapers of large circulation.

Machines for hot type composition are no longer produced in the United States (cf. Winsbury, 1975, p. 9). In relation to this circumstance it is worth mentioning that American newspapers are between one and six years ahead of the European ones with respect to the new technology (op.cit., p. 7)

7.2 The Pressure for New Technology

In discussing the pressures for conversion to new technology, we shall use the model presented in Chapter One (Section 1.2: "An Organizational View"). That model made a basic distinction between customers and providers (personnel, financiers, governments and suppliers).The first explanation of growth derived from this model is simply growing demand, which may be seen as customer-propelled growth. But, although such advantageous conditions are not present in all firms, it can be argued that all firms will be under more or less pressure for growth, in this case a provider-propelled growth.

This second explanation of growth is based on the assumption that all providers want to increase their rewards per input unit. As a result we would expect them to have an interest in increasing their volume of sales. Such demands for increased rewards will be particularly significant in high growth and inflationary economies. In such economies we can expect the firm's providers to attempt to capture their proportional share of the national increase in standard of living, and concurrently to seek to compensate for price increases in their own inputs.

The above arguments may seem primarily related to the employees of the firm. But there are reasons to believe that also other provider groups will be pushing for growth, since they have their own providers seeking larger rewards, which have their own .... etc.

Under provider pressure for growth an organization has mainly three "pure" strategies of response:

1. The Demand Function Alternative
    (a) Passing along the increasing provider demands to customers,
    (b) Seeking new customer groups.

2. The Provider Function Alternative
    (a) Cutting rewards to existing providers by reducing
        (i)   the reward per provider

(ii)   the number of members in different provider groups
(b)   Seeking new provider groups

3. The Production Function Alternative

Of the different strategies, the first implies price hikes for customers or that new customer groups be identified. Movements into foreign markets have been a widely used method as regards this second substrategy (cf. e.g. Engwall, 1973 b). The same has been true with regard to the provider function alternative, i.e. firms have moved their production to foreign countries with cheap labour and low taxes (like Portugal -- before the change of regime in 1974 -- or Taiwan). Substitution within the country may also occur, however.[1]

The provider function alternative may also imply renegotiations among existing providers, and here two alternatives exist: the rewards per provider are cut, or the number of providers in the different groups is decreased. The latter two alternatives are frequently combined with changes in the production function, i.e. efforts to find a better technology and/or rationalization of the existing production organization. The rationalization strategy is particularly important for organizations that are weak on their customer markets, i.e. organizations which cannot pass increased provider demands on to their customers.

Having considered the model, we can now return to newspaper country. Using data from the sample of Swedish newspapers used for the analysis of allocation outcomes, (Cf. Chapter Two, Section 2.4: "Allocation Data Analysis"), we find in Table 7:1 that these firms have been subject to provider-propelled growth, i.e. growth in costs.[2]

---

[1] In Sweden, for example, the increased employment of women in industries like the printing industry, the metal industry and some areas of transportation during the 1950's is considered to be a consequence of the fact that women's wages have been about 20 to 25 per cent below those of male workers (Holmberg, 1963, p. 136 f.)

[2] Cf. also Winsbury (1975, p. 7): "The problem of [newspapers] is not one of income: it is a problem of costs".

	Journalistic	Business
Major	9.32 %	11.47 %
Minor	9.37 %	14.49 %
Total	9.34 %	12.98 %

Table 7:1. *Average Annual Growth Rates in Costs, 1968-1972*[a]

Note:

[a] For a description of the distribution of costs between the journalistic (news and politically oriented groups) and the business group, see the Appendix to Chapter Eight.

While the growth of costs has been relatively similar among major and minor newspapers, it has been somewhat higher among minor papers. In both groups of newspapers business costs have risen faster than journalistic costs. And, both types of costs, journalistic as well as business costs, have risen faster than consumer price and producer price indices, which increased on average by 5.56 and 5.92 per cent, respectively, during the period.[1]

Turning to consider the various approaches to handling provider pressure for growth, the studied newspapers have clearly applied the demand function alternative, charging higher prices. This is shown in Table 7:2, which also shows that price hikes for readers have been greater than those for advertisers.[2] It is also evident that costs (cf. Table 7:1) have grown faster than prices.

	Single Copy	Subscription	Advertisement
Major	6.71 %	6.65 %	6.03 %
Minor	6.86 %	6.85 %	5.58 %
Total	6.79 %	6.75 %	5.81 %

Table 7:2. *Mean Growth Rates of Prices Charged by Fourteen Swedish Newspapers, 1968-1972.*

---

[1] The source for these computations is *Statistisk Årsbok* (1975, Tables 221 and 225, pp. 220-221).

[2] Advertising prices are exclusive of the advertising tax introduced in 1971. All prices have been raised more than the consumer price index, which increased by 5.56 per cent (cf. above).

The second substrategy in the demand function alternative is to find new customer groups. Success in applying this strategy seems to have been limited among the fourteen Swedish newspapers studied. Major papers have experienced a slight annual growth in circulation, whereas minor papers have faced annual declines in circulation, Both groups of newspapers have seen a decrease in the inflow of advertisements (Table 7:3).

	Circulation	Advertising Space
Major	0.69 %	-0.94 %
Minor	-1.19 %	-1.10 %
Total	0.25 %	-1.02 %

Table 7:3. <u>Mean Growth Rates in Circulation and Advertising Space in Fourteen Swedish Newspapers, 1968-1972</u>.

In describing the model it was mentioned that the demand function alternative has often implied the opening up of foreign operations. This approach is of limited importance for newspapers. This is particularly the case for newspapers like the Swedish, which are printed in a language with limited distribution. Foreign operations are important only for a few internationally well-known newspapers such as <u>The New York Times</u>, <u>The London Times</u> and <u>Le Monde</u>.

If there are some, but very limited possibilities for newspapers to find customers abroad, there is almost no chance of finding production opportunities abroad.[1] The main reason of course, is the short production cycle of daily newspapers: despite the possibilities to stock some material (cf. the previous chapter) transportation time will render material obsolete.[2]

---

[1] One possibility, which has not been employed so far, is the electronic transfer of newspapers. Language problems remain a hampering factor, however.

[2] This is in contrast to the printing of books, which can be undertaken abroad. But, neither are such activities without problems: the circumstance that compositors do not know the language they are to compose often leads to a larger number of misprints.

As far as the application of the provider function alternative to domestic providers is concerned, some possibilities exist, but these, too, are limited. Approaches used include printing on thinner newsprint as well as cutting the size of the paper.[1] In addition, the fuzzy technology of newspaper production may facilitate cuts in staff, not necessarily by firing, but by a no-hiring policy as employees leave the newspaper.[2] But, these manning procedures as well as negotiations on monetary rewards are subject to union bargaining, which, due to the strength of newspaper unions, may limit the cost reductions achieved this way.

Of the strategies mentioned above, one still remains: the production function alternative. And, this alternative has been widely used in newspapers, a circumstance described in Section 7.1. The same has also been true for the fourteen Swedish newspapers, for which we have noted that (1) price hikes could not compensate for the increases in costs, (2) the growth in circulation and advertising space was insufficient, and (3) there seem to have been limited opportunities to apply the provider function alternative. In the light of these findings, it is not surprising that ten of the fourteen newspapers converted to cold type composition and offset printing during the period 1968 to 1972.

---

[1] An important restriction for the thickness of the newsprint is that it must not tear.

[2] An example can be taken from The Record, where two vacancies in the news-room had not been filled for some time.

Of course, the need to compensate for increasing demands from providers is not the sole explanation for the adoption of the new technology.[1] An extremely important reason is of course the development of technology which has implied a significant breakthrough in information processing. An illustration of this can be obtained from Figure 7:2, which shows the number of types set per hour using different techniques during the nineteenth and twentieth centuries. Note the extreme growth in the last decade.

---

[1] Economic problems have nevertheless doubtless been important. This was stressed by a British union official, who pointed out the problems arising from the downturn of the economy and the growth of newsprint costs as well as other costs such as post and telephone charges and local taxes. He added that these factors strike particularly hard since, in his opinion, not enough investment was made in more profitable days: "The employers thought a little less about the problem in the period 1960-1975 than we did."

Cf. also Winsbury (1975, p.7): "The fundamental significance of new technology . . . is that it offers the opportunity and the means for cutting costs." This is indirectly corroborated by the words of the President of The New York Times as he wrote to the stockholders: "But major problems of efficiency in producing The Times, arising chiefly from bans on modern equipment and from excess manning, prevented cost reductions necessary to offset wage increases" (The New York Times Co., 1973, p. 2). Changes have since taken place (cf. Pressens Tidning, Mars-April, 1975, p. 32).

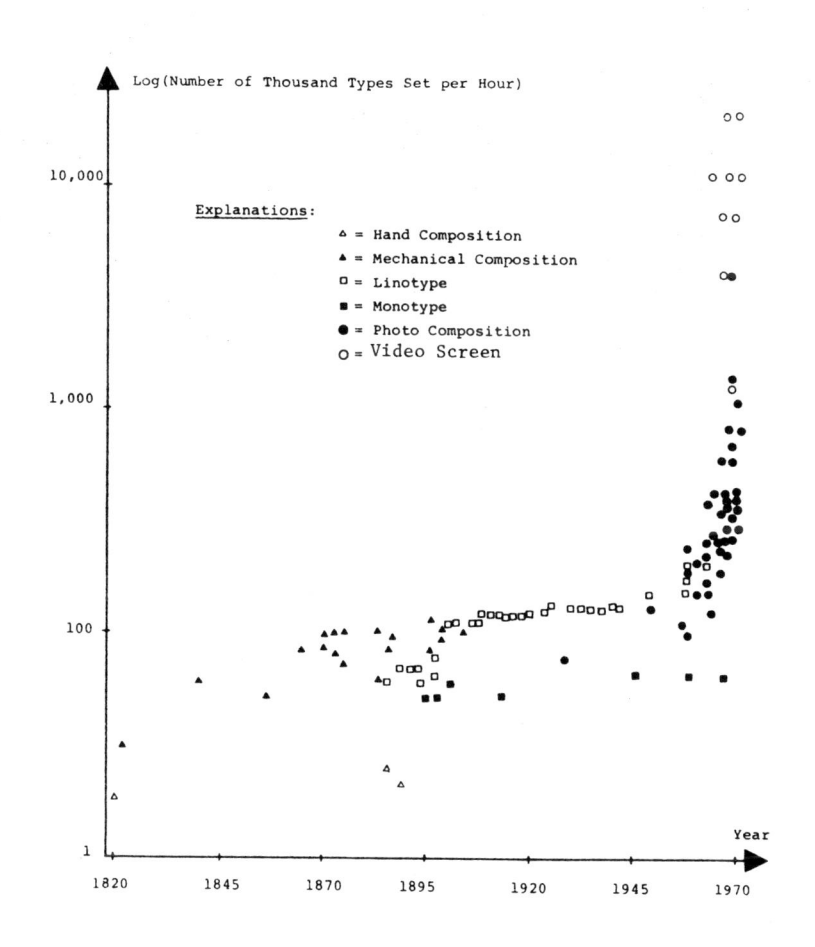

Figure 7:2. The Development of Composition Technology

Source: Esselte Norstedts (1973) and Knoph (1974, p.6)

In addition to being less labour intensive, the new technology provides, as was shown in Chapter One (Section 1A1: "Suddenly the Ground Started to Shake...."), considerable flexibility.[1] This is true for the handling of news as well as advertisements.

7.3 The Procedure of Introduction

There are a number of important subjects that come up on the agenda as newspapers consider converting to an alternative technology. First of all, a decision has to be taken as to <u>when</u> changes should be made. Second, it is of crucial importance to determine <u>what to buy</u>. Both these decisions involve quite a bit of uncertainty and have characteristics which are not present in many other decisions on investment in the new equipment. A basic dilemma is that the old equipment is still usable and could be used for many years to come. In addition, technological development in the field may bring further breakthroughs which may result in better as well as cheaper equipment.

A third and very crucial question in relation to the introduction of new technology is: <u>how</u> to do it? The latter question is often mentioned as "the implementation problem" and as such is sometimes discussed in isolation without any relation to the other two questions. Clearly, there are several important relationships between the three questions, however, so that <u>when</u> and <u>what</u> sometimes will be a result of the answer to the <u>how</u> question.[2] The reason is simple: an economically perfect decision (the answer to the <u>when</u> and <u>what</u> questions) is useless unless executed in an appropriate way (the answer to the <u>how</u> question).[3]

---

[1] A study employing simulation technique in order to investigate the influence of technology on the production flow and production planning is presented in Pettersson (1974).

[2] For discussions on decision-making and implementation in relation to computer systems, cf. Pettigrew (1973) and Mumford & Pettigrew (1975).

[3] A related question which was mentioned in Chapter Four (Section 4.6: "Competitors") concerns cooperation in printing.

The procedures used to answer these questions are different analyses and planning activities. Here we shall consider the procedure used in Times Newspapers Ltd., London, by way of illustration.[1]

As of Spring 1976 a project team in The Times organization was working on the introduction of new technology. In addition to the General Manager and the project coordinator this team consisted of a number of newspaper employees, including editors, printers and managers.[2] The members of the team also participated in a number of investigatory committees, eleven in all, concerning issues such as type faces, advertising, formating, darkroom, wire room, platemaking, etc. Each person took part in at least one group, and some were members of several groups.[3]

The described project team was the result of thoughts about a change in technology which arose in December 1973, leading to more formal discussions about a year later. During 1975 different study groups were sent to the United States to look at applications there, and in June 1975, one company (Harris Intertype) was called in to make preliminary investigations in order to determine the kind of computerized system best suited to present operations.

---

[1] A case from the Swedish scene is given in SOU 1974:34, Chapter Six, Section 6.6. It concerns Värmlands Folkblad, a Social Democratic local newspaper which turned to new technology in 1972. A short passage from the description may be of relevance: "The change first entered the discussion during 1970. The investment decision was made the same year. In the Spring of 1971 the training started, and the first machines for training purposes were brought into the company. The training of personnel for photo composition machines and press was mainly external. The change was made in the course of 48 hours, All Saints' Day, 1972. The day before this weekend the paper was produced in the old technology, the day after, with [the new technology]." (Ibid. p. 123, my translation from Swedish.)

[2] Members were senior editors of The Times and The Sunday Times, the printers of both papers, the development manager, the chief accountant and the advertising systems manager. (For the organizational set-up of Times Newspapers, cf. Appendix to Chapter Five, Section 5A7.)

[3] All groups were able to call in experts from their departments to their assistance.

In October 1975, Times Newspapers called in four more companies to explore conversion.[1] Each of these companies was given an extensive specification book as well as the opportunity to discuss details with various departments. They were asked to present their systems philosophy and cost estimates a month later. At that time two companies (ICL and MGD) were eliminated: one due to lack of proven hardware and software as well as a high price, the other because of misinterpretations of the requirements. From the proposals of the three remaining companies the best parts of each system were then selected. The resulting skeleton was fed back to the companies with a request to report back in January 1976. This reporting led to the decision to ask Systems Development Corporation to make a detailed specification, due at the end of April.

The system envisaged by the company is a full front-end system with "keystroke at source" by means of video screen terminals for reporters and advertising receivers.[2] Their input will then be fed directly into a data base, in which it is subsequently corrected by sub-editors on editorial terminals and edited on page view terminals.[3] This means that the company aims at page fit as well as a story fit.[4]

---

[1] The five corporations were: Harris Intertype, International Computers Ltd., Linotype-Paul, Systems Development Corporation and MGD.

[2] This is in accordance with the American approach "capturing the original keystrokes" (cf. Winsbury, 1975, p. 13).

[3] Excluded from the above system is the material brought in from outside, which will continue to be composed in the central production area. In all, 65 per cent of all set material will be keyed in the central production room, leaving 35 per cent to be originally keystroked.

[4] Story fit: "You key in that you have, for instance, a 14" story across four columns and then press the button." The area fitting and page fit are performed with the aid of page make-up terminals simplifying operations which now are a very complex exercise: "Take, for example, a display advertisement for a food store! Now it takes 580 man-minutes to make, and in the new system we will come down to 192 man-minutes. So the scale of economy is enormous."
As of 1975, the full page systems were not operating. The British International Publishing Corporation has exported a system to Dow Jones, publisher of The Wall Street Journal, however. Other full page systems projects are the IBM-based Newspaper Systems Development Group and The Richmond Group (cf. Winsbury, 1975, pp. 49-51).

The strategy of the company is to introduce the new system in two or more stages, starting with publications where the profits and risks involved are least, viz. one of the supplements.[1] The procedure will thus be that shown in Table 7:4.[2]

Step	Activity
1	One supplement
2	Another supplement
3	All three supplements
4	Classified and display advertising in The Times and The Sunday Times
5	Editorial material in The Times and The Sunday Times

Table 7:4. Steps in Introducing New Technology in Times Newspapers.

The Times case points to some important factors to be considered in the planning and implementation processes. For one thing, the need for cooperation between employees is acknowledged. In terms of Whisler's (1970) classification of change strategies, The Times organization employs a participative or cultural change strategy instead of a bureaucratic strategy.[3] The importance of such "people oriented planning" has earlier been stressed by Mumford (1968), who suggests three phases in planning for computers: strategic planning, socio-technical planning and tactical planning. Of these three phases, the first one should be performed by computer specialists and top management, the second one between computer experts and user department, whereas the third is undertaken in the user department.

---

[1] There is nothing sacrosanct about the publishing day of the supplements. Therefore, it does not matter, if a supplement is delayed in times of introduction of new technology.

[2] Table 7:4 does not include the steps to be taken viz-à-viz labour unions. The format for these steps is that a newspaper makes an announcement and informs the labour unions. Then, negotiations start between representatives of The Newspapers Publishers' Association and top people of the six unions in order to reach an agreement on the introduction of new technology. Important issues in these talks are the construction of a social package for people in the industry as well as the removal of demarcation lines. (Cf. further below.)

[3] The three mentioned strategies are in a way a thesis, antithesis and a synthesis. The first implies that the change is accomplished through a written plan, a technique which may cause problems through lack of motivation. The second strategy is characterized by the participation of many employees in the planning of change, whereas the third one is a combination of the other two strategies: many employees participate, but a basic work is done in a "think tank". The second and third strategies share difficulties in solving arising conflicts as well as obtaining enough time for the problem solving.

A basic problem in all three of the mentioned planning phases seems to be that of communication between newspaper employees and computer specialists.[1] The former often have a limited knowledge of computers, whereas the latter commonly have limited knowledge of newspapers. As a result, newspaper employees sometimes have difficulties seeing the advantages of the new technology, while computer specialists have difficulties understanding specific problems in a particular newspaper. As far as the first difficulties are concerned, one newspaper consultant I talked to considered the analyses made by technical supervisors very conservative. He also mentioned that it is not unusual that cold type composition is investigated under the assumption that the old routines should be maintained. A frequent conclusion, therefore, is that the change to new technology is not profitable.[2] But, knowledge of the experiences of other papers often leads to new analyses, a circumstance which involves the risk that the system of another newspaper is taken over. In most cases such an approach is very problematic, since different companies require different systems. In addition there is the risk that the system selected will not be adequate for further integration of production.

Turning back to The Times case, their employment of people-oriented planning contrasts somewhat to those used in some American newspapers. Winsbury (1975) thus remarks that "the most remarkable omission from the American scene is any attempt at systematic joint consultation, before the event, between management and unions over automation." (Op.cit., p. 23). The same author also describes how several newspaper managements have trained non-organized labour in handling the new equipment, then bringing in the equipment without any consultations.[3]

---

[1] A consequence is that the opportunities for graphical workers to influence the decisions have been reduced: "Earlier a printer could discuss with a producer of equipment -- today it is the financial manager who talks with computer specialists." (Perby, 1976, p. 16, my translation from Swedish.)

[2] During the fall of 1975 a computerized system for a newspaper with a circulation of 30 to 40 thousand copies cost between one and two million Swedish Crowns, a figure which could be compared with the approximate costs for one employee during ten years: 1.5 million SCr.

[3] Examples are given from The Miami Herald, from Richmond, Virginia, from The Washington Post, i.a. Among these, the first newspaper was a "trail blazer" and it is worth noting that Mr. John Prescott, who was in charge of the change at The Post was brought in from The Miami Herald. (For a sum-up of the dispute at The Post, cf. Teste, 1976.)

A second feature of the processes illustrated by the case, is the need for a step-by-step procedure: Times Newspapers has chosen to proceed in a number of different phases, starting with the least sensitive operations (weeklies). In this way different problems which appear in the process may be handled appropriately. This strategy contrasts to what Winsbury (1975) mentions as "the 'big bang' approach", which implies that everything is done in one step. The same author also points to the problems which have appeared as a result of the application of this approach. Since the experience in the new technology is limited, a number of complications may pop up unexpectedly.[1] In addition, the "big bang" approach has often implied that producers of equipment, not the users, have controlled the design of the systems.[2]

One approach which has produced a number of problems is the use of OCR (Optical Character Reader or Recognition), which implies that input is written on an electric typewriter, the type-written text being fed directly into an OCR scanner. This approach has worked for advertisements, at The New York Times, for example, but has not been feasible for editorial copy. For persons with experience of editorial copy the reason is clear: journalists do not write their manuscripts so methodically and carefully that OCR reading would work.[3] In addition, editing is required of most material, and this would require retyping before the input to OCR.

The question of speed in introduction is not only a technical question, however. It is also a question of matching the machines to the people in production. And, in this context a British union official considered the expectations of newspaper publishers with regard to rapid changes a significant problem. He stressed that

---

[1] Cf. Winsbury (1975): "Some of those U.S. papers which once prided themselves on technological leadership are now regretting it. Those who come second or third can benefit from the leader's mistakes." (Op.cit., p. 34)

[2] Cf. again Winsbury (1975): "[it .....] will be clear to anyone with experience of earlier generations of photo composition and copy input devices, [that they] simply in order to get them to work, demanded changed routines and sacrifices of time and scope; that is, imposed their conditions on the newspaper." (Op.cit., p. 35)

[3] At least in Sweden, it is not unusual that journalists "do the index finger waltz" on their typewriters.

his union recognizes that changes must be made but that they also have the feeling that some British publishers of national newspapers seem to be wishing to "take the whole apple in one bite", i.e. to introduce all the modern equipment in one step.[1] The announcements of The Financial Times and The Daily Telegraph have been particularly dramatic in this context, since their publishers want to move very fast, although they have employees covering a broad spectrum of age groups.[2]

Similar thoughts are also expressed by Swedish newspapermen. One working with the new technology thus considers the implementation of new technology as a personnel problem and is quick to stress the need to follow a step-by-step approach: "You have to settle the composing room at a pace agreed to by the unions."[3]

The same interviewee exemplified his reasoning with the issue of video screens. This equipment makes it technically possible to "skip" keypunching and some composing personnel. In practice, however, this is not possible, and the video screens must be gradually moved into the news-room as the number of employees in the composing room decreases.[4] That other strategies fail has, according to the interviewee, been the experience of several newspapers that have tried to go on fast.[5]

---

[1] In the interviewee's opinion this is in contrast to the strategy employed on the Continent, where publishers stick to the strategy "one step at a time", making it possible to solve problems gradually.

[2] "The change is particularly hard for those in their forties or fifties. It's hard for them to give up the earning opportunities they have received after having been promoted to well-paid jobs from lower paid jobs in the commercial printing."

[3] But, even if this strategy is used there may be problems, as the Central Union may step in, imposing a veto with the rationale: "It might be O.K. in this paper, but we have to think of our members in other papers."

[4] Contributing to the use of this smooth approach may be the relative peace on the Swedish labour market. In the newspaper industry this condition is even manifested in a "peace pact" between publishers and unions. The first of these agreements was made in 1937, and a basic provision is that "arising controversial issues are passed to an arbitration court consisting of neutral persons" (Wahlgren, 1970, p. 120). The peace agreement has not been completely successful, however, since a number of wild cat strikes and slow downs have occurred in recent years.

[5] "Mainly the large newspapers are those that make the mistakes."

Quite in accordance with this reasoning, the main problem of implementation in Times Newspapers is considered to be the acceptance of video screens. This constitutes the barrier to be overcome in order for the system to be accepted.

A third point which should be mentioned in relation to the Times case is the need for training of employees as new technology is introduced. And, in this context there is a particular problem to schedule training courses for employees attending to their normal jobs. This problem is of special concern to those newspapers desiring to move very fast.[1] It is also a tricky problem for newspapers with small personnel reserves, like The Record; smaller papers may have real difficulty keeping up the quality of the paper during the training period.[2]

In addition to training outside the company, implementation often also involves experiments with the new technology. These experiments give employees some idea of what can be expected, but they are seldom very realistic, since the time pressure of real life is absent: "In an experiment nothing is at stake. People are used to having an irregular job. They are prepared to stress themselves in order to get the paper out."[3]

---

[1] "How do you manage to retrain fifty to sixty per cent of the labour force ?" (A common solution is to engage unemployed people temporarily for shorter periods up until a year. But, this procedure is not always successful because it is difficult to cater for sickness and other contingencies.)

[2] "During the training period we made a thin paper. Actually we made a rather poor product." (A journalist.)

[3] Cf. here Chapter Six, Section 6.6: "Human Relations Aspects on the Flow Issue".

7.4 The Distribution of Benefits

A second question which is important in introducing new technology is: Who should reap the benefits of technological change? The company? The present employees? The employees who remain? As was pointed out in Section 7.2, a basic motive for the introduction of new technology is to improve the economics of newspaper production. Thus, managements have expectations that their companies should benefit from the change. It is evident for most managements, however, that the companies will have to share these economic benefits with the employees.[1] But how? How much can the companies benefit from the change, and how much should be transferred to employees? A second issue in the same context concerns the distribution of benefits between employees who leave the company and those who remain. All these questions are concerned with manning and pay structure in the new technology: How many are to be employed in the production process, and how should they be paid?

These two problems emerge since there will be fewer employment opportunities in the new technology, and new skills have to be learned.[2] Therefore, establishing new wage scales is a difficult task: "You cannot just translate the scales from the old technology into new ones for the new technology." (A union official.) An illustration of these difficulties is the agreement in the Times Newspapers organization concerning the composition of City and Wall Street stock prices, which are handled by means of computer and photo composition. The agreement implies that compositors are paid for the composition of the stock prices although they do not do the composition.[3] This agreement has been

---

[1] In Sweden, there is a historical background provided by the change from hand composing to machine composing: "The hand compositors who became machine compositors got, through the intervention of their union, shorter working hours and a pay rise. The typographers elevated the position of workers by collecting part of the rationalization profits through a union dispute." (Ring, 1976 a, my translation from Swedish).

[2] Note the remark of an ANPA official: "[new] technology is useless without eliminating people" (Winsbury, 1975, p. 19).

[3] This system started in 1970. A similar arrangement applies to advertisements composed outside the company. (The British arrangement contrasts with that in some American newspapers, where the ready-made material used to be composed once more!)

possible, since the system is to the advantage of the company: it saves money and reduces the number of errors in the price lists.[1] It seems doubtful, however, that similar agreements will be reached as the complete system is introduced.[2]

It seems quite clear that union negiotiators have tried to secure benefits for everyone employed in newspapers. The over-manning problem is thus solved through "natural attrition" as well as "buying out" individual employees.[3] In the front-running newspaper in Fleet Street, The Daily Mirror, an agreement on the fundamental principles for change was reached in 1975. This agreement will be followed by negotiations on job security, changes in positions, etc. The Manpower Director has outlined four schemes to be used:

1. voluntary redundancy
2. voluntary early retirement
3. voluntary retirement of staff over 65
4. a policy of non-automatic replacement and non-recruitment

(Mirror Group, 1975, p. 2)

"Voluntary redundancy" implies that the economic benefits are not reaped immediately, and this approach may, according to one union official, cause considerable unhappiness among employees, but shorter working weeks and increases in the number of holidays may help.[4]

---

[1] The errors are caught by a built-in software check that price changes are not "abnormal".

[2] The stock price system is completely different from the planned system and will not be intregrated into the new system, since it is an efficient operation as it stands. The fact that some computer composition has been used is considered to be a psychological advantage as the new technology is introduced, however.

[3] Similar arrangements can be found in other industries where new technology has been introduced. One example is containerization in the handling of cargo, which implied radical changes in manpower needs (cf. e.g. Johnson & Garnett, 1971, p. 79 ff).

[4] "That's our policy. And, we have always taken a considerable interest in the Continent, since they appear to have more holidays than we have."

With respect to the possibilities of making manpower cuts, the age structure of the employees is of extreme importance. It is therefore common that newspapers on the way into the new technology make studies into the length of service as well as the age profile of employees. In Times Newspapers, for instance, these investigations have indicated that a fairly significant number of employees are likely to leave within the near future.[1]

According to a Swedish interviewee, the newspapers that kept statistics on age distribution and attrition were exceptions. It has therefore been necessary to collect such data at an early phase of most conversions to new technology. The same informant also stressed that such statistics will be particularly important in the future, as newspapers (like The Daily Mirror) employ a policy of non-automatic replacement and non-recruitment. Such a policy is likely to lead to considerable personnel problems within the next ten or fifteen years as a result of the non-representation of certain age groups within the company.[2]

In addition to the four strategies employed by The Daily Mirror, employees are commonly transferred to other jobs as the new technology is introduced. At The Record, for instance, such an approach has been used, several of the compositors having moved to sales, advertising as well as to custodial jobs.[3] A similar course of events has been observed in another Swedish local paper, where 37 jobs disappeared as the company changed from hot-type to cold-type composition.[4] Of these jobs, 19 were held by hand compositors, 14 by machine compositors and 4 by stereo-typists. Since the company employs a no-firing policy, persons laid off were invited to apply for different jobs within the company. The result of this procedure is shown in Figure 7:3.

---

[1] Despite this "natural attrition" the company will find it difficult to reach an acceptable level of employment. The speeding up of attrition will therefore be a significant area for negotiations between management and unions. A quite different experience was made at The New York Times: "The paper never expected so many people to leave all at once under their special retirement scheme and was seriously embarrassed, at least temporarily, by a shortage of labour to produce its mammoth Sunday edition." (Winsbury, 1975, p. 38)

[2] "You end up with too many older people, since it is easier for the young ones to move."

[3] These replacements and natural attrition were not sufficient to cut the overcapacity in the composing room, however.

[4] The description is based on Henriksson-Jönsson et al. (1975).

In relation to this figure it is particularly worth mentioning that the two proof-reading jobs were considered exceptions to the rule, since the local chapter of the Union of Journalists considers this to be a job for journalists.

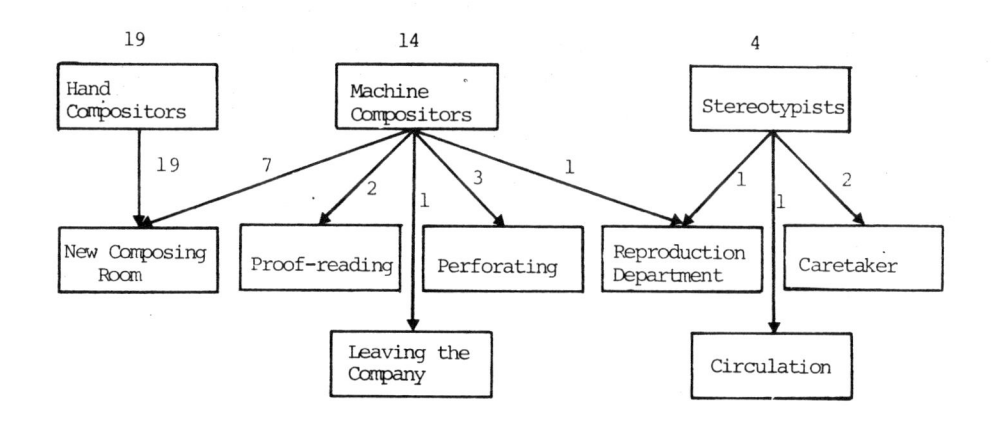

```
    19                    14                      4
┌──────────┐         ┌──────────┐          ┌──────────────┐
│  Hand    │         │ Machine  │          │ Stereotypists│
│Compositors│        │Compositors│         │              │
└──────────┘         └──────────┘          └──────────────┘
     │19         7  / 2│ 3  \ 1                1 /  \ 2
     ▼              ▼  ▼ 1  ▼                   ▼    ▼
┌──────────┐  ┌─────────┐ ┌──────────┐ ┌────────────┐ ┌─────────┐
│New Composing│ │Proof-   │ │Perforating│ │Reproduction│ │Caretaker│
│    Room    │ │reading  │ │          │ │ Department │ │         │
└──────────┘  └─────────┘ └──────────┘ └────────────┘ └─────────┘
                              │                │
                              ▼                ▼
                        ┌──────────┐     ┌──────────┐
                        │Leaving the│     │Circulation│
                        │ Company  │     │          │
                        └──────────┘     └──────────┘
```

Figure 7:3. The Transition of Employees into News Jobs in a Swedish Newspaper.

An important issue in relation to transfers between jobs concerns economic compensation. One example of an agreement on this issue is that between the management of _Dagens Nyheter_ and the unions of the paper.[1] A basic principle of the agreement is a no-firing policy. Starting, then, from the length of service in the company, the system of economic compensation shown in Table 7:5 was drawn up.

Length of Service	Employees Leaving	Employees Moving to Less Well Paid Jobs
5 to 9 years	6 months' pay	New pay + 40 % of difference from old pay
10 to 19 years	12 months' pay	New pay + 70 % of difference from old pay
20 years or more	24 months' pay	Same pay

Table 7:5. Economic Compensation to Leaving and Remaining Employees of Dagens Nyheter.

---

[1] The source for the description is _Pressens Tidning_ (May, 1976, p. 20).

In addition to the benefits shown in Table 7:5 the agreement includes provisions for employees aged 63 or over to receive seventy per cent pay until the age of 65, if they choose to leave the company. Partial retirement is another alternative offered.

For employees who choose to stay despite the fact that their job has disappeared, the agreement includes a guarantee for training during 180 working days within a two-year period. All employees are also guaranteed compensation for training in which they participate in their leisure time.

7.5   The Demarcation Problem

The demarcation problem arises from rules stipulating that certain jobs be done by certain employees exclusively. Ron referred to such a rule in the case of "The Neartown Car Dealer" (Chapter One, Section 1A4): "I'm not really supposed to do this. It's the compositors' job." The discussions on such demarcation lines have become particularly sensitive as new technology has been introduced into newspapers, making the question, "Who should do what?" a key issue.

The most important question in relation to demarcation seems to be manning of the video screens: should the work with this equipment take place in the composing room or in the news-room? Or, is a compromise possible between these two alternatives? In Sweden negotiations between the Newspaper Publishers' Association and the Union of Graphical Workers have centered around this question. The graphical unions have from the outset opposed placement of any video screens outside the composing room.

Looking at local solutions, it may be noted that the union of graphical workers at The Record, has made it clear that its members alone should be allowed to man video screens for proofreading. This has also been the case with one exception: one journalist has been given a job at a video screen.[1] Otherwise, only

---

[1] Note here the difference from the newspaper mentioned earlier, where graphical workers were given jobs as proofreaders!

graphical workers man the video screens, proofreading, making corrections, feeding in programs and running the computer.[1] A somewhat more extensive agreement has been made at Dagens Nyheter, where it has been agreed that late news may be keyed in by journalists (Journalisten, November, 1976, p. 33).[2] For examples of more "complete solutions" we have to turn to the American scene, however: there graphical workers have been "bought out", being given economic compensation under the condition that management be free to decide on use of video screens (cf. Perby, 1976, p. 7).

The demarcation problem is not only a question of manning of the video screens, it also involves the integrity of journalists: Who should have access to the contents of the data bases? The new technology permits the storage of large data bases of manuscripts, and great fears have been expressed: "To what extent will it be possible for management to unlock the computer in order to make changes in manuscripts or to check the performance of individual journalists? Fears of this sort point out the need for the inclusion of appropriate checks in the software in order to secure journalists' integrity.[3] It is also important for the success of the system that employees believe in the security of this system.

The discussion has hitherto focused on cases of certain groups wanting to defend their rights to do certain things. The demarcation problem has other implications, too. As new technology is introduced into the newspaper, there may also be efforts to thrust certain jobs onto other groups. An example of this can be taken from The Record, where the coding of manuscripts was a job neither the journalists nor the typographical workers wanted to do.[4]

---

[1] Moving more journalists to video screens was contemplated as a couple of journalists are underemployed, but the local chapter of the Graphical Union was against the idea, and another solution was chosen.

[2] An agreement was first reached between the local chapter of the employee unions. Then, management was introduced into the discussions.

[3] This has been stressed in a recent report from the Union of Swedish Journalists: "The new technology implies obvious risks for the integrity of journalists. Unless the necessary checks are created, technically advanced rapid access may be misused for control purposes by the employer. It is also easy to manipulate the text of manuscripts." (Pressens Tidning, Juni-Juli 1976, p. 5, my translation from Swedish)

[4] "Coding" implies adding codes indicating typographical style to the manuscript.

The former did not want to have too much technology in their work, whereas the latter wanted to limit the desk work. The solution has been that the copy editors, i.e. journalists do the coding of editorial copy, whereas advertisements are coded in the composing room.[1]

It should be noted that demarcation problems among technical personnel in Sweden decreased somewhat in importance following the merger of three unions -- the lithographers, typographers and book-binders -- in 1973.[2] Some interviewees indicate that cartels and additional mergers may be expected in the future, which might ultimately result in one single union of newspaper employees.[3] A similar development is also reported from the United States, where mergers imply a reversion toward an earlier system, when all printing workers were affiliated with the International Typographical Union (cf. Winsbury, 1975, pp. 32-33).[4]

Within individual newspapers, too, the new technology often implies removal of barriers between the different groups. An employee of The Record: "The borders between the composing room, the news-room and the platemaking room have become less distinct. In that way

---

[1] In addition to coding, journalists draw mock-ups of the pages. (These make the job of compositors much easier.)

[2] Before the merger there seem to have been intensive conflicts between the three unions. But, as one interviewee told me: "The Lithographers' Union could not manage economically by themselves. In addition, the new technology rendered the old organization principle totally obsolete."

[3] Such an arrangement would seem plausible, since newspaper employees experience a strong identification with the final product (cf. Chapter Six, Section 6.6: "Human Relations Aspects on the Flow Issue").

[4] The result may in due course be mass media unions. This has been indicated by Winsbury (1975), who stresses that the present differences between editorial and printing works may disappear: ....in practice editorial and printing tend to be separate departments, separately managed, with a separate ethos and separate rules, and indeed different types of people with different backgrounds. That distinction is being erroded and in time abolished by the new technology." (op.cit. p. 45).

we we see more of each other."[1] Some observers (cf. e. g. Ring, 1976 b), however, point to the risk that the new technology may also lead to an increasing degree of differentiation: between those who have to sit at a video screen and those who can hand over their material to a video screen operator.[2]

The new technology may also imply an increase in horizontal and spatial differentiation, since computer-based systems take over quite a bit of the interaction between individuals. Thus, instead of delivering material to other departments or other desks, persons delivering copy feed it directly into the computer. It is then taken over by other employees, who are likely to have limited personal communication with the author.[3] This lack of communication, in turn, may significantly inhibit these groups' understanding of each other's problems.

Similarly, the spatially differentiated employees may lose communication links with the editorial office. This will probably be particularly the case for journalists reporting late news -- e.g. sports reporters -- as they will report from the news scene via portable video screens.[4]

---

[1] Similarly, employees in the composing room of The Times are likely to be brought more together in the new system, which will imply the introduction of the principle of common lift, i.e. that any man could pick up any material from any newspaper published by the company.

[2] Others see a need for a link between journalists and computers: technical journalists or journalistic typographers. Furhoff (1976) has pointed to the risk that video screen manning will tend to hamper "old journalistic qualities such as creativity, linguistic ability, carefulness, exactness, patience and integrity". (my translation from Swedish)

[3] For an example of how such communication is carried out today, see the short talk between Phil and Chris as Phil delivered his story on Pankab (Chapter One, Section 1A2: "The Pankab Bankruptcy"). It may be noted that in spite of this conversation, Phil was not completely content with Chris' handling of the story.

[4] A prototype of such equipment is already available, viz. the Teleram, developed through joint research undertaken by the American Newspapers' Publishers Association and The New York Times (cf. Winsbury, 1975, p 41).

7.6 Human Problems

The introduction of new technology implies a number of psychological and physiological problems for the individual employee. In the short run, interviews have indicated general problems associated with organizational changes. Employees have been suspicious of changes and the possible consequences thereof.[1] This uncertainty has in some cases resulted in acute physiological ills, including heart attacks and strokes. It is not unusual that a number of employees choose to leave newspaper companies as new systems are launched. This is even true in cases when training time is paid by their company.

But, employees also experience more long-term uncertainty concerning working conditions: How do human beings react to the materials and equipment used? There is great uncertainty in this regard, and eventual physiological effects may not turn up until much later, since knowledge of the materials is so far quite limited.

At The Record some people have been nauseated by the wax used to attach the composed text, but little else has been reported as yet. The uncertainty concerning the liquids is great, however. The same is true with respect to working conditions at video screens. A proofreader thus remarked: "So far, we haven't noticed any problems. Of course, many of us wear glasses, but we probably would have had to wear glasses anyway."[2]

The chemical substances used have not been completely tried out, and allergies to them are occasionally detected. The response of management is often to relocate workers, but not to switch to other substances (Ejvegård, 1976, p. 17). A consultant on technical change, however, remarked that it may be possible to induce such changes by pointing to the stands on work environment taken on the editorial pages of the newspaper.

---

[1] "This development not only implies disadvantages for those who are laid off but also for those who remain in the jobs." (Ejvegård, 1976, p. 17, my translation from Swedish.)

[2] The same person also mentioned the problems to handle questions on working conditions in economically weak newspapers: "Everybody wants to keep their job, so they don't say much. They don't know where to go with complaints."

A basic question in relation to the new technology is also whether the remaining employees will have meaningful jobs. And, here a big problem presents itself in the need to transfer skilled craftsmen to less skilled, more routine jobs.[1] This transfer may lead to stress, uncertainty and dissatisfaction.[2]

A Swedish study (Björk et al., 1974), provides an impression of the attitudes of newspaper employees to working conditions in the new technology, compared to the old. A nine-point scale, was used to determine minimum requirements, aspirations, present possibilities and future possibilities for ten aspects of working conditions.[3] The results of this study appear to indicate that interviewees see a number of advantages in the new technology, among them possibilities for improvement of work environment. One important improvement in that context is that the noise level in newspaper production has declined considerably.[4] Another is that photo composition is cleaner, since lead dust, oil, etc. are no longer present. Third, the risk of lead poisoning is removed. And, fourth, the work does not require the same amount of physical strength.[5]

---

[1] "The professional feeling is disappearing -- it doesn't help that pride in the profession is still there." (Perby, 1976, p. 15, my translation from Swedish.)

In a radio discussion ("Vår grundade mening", April 7, 1976) a union representative stressed the need for union members to secure meaningful jobs. The representative of employers responded that some people may have to give up meaningful jobs in order to be employed.

[2] "Ever greater mechanization raises the working pace. Haste is becoming more and more of a problem." (Ejvegård, 1976, p. 17, my translation from Swedish.)

[3] The ten items were: employment security, level of earnings, work environment, variations in the job, opportunities to produce work of good quality, freedom on the job, psychological atmosphere in the job, opportunities for training, opportunities for development in the craft, and participation.

[4] This is true in the composing room as well as in the press room. In the latter, however, printers still need protection for their ears.

As for the composing room, it is technically possible to use completely silent keypunching machines, but such equipment causes problems for those who use them, since they need an acknowledgement that each letter has been punched. At The Record a "click" has therefore been built into the keypunching devices.

[5] The four advantages are discussed in Björk et al. (1974, pp. 10-12). The same authors also mention that most typographers "are happy to move from a hard, dirty and often hectic job to one which is felt to be modern and which has opportunities for development." (Ibid. p. 30, my translation from Swedish).

Note however, the disadvantages mentioned earlier.

7.7 Concluding Remarks

A number of sub-problems have been identified in relation to the technology issue: (1) the procedure of introduction, (2) the sharing of benefits, (3) demarcation lines, and (4) human problems. In relation to the model of newspapers used here, the first two problems involve conflicts between the business oriented group, on the one hand, and the news and technically oriented groups on the other. The third problem may add a conflict between the news and technically oriented groups, whereas the fourth problem is more individual in nature. In terms of our newspaper model, the technology issue can thus be summarized as in Figure 7:4.

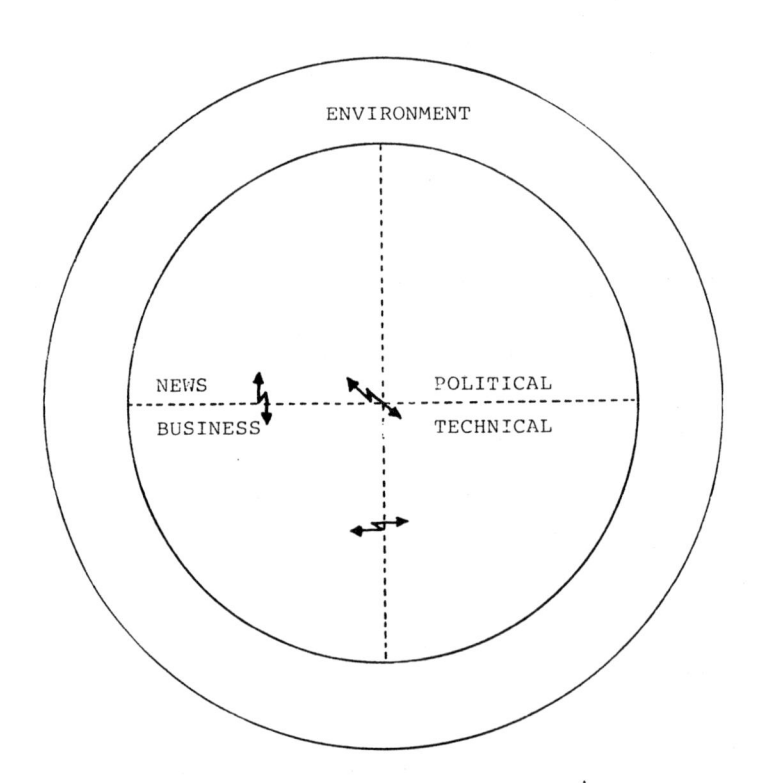

Figure 7:4 Technology Conflicts between Groups

The technology issue is a fairly new one in newspapers, but it seems quite evident that it is bound to stay on the agenda. Different forecasts of future printing methods point to rapid technological development as well as to the need to rationalize production for reasons of cost.[1] As new technology is introduced into newspapers, employment opportunities decrease. Table 7:6 shows the demand for employees working in keypunching, composing, printing and computer maintenance as a newspaper advances to increasing degrees of automation.[2]

Level of Automation	Index Value
Automated Syllibification, Evening Margins and Formating	100
Storage on Magnetic Plates	91-93
Integration of News-room and Composing Room	77-82
Page-fit	68-75
Platemaker Direct from the Computer	57-67

Table 7:6　Employment in Composing and Printing at Different Levels of Automation.

Source: Nilsen (1975, pp. VIII-XII and p. 47)

It is quite evident that such drastic reductions in manpower as those indicated by Table 7:6 cannot be made in one step.[3] This has been stressed above and should be stressed again. Indeed, the need to employ people oriented strategies will probably grow in years to come as the issue of employee participation develops.

---

[1] Examples of such forecasts are International Comprint (1971) and Esselte-Norstedts (1973). Discussions of future technological trends are also provided by Knoph (1974).

[2] A forecast of employment within the whole printing industry in Sweden until 1980 is more optimistic as regards employment opportunities. There will be drastic declines in certain areas, such as hot type composing (a decrease by two-thirds), but the total decline in employment within the industry will only be about five per cent. (SOU 1974:34, p. 146, Table 7:1.)

[3] There will also be clear differences in adaption behaviour. Some newspapers are likely to stick to the old technology for some time to come. At Le Monde, for instance, I was told that the paper will stick to the old technology for the sake of quality.

It is therefore conceivable that those who are going to use
the equipment will be increasingly involved in the analyses
preceding decisions on installations of new technology.[1]

The development of mass media technology may imply a threat to
more than employment opportunities in newspapers. In the opinion
of some forecasters, it may also imply a threat to newspapers
as such. Several scenarios which imply that television and
on-line systems will take over the functions provided by newspapers have been advanced. It may sound all very rational that
an individual submits a personal interest profile to an information collecting company, which, in turn, provides him with
his type of information. There are a number of complications,
however. For one thing, it is difficult to design appropriate
profiles. (Persons with experience of literature search and
information retrieval systems certainly realise this.)[2] Second,
man is not that rational: it is not unusual that individuals
jump between different subjects, something which has apparent
advantages for innovative processes.

There are also other reasons to believe that newspapers will survive.
One basic strength of newspapers is accessibility of information.[3]
The relation of newspaper reading to television watching is similar
to that between a magnetic disc and a magnetic tape, the former
being a direct access memory and the second a sequential memory.
In other words: reading a newspaper, it is possible selectively
to scan several subjects in a short time, whereas a TV program
requires a longer attention.

---

[1] Cf. Winsbury (1975, p. 46): "The result has been a general move .... by the journalists and editorial departments to take charge of both the planning for new technology, and the actual use of new equipment once installed."

[2] One problem, for instance, is that different words have different meanings, depending on the context where they are used.

[3] For discussions on the advantages of newspapers, see Bagdikian (1971) who adds that "the price the citizen pays for this advantage is that he gets his news later, as much as a whole day later in the case of communities with a single daily." (Op.cit., p. 154)

Another basic strength of newspapers is that they can be consumed anywhere at any time.[1] Commuting to and from work, for instance, newspaper reading is entirely feasible, whereas access to television during these trips is barred.

---

[1] Or, in other words: the newspaper provides a permanent memory. This advantage has also been mentioned by Bagdikian (1971, p. 191), who adds, however, that "....in the last twenty years men have become nervously aware that this is also one of print's great disadvantages: it does not go away."

CHAPTER EIGHT. ALLOCATION

8.1 Introduction

Chapter Five distinguished different groups of employees who perform different tasks and who have different views as to the purpose of newspaper operations (cf. Section 5.2: "Differentiation"). All these groups have one desire in common, however: to acquire a "fair" share of the joint resources in the organization. Quite often this implies that they feel a need for more financial resources and more employees. Different desks in the news-room also desire more space in the newspaper.

This is the background to the allocation issue, which concerns the distribution of scarce resources. It involves, as mentioned above, three sub-issues, i.e. those concerning the distribution of financial resources, number of providers and space, which will be treated in the following three sections. We shall then focus on the outcomes of various allocation decisions.

8.2 Allocation of Financial Resources

In the distribution of financial resources previous outcomes and outcomes in similar organizations play an important role in the budget procedures employed in organizations.[1] These procedures are made up on the basis of internal providers' own demands as well as forecasts from external providers. We may thus expect different departments and sub-groups to play "the game of budgeting" (cf. Hofstede, 1967) in order to obtain more resources. The process may be of the bottom-up type or the top-down type, but irrespective of the procedure, it is basically a negotiation for economic resources in compensation for the services rendered by the different organizational units.

---

[1] Note here Wildavsky's remark that "the largest determining factor of the size of the content of this year's budget is last year's budget." (Wildavsky, 1964, p. 13)

Important negotiations in newspapers are those between managing editors and top management. These may lead to budgets for the different editorial activities, but according to one interviewee, it is somewhat difficult to employ budget procedures in organizations like newspapers.[1] This is particularly the case in economically successful newspapers.[2]

In economically weak paper, such as The Record, the situation is somewhat different: the scarcity of resources leads to the observance of strict economy. The basis for this practice is annual discussions in a budgetary committee, which starts its work in September-October. This committee, basing its work on several years' preliminary budgets, produces budgets for revenues, costs and liquidity.[3]

Budgets constitute, in a way, forecasts of future activities in organizations, and like most forecasts they involve quite a bit of uncertainty. In order to take care of this, different control procedures can be used to allow revision of budgets or to let different persons know when they are not running according to plans. A particular problem in employee intensive operations such as newspaper production is that immediate cost reductions are difficult to achieve since a large proportion of the costs is fixed.

A rough picture of the outcome of the budgetary process in newspapers is presented in Table 8:1, which summarizes the results from

---

[1] This has to do with the differences between journalists and businessmen mentioned in Chapter Five. The problem is stressed by Tingsten (1971 a), who pointed to "the strain between the group which edited and wrote the paper, and the group which handled its economy, between editors and directors." (op.cit. p. 76, my translation from Swedish.)

[2] A manager in a successful newspaper mentioned in an interview that a big problem of the paper was its earlier success, which had had the effect that the desire to run the company as a business had decreased: "Employees have been spoilt. They never put price tags on things. They never think about the costs." The same interviewee also pointed to the need for a change in attitude in order for the budget system to work well.

[3] In the budgetary process of minor papers in countries with public support to the press the outcome of political decisions plays an important role, and such papers therefore find it difficult to plan their budgets in a longer perspective. In The Record, for instance, the 1976 budget was very much dependent on the Parliamentary decision on subsidies. Since this decision was not taken until mid-Spring of 1976, the paper could not determine its definite 1976 budget until that time!

three Swedish studies.[1]

Expenses\Year	1924[a]	1934[a]	1946[a]	1958[b]	1972[c]	Average
Editorial Office	24.1	22.4	20.3	23.5	24.0	22.9
Technical Departments	21.9	22.9	19.6	17.4	17.0	19.8
Newsprint	26.2	23.0	25.3	13.3	10.0	19.6
Circulation	7.8	11.2	10.9	16.6	20.0	13.3
Administration	11.3	9.4	10.8	14.1	15.0	12.1
Advertising	8.7	11.1	13.1	15.1	14.0	12.3
Total	100.0	100.0	100.0	100.0	100.0	100.0

Revenues\Year						
Advertisements	--	--	--	61.0	63.4	62.2
Circulation	--	--	--	39.0	36.6	37.8
Total	100.0	100.0	100.0	100.0	100.0	100.0

Table 8:1. **Percentual Distribution of Resources in Samples of Swedish Newspapers**

Notes:
[a] The data refer to 32 newspapers. Source: Carlsson (1948).

[b] The data refer to 18 provincial newspapers. Source: Tollin (1960).

[c] The data refer to a hypothetical company having a circulation of 30 000 copies. Source: Tollin (1972).

Although the data in the table are derived from different samples, they indicate some characteristics of the outcome of the budgetary

---

[1] A similar distribution can be observed for Le Monde in 1974. Printing costs were the largest -- about one-third -- followed by costs for the editorial office and newsprint -- about one-fourth, respectively. The remaining resources are absorbed by general and social costs (10 %), administration (9 %) and profit (3 %). (Le Monde, 1975).
It should be noted that in terms of type of costs, wages and salaries are the far most important in newspapers. In Dagens Nyheter, for instance, these amount to fifty per cent of total costs. (Dagens Nyheter, 29 augusti, 1975, p. 32.)

process in newspapers.[1] It is particularly noteworthy that
the share allotted to the editorial office has been fairly
stable over time. Furthermore, we note increases for administration (circulation, business office and advertising), whereas
the share to newsprint and the technical departments has
shrunk.[2]

In order to illustrate the allocation of financial resources
somewhat further, resource allocation data for the sample of
fourteen Swedish newspapers have been analyzed with reference
to the basic distinction of values in newspapers, i.e. that
between journalistic and business goals.[3] In doing so, the
news oriented and the politically oriented employees have been
referred to a journalistic group. The technically oriented group
has been counted as a service unit to the journalistic and business
groups. As a result, the resources allocated to the technically
oriented group have been divided between the journalistic and
business groups according to their estimated use (cf. Appendix).

<u>Size of circulation</u> has been a basic variable in the ana-
lysis. As pointed out by Pondy (1969) among others, the size
variable can be taken to reflect technology and specialization.
An analysis with reference to size does not seem to be enough,
however, when dealing with newspapers. Another important variable
is the <u>market position</u> of a newspaper, i.e. whether or not the
newspaper is the leading one within its distribution area. The
importance of this variable is stressed in several earlier discussions of the advantages the major paper in an area enjoys over
a minor one (cf. Furhoff, 1967; Thomsen, 1968; Nussberger, 1971, i.a.).

---

[1] There are of course, differences between different types of newspapers. Reddaway (1963, p. 209) for example, points to the differences in editorial costs between popular and quality papers, the former spending "three times as much as the typical quality because of the emphasis which it puts on such things as the speedy col-lection of all possible news and pictures, preferably of an exlusive nature." The same author also raises the question "Is it <u>really</u> necessary for a national paper of wide appeal to spend such vast sums on 'editorial'?" (<u>Ibid.</u>, p. 217)

[2] This is somewhat in contrast to the developments of the past several years, during which time newsprint prices have increased rapidly. In <u>Le Monde</u> the share of news-print costs thus increased from 21 per cent in 1972 to 25 per cent in 1974.

[3] For a description of the sample, see Chapter Two (Section 2.4: "Allocation Data Analysis").

Looking at the relationship between circulation and the journalistic share of financial resources, we find (Figure 8:1):

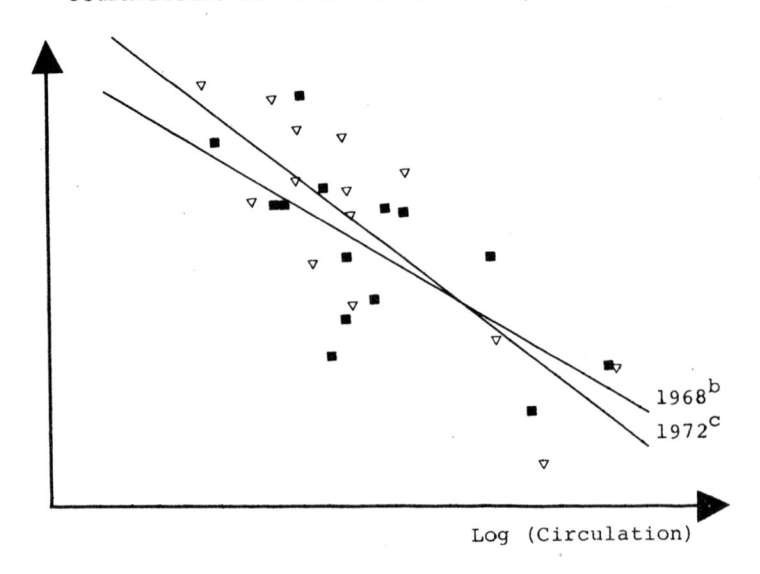

Journalistic Share of Financial Resources

[Scatter plot with two regression lines labeled 1968[b] and 1972[c], x-axis labeled Log (Circulation)]

Figure 8:1. Journalistic Share of Financial Resources in 1968 (■) and 1972 (▽) Plotted Against Circulation in Semi-Logarithmic Scale.[a]

Notes: [a] The scales have been omitted in order to preserve the anonymity of the newspapers.

[b] The regression line follows the equation Y = 93.00 - 12.31 log X. The b-coefficient is significantly different from zero on 1 per cent level of risk (t = 3.31, d. f. = 12). The equation explains 47.7 per cent of the variation in the share of financial resources.

[c] The regression line follows the equation Y = 110.33 - 16.69 log X. The b-coefficient is significantly different from zero on 1 per cent level of risk (t = 5.17, d. f. = 12). The equation explains 69.0 per cent of the variation in the share of financial resources.

The results imply a negative relationship between circulation and the allocation outcomes for the journalistic groups. This is further evidenced by the values of the rank correlation coefficient between circulation and share of financial resources: -0.723 in 1968 and -0.752 in 1972. Both these values are significantly different from zero on a one per cent level of risk.[1]

Turning to consider the second variable mentioned above, market position, we obtain the results exhibited in Table 8:2.

	1968	1972
Major	44.3 %	44.1 %
Minor	53.8 %	58.7 %
Total	49.0 %	51.4 %

Table 8:2. <u>Share of Total Revenues Allocated to the Journalistic Group in 1968 and 1972</u>.

The share of financial resources allocated to journalistic activities has thus been fairly constant in major papers, about 44 per cent, while it has increased in minor papers. In both years the minor papers spent a larger part of their total revenues on the journalistic group than on the business group. Two interpretations of this result are possible: (1) minor papers have larger editorial costs per copy, or (2) minor papers have smaller revenues per copy. And, of these two explanations, the first mechanism seems to be the case, since revenues per copy were somewhat larger in minor papers even before production subsidies were introduced: in 1968 they were SCr. 1.11 for minor papers and SCr. 1.02 for major papers.[2] Editorial costs per copy, on the other hand, were, as shown in Table 8:3, considerably larger in the group of minor papers: in 1972 they were SCr 0.96 vs. SCr 0.60 for major papers.

---

[1] For a formula for the derivation of critical values, see Cramér (1961, p. 188).
[2] Production subsidies were introduced in Sweden in 1971.

	Journalistic		Business	
	1968	1972	1968	1972
Major	0.43	0.60	0.57	0.87
Minor	0.64	0.96	0.69	1.29
Total	0.53	0.78	0.63	1.08

Table 8:3. Costs per Copy (SCr) in the Two Groups in 1968 and 1972.

Similar conclusions can be drawn for the business group irrespective of whether costs per copy or costs per column-meter are used for the analysis (cf. Table 8:3 and 8:4). The journalistic costs per column-meter, however, are larger in major papers than in minor papers. The latter is probably an effect of specialization efforts in larger newspapers, i.e. that more resources are allocated to different specialities.

	Journalistic		Business	
	1968	1972	1968	1972
Major	0.34	0.46	0.96	1.56
Minor	0.32	0.38	0.97	1.86
Total	0.33	0.42	0.96	1.71

Table 8:4. Costs per Column-meter (SCr) in the Journalistic and Business Groups in 1968 and 1972.

8.3 Provider Allocation

The most important allocation of providers is the allocation of employees. Whereas technology in most cases defines the input from other provider groups within quite narrow limits, the input of human work is more difficult to determine.

That manning can be an issue in newspapers has already been pointed out in the previous chapter. There, the manning issue was touched upon in relation to the introduction of new technology, i.e. when the rules of the game are changing. Under other circumstances manning is quite stable, and changes occur gradually as responses to economic problems or success. Similarly, gradual changes may occur in the manning of different departments and desks.

One tool of personnel planning is a manning list, showing the number of persons working in different parts of a newspaper. Changes in this list often reflect policy changes. An example is Dagens Nyheter, which some years ago cut down on its police reporter staff. This was done by a no-hiring policy as employees left the paper for one reason or another. In addition, some transfers occurred in response to internal advertisements of vacancies.[1]

The same paper also offers an example of how business operations influence hiring policy. In recent years Dagens Nyheter has according to an interviewee, had too few employees in certain jobs such as night editors and copy editors.[2] This situation has, according to the same source, probably arisen as the result of a non-active hiring policy. During a period of expansion the hiring policy was rather liberal, but as the inflow of advertisements started to decline a couple of years ago, a no-hiring policy was introduced. As a result the personnel structure was frozen. This was compounded when a law enforcing job security was introduced.[3]

Exceptions to the no-hiring policy have been openings arising as a result of product developments. Recruitment to these positions is often internal, which, in turn, leads to an inflow of outsiders. Examples are Dagens Nyheter's weekly supplement, På Stan, and some local weekly supplements for certain distribution areas.[4]

---

[1] "Now and then members of the staff came in and told me they wanted another job within the paper. But, sometimes I couldn't help them, there were no openings." (A managing editor.)

[2] "The resource problem is getting enough people to do the job."

[3] "The law has been devastating for newspapers." (An editor)

[4] It is worth noting that local supplements are more profitable than the main paper, since they have a 50/50 relation between ads and news, whereas the main paper holds a 40/60 per cent ratio. (Cf. more on this issue in Section 8.4).

Looking at the data for the fourteen Swedish newspapers, plotting the journalistic staff in 1972 against circulation produces the following result (Figure 8:2):

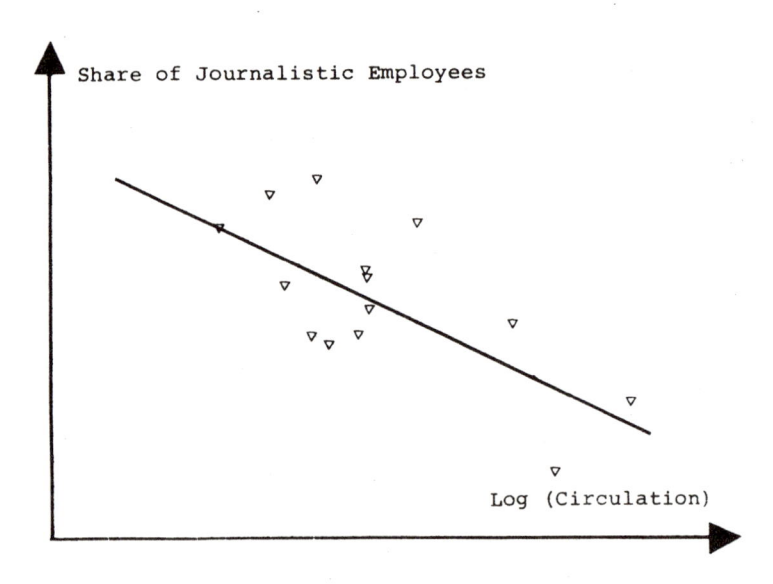

Figure 8:2 Share of Journalistic Employees in 1972 Plotted Against Circulation in Semi-Logarithmic Scale[a].

Note: [a] The scales have been omitted in order to preserve the anonymity of the newspapers.

The regression line follows the equation Y = 97.60 - 10.02 X. The b-coefficient is significantly different from zero on 1 per cent level of risk (t = -3.362, d.f. = 12). The equation explains 48.5 per cent of the variation in employee share.

Figure 8:2 demonstrates the negative relationship between circulation and the share of journalistic employees. This holds true for major as well as minor papers, although the relationship is weaker for the latter: the value of the rank correlation coefficient is -0.500 for major papers, -0.250 for minor papers and -0.490 for the total sample.[1]

---

[1] None of the values are significant on 5 per cent level of risk.

We find, then, that the relative shares of employees in the journalistic and business groups average roughly 60/40 per cent, major papers allocating a smaller share, 58.7 per cent, to the journalistic groups, compared to 65.7 per cent among minor papers. In these figures technical personnel have been distributed between the two groups according to the procedure described in the Appendix to this chapter.

By way of illustration it may be useful to diverge from this dichotomy for a moment and consider all three groups. Toward this end Table 8:5 shows the share of employees in the journalistic group, the business oriented group and the technical group.

	Journalistic	Business	Technical
Major	35.9 %	31.0 %	33.1 %
Minor	41.7 %	27.8 %	30.5 %
Total	38.8 %[a]	29.4 %	31.8 %

Table 8:5. Share of Employees in the Three Groups

Note:
[a] 15.5 per cent were employed in local branch editorial offices, while 23.3 per cent were employed in the main editorial office.

Thus, the three groups each account for about one-third of the employees, with the journalistic group somewhat more. Partitioning the newspaper into major and minor papers, we find that the share of the journalistic employees is larger in the latter. This circumstance probably reflects efforts on the part of minor papers to keep journalistic standards on a par with their larger competitor. A further illustration of the same fact is the average difference in the size of the three groups between the seven pairs of competing major and minor papers (Table 8:6).

	Journalistic	Business	Technical
Number of Employees	8.9	15.8	14.8
Per Cent	12.5 %	27.3 %	24.6 %

Table 8:6. Average Difference in Number of Employees Between Pairs of Newspapers in the Same Distribution Area.

Thus we find that the difference in number of employees is much more pronounced with regard to business and technical personnel than among journalistic personnel. The circumstance that minor papers sometimes have even larger editorial staffs than their larger competitor is particularly worth noting in this context.

The size of the business and technical groups thus varies more closely with circulation than the size of the journalistic group, a fact verified by the values of the rank correlation coefficient between circulation and the size of the three groups. The values are 0.538 for the journalistic groups, 0.718 for the business group and 0.859 for the technical group.[1]

If we then look at productivity in the fourteen newspapers in terms of column-meter per journalist and day, we obtain an estimate of 0.96 for the group as a whole. Distinguishing, then, between major and minor papers, we find that productivity is lower in the major papers than in the minor ones: 0.88 compared to 1.04. This circumstance is also consistent with the findings with respect to costs per column-meter (cf. above Table 8:4), which indicated higher costs in major papers. Both results are probably a result of a greater degree of specialization in major newspapers. An indication of this mechanism is a statement of a managing editor of a large Swedish newspaper, who said in an interview: "All in all, the editorial office is oversized. But, you need the specialists for certain jobs. The problem is not increasing productivity, but rather making people satisfied with their job despite the fact that only a small portion of their material is published.[2]

---

[1] The three values are significant on 5, 1 and 0.1 per cent levels of risk, respectively.

[2] A member of the editorial staff in the same newspaper, a business specialist, mentioned that he considered employee productivity fairly low: "I took measurements. They indicate that a journalist on this paper produces on average between 0.1 and 0.3 column meters per day." (Compare the figures 0.88 and 1.09 above for major and minor papers in the present sample.)
The competitor of this newspaper provides an illustration that employee productivity -- measured in column-meters per journalist and day -- is greater in the minor paper. The competitor has only half as many journalists as the major paper. Nevertheless, they produce almost as many columns a day as the major paper (the minor competitor being eight columns shorter).

Some further ideas of staffing mechanisms can be obtained by relating the analysis to the findings of Deutschmann (1959) and Polich (1974) concerning size of editorial staff and circulation. Regression lines for the number of journalists plotted against circulation in double logarithmic scale have been derived in accordance with their methodology. The results are shown in Figure 8:3 and Table 8:7.

Log (Number of Persons in Editorial Office)

Major Papers
Total Sample
Minor Papers
Deutschmann and Polich

Log (Circulation)

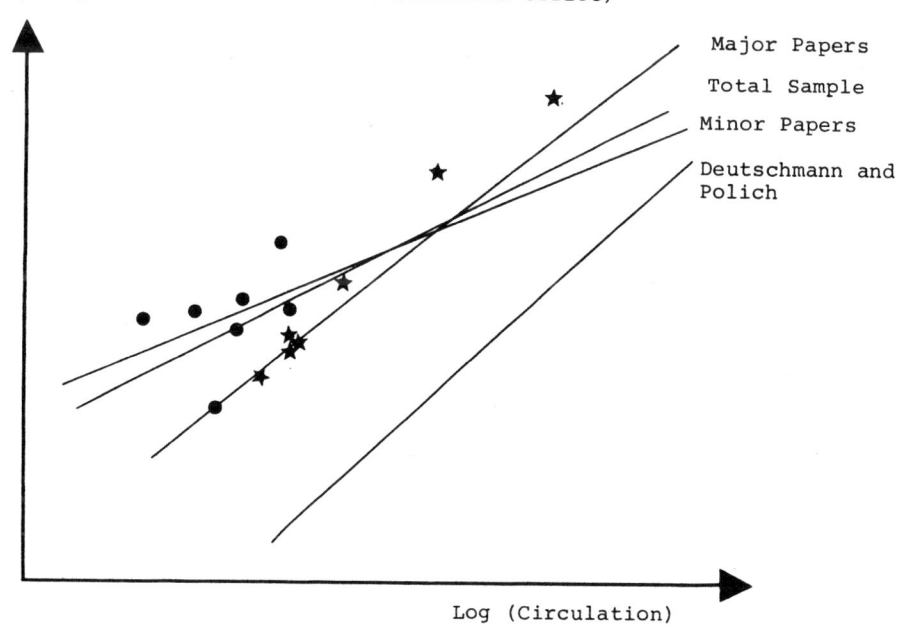

Figure 8:3. <u>Number of Persons in Editorial Office Plotted Against Circulation in Double Logarithmic Scale</u>.[a]

Note:
[a] The scale of the axes has been omitted in order to preserve the anonymity of the newspapers, ● refers to minor papers and ★ to major papers.

	α	β	t	R^2
Major[a]	1.319	0.767	3.63	0.725
Minor	2.856	0.393	0.98	0.162
Total	2.445	0.497	3.59	0.518
Deutschmann	1.200	0.872	--[b]	0.903
Polich	1.172	0.880	--[b]	0.935

Table 8:7. <u>Parameters in the Regression Equations for the Number of Journalists on Circulation in Double Logarithmic Scale.</u>[c]

Notes: [a] The coefficients refer to the equation: log (Number of Persons in Editorial Office) = α + β log (Circulation)

[b] Data unavailable.

[c] The coefficient for major papers and the total sample is significantly different from zero on the 2 per cent level of risk, whereas that for minor papers is not significant on even the 10 per cent level of risk.

The slope of the line for major newspapers in the Swedish sample is very similar to those estimated by Deutschmann and Polich, while the slope of the line for the whole sample is less steep. It is also striking that the intercepts are much larger for the Swedish newspapers. This result can to some extent depend on the definition of editorial staff: Deutschmann uses "full-time editorial staff", and it is not clear whether or not part-time employees have been "translated" to full-time employees as was done in the present study.[1] But, even if we only consider journalists employed in the main office of the newspapers, editorial staffs would appear to be larger in the Swedish sample. One possible explanation for this state of affairs is that Swedish newspapers produce more articles internally than their American counterparts. American papers make greater use of news bureau material and syndicated columns. Another explanation is the difference in space allocation practices in the

---

[1] Nor is it possible to determine how Polich defines editorial employees.

two countries.[1] Whereas about thirty per cent of Swedish newspapers is devoted to advertisements, ads occupy as much as sixty per cent or more of the space in American newspapers.

8.4 Allocation of Space

The sub-issue concerning allocation of space has to do with the mix of news and advertisements in the newspaper. This problem is particularly important, since, as has been mentioned several times, the revenue derived from advertising is in most newspapers greater than revenue from readers. This means that the business group may consider an increase in advertising space an attractive alternative as they look for sources of greater revenue.

In order to handle space allocation most newspapers use budgets and quotas. The design of these instruments differs somewhat between different newspapers, however. Looking at the four American newspapers studied, we find that The Boston Globe uses lower and upper limits (minimum and maximum space) for the news department, The New York Post allocates a fixed proportion of each issue (45/88) to news, The New York Times assigns a basic daily quota (208 columns), whereas newsspace in The Washington Post is allocated on the basis of a yearly budget which is broken down into weekly budgets. In all cases leeway is given for unforeseen events and daily space allocation decisions are made in meetings between people from the news-room and the advertising department.

Data from the French newspaper Le Monde illustrate the dynamics of space allocation. The size of this paper is determined by a ready-reckoner (un barème), which, assuming certain volumes of advertisement inflow, prescribes for each day of the week: (1) the number of pages to be printed, and (2) the distribution between

---

[1] Yet another explanation is that the American newspaper market is more locally monopolized.

news pages and advertising pages. This lineage guide implies that
the number of news pages increases with the inflow of advertisements, but they do not increase as rapidly as the advertisement
pages. Thus whereas the news pages on average make up 68 per cent of
a 24-page paper, "le barème" allocates only 53 per cent of a 36-page
paper and 48 per cent of a 48-page paper to news.

At The Record the size of each issue is determined by the news
editor, who applies a general rule from management to the volume
of ads received in the morning.[1] He then obtains up-to-date
figures later in the day (3.00 p.m. and 5.00 p.m.), and if the inflow of ads is unexpectedly heavy he goes up to the Managing Director for consultations.[2] The decision they take is very seldom
changed, but if late ads are in extremely large number, changes may
also be made late at night after consultations between the night
editor and the foreman of the composing room. But, most of the time
inflow of additional ads instead leads to the deletion of some
stories.[3]

In addition to being a problem between the news oriented and the
business oriented groups, space allocation is also a problem within
the news oriented group, since different desks and journalists
fight for space in the paper.[4] The executive editor of The Washington Post, however, characterized this conflict as a "creative tension", acting as a stimulus in the production of the newspaper.

---

[1] The rule prescribes that the paper hold a minimum format, irrespective of the inflow of advertisements. As the inflow of advertisements passes a certain limit, pages are added according to certain rules.

[2] Cf. here Chapter One (Section 1A5: "The Policy Discussion").

[3] Section 1A5 of Chapter One pointed to the fact that The Record due to the rising prices of newsprint, has decided to cut down the number of pages. This has caused certain frustrations among the journalists: "Just imagine you've been doing a job. Then several days go by before it's published. And, when it's published it's severely cut down. -- There is also a risk that the stories become out-of-date. A story on a demonstration on May 1, for instance, cannot be published in mid-May." Postponement of publication and deletion are a particular problem for authors of series, when some of the first articles have been published but the following ones have to wait and therefore become out-of-date.

[4] Important in this context is also whether or not a story makes the front page. (Cf. Adler, 1971, p. 139 and p. 150; Sigal, 1973, p. 12.)

The fight between different desks is also the major allocation conflict in some newspapers[1]. And, since the amount of news within different areas varies over time, bargaining for space is a continuous process. Quite often bidding for space cannot be based on factual events, since the bids have to be submitted quite early in the day (or the day before), long before the respective desks know what will come up. As one journalist expressed it: "We have to guess quite a bit. Look at to-day's paper, for instance! We didn't know any of our stories before 4 p.m. But, we had to ask for space at 11 this morning."

The space demands of the different desks are used as input to allocation decisions taken in meetings between editors. The variations between different days are in most cases small, however. Thus, some papers have certain predetermined space quotas for different desks per day or per week.[2] These may then bargain for more space as special events occur. A problem arises when special events fail to develop according to expectations. This was particularly stressed by a sports journalist, pointing to the fact that success for the home team requires more space than a failure: "Take the soccer game against Yugoslavia, for instance. We thought the Swedes would win and had one and a half pages ready. Then, they lost, 3-0. That's not so interesting!"

It was mentioned earlier that the outcome of the space allocation decisions between news and ads is dependent on the profile a paper chooses to strive after. The same is also true of the allocation between different desks. At The Record, for instance, priority is given to sports and local news. This is illustrated in Figure 8:4, which shows the share of space allocated to different content during one month in 1974.[3]

---

[1] Papers having a good inflow of ads can use the ads as "fuel" since more ads give more money for news coverage. Others need to hunt for ads for revenue and to fill a minimum space of advertising. A particular restriction in allocating space is the predetermined allocations to local pages, etc.

[2] Such predetermined space quotas tend to reinforce differentiation and the creation of "separate kingdoms" (cf. Chapter Five, Section 5.2: "Differentiation").

[3] Similarly, but with another orientation, Le Monde gives priority to foreign news, economic issues and domestic politics, which occupied an average of fifty per cent of that paper's news space in 1974.

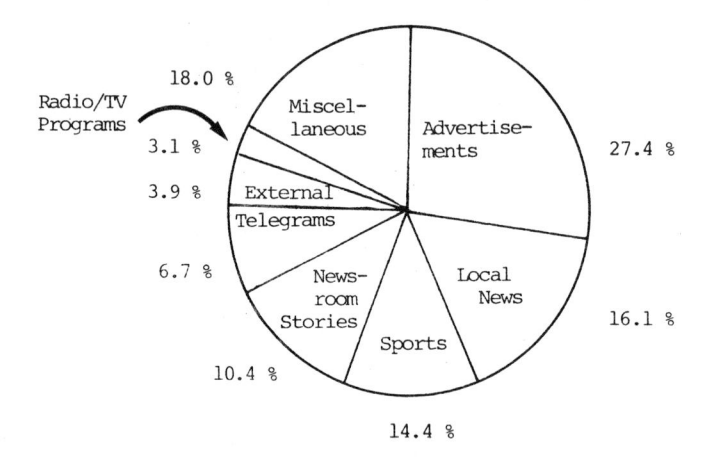

Figure 8:4. The Outcome of Space Allocation in The Record During One Month in 1974.

Note: [a] These are all items accorded two per cent of the space or less. They include Letters to the Editor, editorials, cartoons, reviews, etc.

Pursuing the space allocation issue on a lower level, we may note competition for space between different local editors, each of whom are under continuous pressure from their respective communities where the general feeling is that the paper contains too little news from the neighbourhood.[1]

The previous chapter showed how increasing aspirations and wishes for compensation are likely to lead to pressures for growth. In this context new technology has implied a way out, as increasing demands for rewards on the part of providers have been difficult to transfer to customers. The new technology will not help with respect to the allocation of space, however.

---

[1] Statistics on the allocation of local pages have been compiled in The Record in order to provide local editors with figures demonstrating that their respective communities were not under-represented.

Earlier, demands for more space were met by increases in the size of the newspaper, but such arrangements are likely to become difficult in the future due to newsprint shortages and increasing costs for newsprint and distribution.[1] Therefore, space allocation decisions in the future are likely to become more difficult than earlier. Probable courses of action are selectivity with respect to the news printed, the cutting of stories, cuts in the size and number of pictures.[2]

Looking at the data for the fourteen Swedish newspapers, plotting of the journalistic share of space against circulation produces the following result (Figure 8:5)

Figure 8:5 demonstrates the negative relationship between circulation and share of journalistic space. This is further evidenced by the values of the rank correlation coefficient between circulation and journalistic share of space: -0.723 in 1968 and -0.773 in 1972.

---

[1] In 1950 the size of The Washington Post was thirty pages; today it is double that size.

[2] In the United States at least, there are limits on the possibilities to cut down on news space, since some papers already are nearing the minimum requirements for second class postage by U.S. mail, twenty-five per cent news. The percentage news space in the four American newspapers interviewed was:

The Boston Globe	30-40 per cent (Sundays: 30% and weekdays: 40%)
The New York Post	51.1 per cent
The New York Times	33.3 per cent
The Washington Post	26.0 per cent

By way of comparison it can be mentioned that the average for Swedish newspapers in 1967 was 69.1 per cent (SOU 1968:48, p. 106, Table 5).

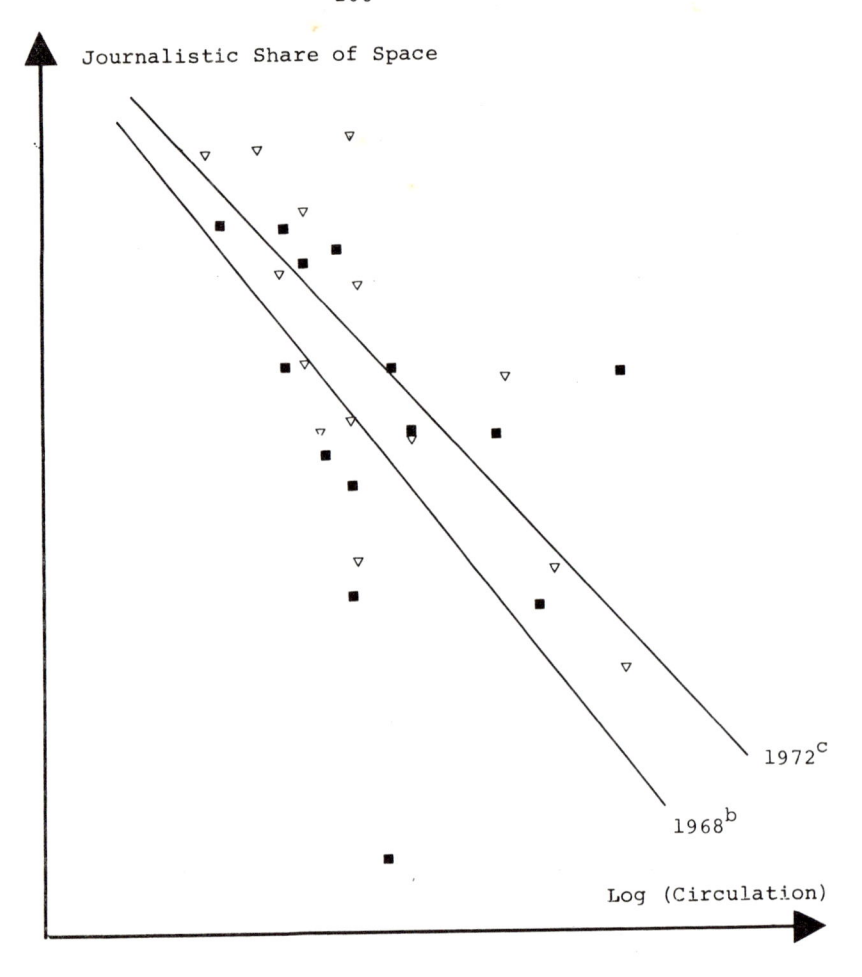

Figure 8:5. <u>Journalistic Share of Space Plotted Against Circulation 1968 (■) and 1972 (▽).</u>[a]

Note: [a] The scales have been omitted in order to preserve the anonymity of the newspapers.

[b] The regression line follows the equation $Y = 109.17 - 9.45 \log X$. The b-coefficient is significantly different from zero on 1 per cent level of risk ($t = 3.18$, d.f. = 12). The equation explains 45.8 per cent of the variation in the share of space.

[c] The regression line follows the equation $Y = 107.09 - 9.45 \log X$. The b-coefficient is significantly different from zero on 1 per cent level of risk ($t = 4.03$, d.f. = 12). The equation explains 57.5 per cent of the variation in the share of space.

Both these values are significantly different from zero on a one per cent level of risk.

The fourteen newspapers studied exhibit a 70/30 per cent relationship between news and advertising space, a relationship which, as indicated in Table 8:8 has changed to the advantage of journalistic copy in the interval between 1968 and 1972.

	1968	1972
Major	67.7 %	69.3 %
Minor	72.2 %	78.1 %
Total	70.0 %	73.7 %

Table 8:8. **Space in Per Cent Allocated to the Journalistic Group in 1968 and 1972.**

The change to the advantage of journalistic copy is true of both major and minor newspapers during this period, a circumstance corroborated by the growth rates shown in Table 8:9.

	Journalistic	Business	Total
Major	0.73 %	- 0.65 %	0.05 %
Minor	3.20 %	- 1.10 %	2.19 %
Total	1.97 %	- 0.88 %	1.12 %

Table 8:9. **Annual Average Growth Rates in Space in the Period 1968 — 1972.**

Thus, the journalistic group has gained space, whereas the business group has lost. Since Table 8:9 shows growth rates in colomn meters, this result -- growth for one group and decline for the other -- is far from self-evident. As has been mentioned above, many papers have responded to pressure for more space by increasing the total size of the paper. This has been the case among minor newspapers (a growth in space of 2 per cent per year), whereas the growth is insignificant for major papers. It is also in minor papers that news space has grown the most, 3.2 per cent, while the business group in such papers has lost the most, 1.1 per cent.[1] Production subsidies are the likely explanation to the growth of journalistic space in minor newspapers.

8.5 Concluding Remarks

Like all other organizations newspapers face the problem of how to share scarce resources among participating members. This issue has, as we have seen, three dimensions: financial resources, providers (mainly employees) and space. There are thus a number of conflicting interests with respect to the allocation issue.

There is competition between external and internal providers (the latter represented by the business oriented group) concerning financial resources. There is competition between the business oriented group and the other internal providers for financial as well as personnel resources. And, there is competition between the news oriented and business oriented groups concerning space. In addition, finally, there is internal competition within the news oriented group for the allocation of space. A graphic summary of the allocation issue would therefore look like Figure 8:6.

---

[1] The rank correlation between space in column-meters and circulation is lower for journalistic space than for advertising. The values of the coefficient are 0.305 and 0.815, respectively. For a sample of the size used here, significant values are 0.53 on 5 per cent level of risk, 0.66 on 1 per cent level of risk, and 0.78 on 0.1 per cent level of risk.

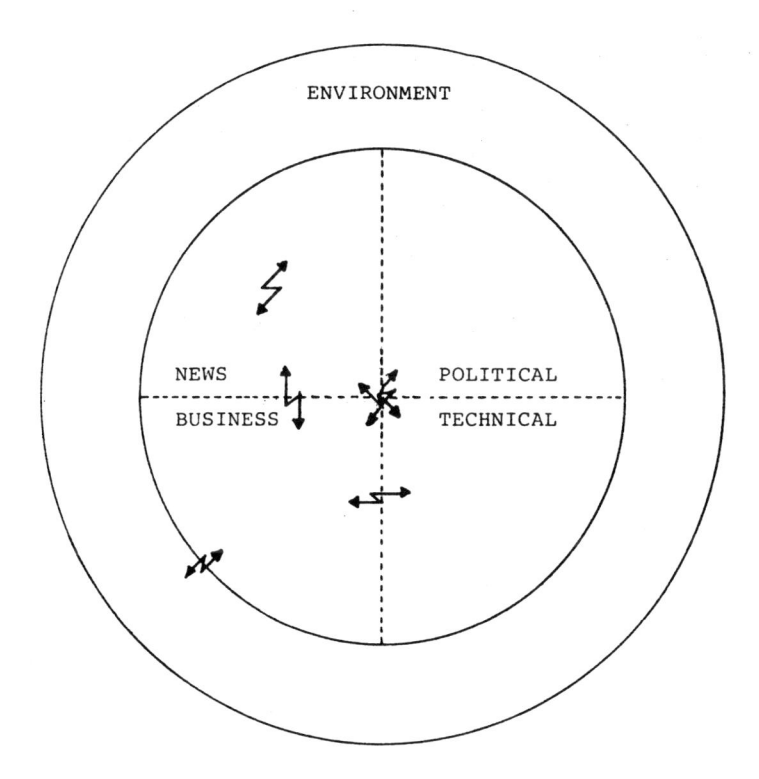

Figure 8:6. Allocation Conflicts between Groups.

We have noted that different budget procedures are used in newspapers to handle problems of allocation. Empirical data from a sample of fourteen Swedish newspapers also illustrated the outcome of some allocation decisions. And, we note certain similarities between the results for the three types of decisions. These similarities are also corroborated by the values of the rank correlation coefficient between the different outcomes, as shown in Table 8:10.

Share of Space vs. Share of Employees 0.726^{xx}
Share of Financial Resources vs. Share of Employees 0.618^{x}
Share of Financial Resources vs. Share of Space 0.625^{x}

Table 8:10.   Values of the Rank Correlation Coefficient between Three Allocation Variables.[a]

Note:
[a] Significant values for a sample of the size used here are 0.53 on 5 per cent level of risk (x) and 0.66 on 1 per cent level of risk (xx).

In reading the table it should, of course, be remembered that technical personnel and expenses for the technical department and newsprint have been distributed according to space allocation figures. This procedure has only raised the values of the correlation coefficient from about 0.5-0.6 to 0.6-0.7, however.

They are also demonstrated by the profiles of allocation outcomes shown in Figure 8:7. Thus, although on different levels, the profiles for different groups of newspapers are very similar.

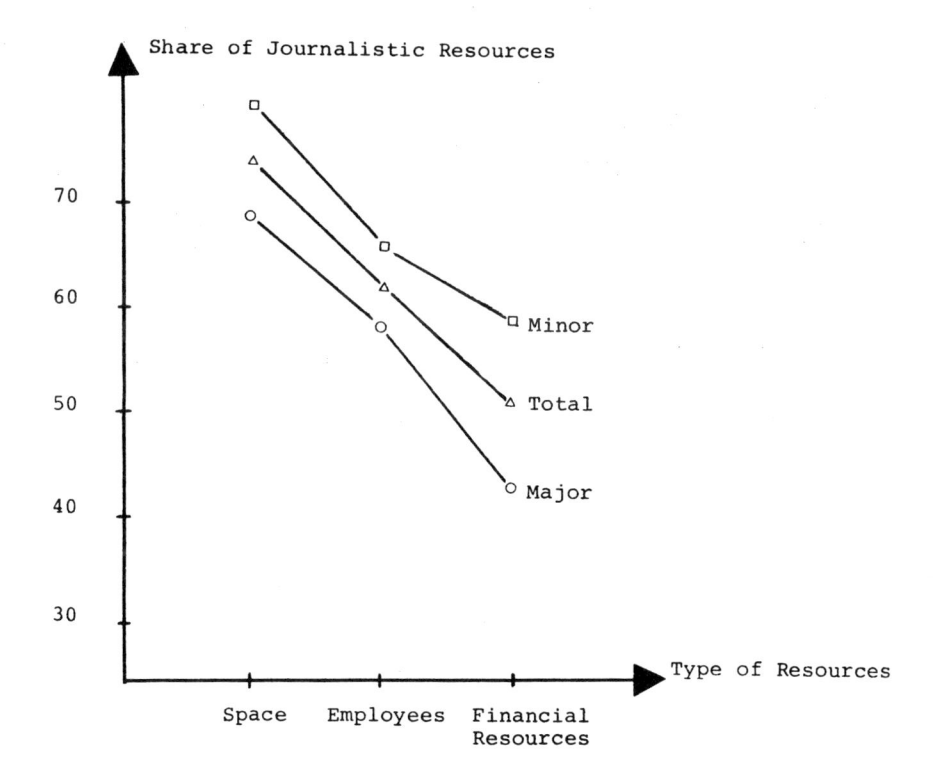

Figure 8:7. Share of Journalistic Resources for Different Groups of Newspapers in 1972.

Summarizing the results, we found that major papers differ from minor papers in that they
- allocate a smaller share of space, employees and financial resources to the journalistic group
- have higher journalistic costs per column-meter, but lower business costs
- have smaller costs per copy of both journalistic and business activities

In addition, we have found that the share of resources allocated to the journalistic group is negatively related to circulation.

Finally, it would appear that Swedish newspapers produce journalistic material internally to a greater extent than their American counterparts.[1]

---

[1] The generality of the above conclusions is, of course, very much dependent on the sample used. Indeed, the results refer only to the fourteen Swedish newspapers selected. But, as was mentioned in Chapter Two (Section 2.4: "Allocation Data Analysis"), these papers have an average weekly circulation similar to that of the total population. Moreover, they have been chosen so as to provide wide geographic distribution throughout Sweden.

APPENDIX TO CHAPTER EIGHT. VARIABLES USED.

In the analysis space allocation was measured in terms of the (percentage) shares of total space devoted to news and advertising, respectively. The measure of circulation was the daily circulation reported in the Year-Book of Swedish Audit Bureau of Statistics (TS-boken).[1]

With regard to allocation of employees, all employees were considered, viz. employees in the main office as well as externally located ones. The following procedure was followed in assigning the different employees to the two groups: employees working in administrative functions, in advertising and circulation were brought to the business group, whereas employees in the editorial office were brought to the journalistic group. Employees in the mechanical department, finally were divided between the two groups according to space, a proxy of the extent to which the services of the technical group have been used by the journalistic and the business group.

The analysis of the allocation of financial resources is more complicated than that of the other allocation outcomes, since cost figures were only available for the editorial office, circulation and advertising. Of these, editorial office costs were referred to the journalistic group, and circulation and advertising costs to the business group. Estimates must be used in taking other costs into consideration. This seemed possible, since the quota costs/revenues for the editorial office and circulation and advertising departments were very similar to those shown in Section 8.2 (Table 8:1), where, taking an average of five studies of distribution of expenses, it was found that 22.9 per cent of the expenses were allocated to the editorial office and 25.6 per cent to circulation and advertising. The corresponding figures for the sample used in this study were 22.6 per cent and 28.5 per cent, respectively. In view of these similarities, the remaining expenses

---

[1] An alternative would have been to use weekly circulation (daily circulation times the number of publication days per week), which was the measure used in Engwall (1974 a), but as the papers in the present sample do not vary very much with respect to periodicity, daily circulation can be used.

were estimated for each newspaper in accordance with the results in the previous study. The expenses for the technical department and for newsprint were then distributed betwen the two groups according to space allocation ratios. Administrative costs were assigned to the business group.

Measuring costs per output of the papers, finally, two indicators were used: <u>costs per column-meter</u> and <u>costs per copy</u>. The values of the indicators have been computed for the two groups separately, journalistic costs per column-meter equalling journalistic costs, divided by the number of column-meters devoted to news, and so forth.

CHAPTER NINE. PUBLICATION.

9.1 Introduction

Section 1A2 of Chapter One recounted Phil's work with a story on a bankrupt company. This case demonstrated a common issue in newspapers: that concerning <u>publication policy</u>. It featured differences in opinion between the President of the bankrupt company and <u>The Record</u> concerning the ethical fairness of publishing a story, i. e. a conflict between an interviewee (a person in the environment) and internal providers. The publication issue may also arise between different groups of employees and may even appear within groups (particularly within the news oriented group).

The purpose of the present chapter is to discuss such conflicts as well as to elaborate on the checks applied in this context. Section 9.2 describes the conflicts involved, whereas Sections 9.3 to 9.5 are devoted to the different checks. Section 9.6, finally discusses some results of publication decisions.

9.2 The Conflicts Involved

News concerns events (or processes) which, as has been pointed out by Berger and Luckman (1966), give rise to different interpretations of "reality". These interpretations will differ among different "insiders", i.e. those involved, among "outsiders", as well as between outsiders and insiders. It is therefore not surprising that Phil, an outsider in the Pankab affair, had a completely different image of the bankruptcy than the President of the company. As a result, the latter rejected Phil's story from the beginning and even tried to prevent its publication. This divergence of views was reinforced by the work of the copy-editors, who edited the story, added the headlines and decided to feature the story on the news bill.Their work annoyed not only the company President, but Phil, too, who at first resented some of the formulations in the headlines.

The reasons for these various "misfits" differ somewhat: in the case of the President, the company had a commercial interest in suppressing an unfavourable story. Phil, for his part, had a professional interest in revealing what he saw to be unfair practices, so he was unwilling to check the story with the company President before publishing it.[1] In the case of Phil versus the copy-editors, it was rather a question of the difficulty of summarizing a long story, compounded by the copy-editors' difficulty in reaching the author of the story for consultation.[2]

Leaving the internal conflict for the moment and concentrating on the external conflict, we may note that journalists cannot always -- as Phil could -- withstand pressures not to publish a story. The experience of one interviewee, a journalist working in a local editorial office, is significant in this context: "I had produced a good story on a planned construction project. I wanted to wind up my work by checking with the construction company. But, the employees were gagged. Finally, I got to talk to the President himself. He gave evasive answers. A quarter of an hour later, the main editorial office phoned and told me to throw away the story! I had a good story, but I couldn't do anything."[3]

Pressures are especially likely to be put on small community papers, which are most dependent on their local environment for information as well as commercially. Sources of information are very important for a local paper, and it is thus difficult to write unflattering stories on useful informants.

---
[1] We will recall that, as a matter of fact, he had also hoped to be able to avoid talking to the President before writing.

[2] Criticism often concerns the formulation of headlines. A striking example occurred on The Record during my visit. A local correspondent had written a story in which he stated that a poster had been set up "in order to inform, not to warn". When the headline opened with the words: "Poster warns ....", he was quite unhappy.

[3] For another example, see Hammenskog (1969, p. 124), who describes the pressure put on an editor-in-chief by a local union leader, who wanted the paper to "kill" a story he considered unfavourable to the union.

We may also note that external publication conflicts include numerous cases, when the external party is not a business firm or an organization, which are able to put pressure on the newspaper, but a private person. In such cases the issue of publication may be very touchy and may even lead to tragic consequences due to the individual's difficulties to rebut the printed text.[1]

The conflicts between a newspaper and elements in the environment may lead to different conflicts inside the newspaper. Conflict frequently arises between the news/politically oriented groups and the business oriented group as a result of the latter's fears of economic retaliation as a result of news coverage or political stands which may displease persons or groups in the environment. Evidence in Sweden that such fears may be well-grounded includes the cancellation of advertising by two big companies -- Algots and Swedish Philips -- in response to negative publicity (cf. Ortmark, 1969, p. 327). As Ortmark notes, however, such drastic actions are not very common, since there are more sophisticated means by which to exert pressure on newspapers.

Conflicts between the journalistic and business wings may also arise without any external pressure: in one large Swedish newspaper, for instance, such a conflict arose as a group of feature journalists started a series of critical stories on different phenomena in society, among them advertising. These articles led to immediate protests from the advertising department: "Do you want to cut off the hand that feeds you?" An example of irritation on the part of journalists, on the other hand, is the planning of "special" issues on certain themes. In these cases marketing people try to solicit advertisements of a certain type for publication in an issue containing stories related to the common theme of ads. Journalists argue that the initiative ought to arise in the news-room.

---

[1] This problem has been treated by many novelists, among whom the most notable in recent years is Heinrich Böll, who in his novel "Die Verlorene Ehre der Katharina Blum" ("The Lost Honour of Katharina Blum", 1974) recounts the problems faced by a young women as a big evening paper runs a series of articles on her contacts with a wanted person. Their meetings have been very innocent, but as the paper gives another impression entirely, she is condemned by the public opinion with no chance to defend herself.
Other works elaborating on the mistreatment of private persons by daily newspapers include Gustafson (1968), Sandgren (1968), Hammenskog (1969) and Rifbjerg (1974).

As for political stands, conflicts may develop as editorials criticize people or institutions of economic importance to the newspaper. A particular problem arises in this context if there are ties between the newspaper and other corporations. Argyris (1974, p. 176 and p. 194), for example, points to the problems of the President of The Daily Planet in trying to maintain good relations with members of the board of the paper whose activities had been criticized in editorials.[1]

The interviews undertaken in the present study suggest that the possibilities for owner intervention are much larger in American newspapers than in Swedish newspapers.[2] The possibilities for management to step in and criticize reporting are in some Swedish newspapers quite limited As one Swedish newspaper manager expressed it: "It's a funny situation. You manage the company, but you can't influence the design of the product!" And, another interviewee, a journalist in a metropolitan newspaper, stressed that it would be considered most improper if management even hinted to people in the news-room that a president of another company had complained about the reporting in the paper.

In the relations between the <u>news oriented</u> and <u>the politically oriented groups</u> irritation may arise in either of the two groups. Conflict is particularly likely when a newspaper is run with the express purpose of representing certain opinions. In many cases, however, dictates from the owners in this respect are met with opposition on the part of the editorial staff, who support their objections with references to freedom of the press.[3]

---

[1] Adler (1971, p. 97) notes a similar conflict in that one and the same issue of The New York Times contained advertising <u>for</u> cigarettes as well as an editorial <u>against</u> smoking.

[2] In British newspapers, on the other hand, The National Union of Journalists claims the right of editors to determine the contents of the newspaper free of any pressures from owners and other groups. This issue has been under negotiation between journalists and newspaper publishers for some time.

[3] Cf. here e. g. Tingsten (1947 <u>a</u>, 1971 <u>a</u>, pp. 83-90; 1971 <u>b</u>, pp. 215-240).

It is worth noting that Tingsten left his post as editor-in-chief of Dagens Nyheter after a controversy with the owners on a political stand. An analysis of this conflict and earlier ones between Tingsten and the owners is provided by Berg (1967).
A related case occurred in the United Kingdom in 1970 when Cecil King suggested that Mr. Wilson should step down from the office of Prime Minister. This stand caused a conflict with the owners, which finally resulted in Cecil King's leaving The Daily Mirror.

The circumstance that the publication conflict sometimes is an
internal conflict within the news oriented group has already been
mentioned. A conflict between different individuals may thus arise in
the processing of copy.[1] Conflict is particularly common between
editors and reporters, the former having a restraining effect on
reporters.[2]

Hitherto, only three of the four organizational groups have been mentioned in relation to the publication issue. There are also examples
of the involvement of the technically oriented group in conflicts concerning publication. One of these occurred in The Financial
Times in relation to the paper's presentation of the interim report
of the Royal Commission on the Press during mid-Spring of 1976. The
editor, considering the information incorrect, deleted a line concerning a group of top-salary journalists, whereas he kept a line on
high-wage printers. The printers argued that The Financial Times presented a biased view, and the ultimate result was that the paper was
not published on the following day, when the editor refused to revise
the paragraph in question.[3]

Another example, which has business implications as well, is a conflict at Dagens Nyheter in early October 1975. This conflict arose
as a result of an appeal from the Swedish National Graphical Association to boycott ads for travel to Spain after the execution of five
resistance men by the Franco regime. Representatives of the local
union at Dagens Nyheter therefore approached management trying to
arrange such a boycott. No agreement was reached, and during a couple
of days the printers removed all Spanish place names appearing in
ads (cf. e.g. Dagens Nyheter, October 4, 1975, p. 38). The conflict
caused an intensive debate inside the house as well as on the editorial
page.

---

[1] This issue will be further discussed below in Section 9.5.

[2] For a discussion of this conflict, cf. Gieber (1964) and Flegel & Chafee (1971). The former provides a general discussion, whereas the latter presents an empirical study of two newspapers in Madison, Wisconsin. The empirical study points to consistent and rather broad political divergences between reporters and editors.

[3] A similar event happened in The Evening Standard some years ago. But, on that occasion the copy was set, together with a comment by the editor on the view of the labour union.

A less dramatic example can be taken from The Record, where it once happened that the non-journalist unions went to the Board of Directors complaining about the paper's reporting of a specific issue. In the opinion of these unions, the journalists had damaged The Record commercially. The reporting was discussed in a board meeting, but no further action was taken.[1]

In a minor paper, like The Record, the publication issue is also reinforced by the need to set priorities. These, in turn, create dissatisfaction among certain employees, since they consider some topics mistreated: "The editorial office is not producing the stories people would like to have. There is too much politics and too little about the little things that affect people. As a matter of fact, they don't listen to tip-offs or our criticism." (An employee working in circulation.)[2]

In comparison with the other three issues discussed, the publication conflict has implications for more of the relations between different groups of newspaper employees. As a matter of fact, it is an issue bearing upon the relations between all groups. In addition, it is important for the paper's relations to the environment as well as for relations within groups. A summarizing diagram of the publication conflict thus looks like Figure 9:1.

---

[1] It should be mentioned, however, that the reporter who wrote the stories in question obtained positive comments from colleagues in non-Socialist newspapers: "You are in a good situation. You, who are able to do a frank story!"

[2] This remark touches upon the crucial question in the reporting of a newspaper: What should be covered? Which stories interest the average reader? What stories is he able to understand?
In relation to the last question it is worth noting that there is empirical evidence that the language used in Swedish daily newspapers is quite difficult for average readers (cf. Frick & Malmström, 1976).

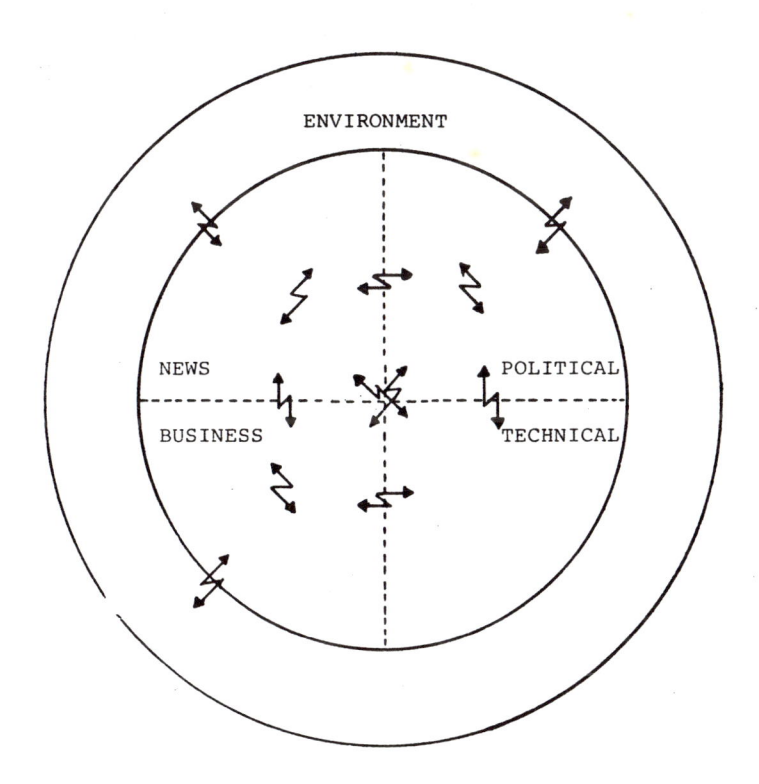

Figure 9:1. Publication Conflicts between Groups

There are a number of integrating mechanisms in relation to the publication conflict. First of all, there are external rules of the game. Second, recruitment involves considerable screening of applicants. And, third, the flow of news and stories is continuously controlled.

9.3 External Rules of the Game

The ultimate boundaries for publication activities in a country are the laws governing the work of the press. These, in turn, can be regarded as a reflexion of the theory of the press dominating the country (cf. Chapter Four, Section 4.5: "External Providers III: Governments"). In addition, they aim at protecting certain interests such as the privacy of individuals and secrets of national defence.[1]

Thus, the easier it is for outsiders to sue the newspaper, the more cautious it will be. And, in this context, complicated laws may make editors overly cautious and cause them to play it safe. This cautiousness may even be reinforced as newspapers hire legal advisers to guard against the possibility of libel suits. A London Times journalist in discussing such legal advisers thus exclaimed: "He doesn't take chances when you ask him. Every time you ask him, he says you are breaking the law."[2]

Other external checks on publication reside in the publication norms set up by journalists and newspaper publishers. In Sweden there are rules of publication formulated by the National Press Club as well as a professional code of the Union of Journalists. The former rules stress the need to maintain the credibility of the press and

---

[1] An example of the latter case which aroused much debate in Sweden was the "IB-case". Two journalists managed to reveal too much of the Swedish "Secret Service". Both were tried for espionage and sentenced to prison, the public prosecutor having chosen not to try the case on the basis of the freedom of the press legislation valid at that time.

[2] In addition to putting questions to the legal advisors, The Times has a lawyer come in every day at 5 p.m. to read the proofs in order to check for libel.
It could be added that the interviewees considered the legal situation for the British press much more difficult than that in some other countries. It was, for instance, felt that the British press would have found it quite difficult to break the Watergate story. (Cf. also Tuchman, 1972, who writes on libel suits: "they are more frequent in England than in the United States. In [the U.S.] libel suits tend to be sensational.", ibid., p. 664.)

argue for such ideals as striving to provide correct information, maintaining a critical attitude toward news sources, the suppression of confidential information and respect for the privacy of individuals. The code of journalists points, among other things, to the integrity of the journalist and prescribes appropriate behaviour in relation to news sources.[1]

In addition to these professional codes, in Sweden there are The Ombudsman for the Press and The Press Review Board. The former receives complaints from persons regarding stories they find libelous, offensive or unethical (cf. again The President of Pankab in Chapter One, Section 1A2), but the Ombudsman can also examine stories on his own initiative. His work aims primarily at bringing about voluntary agreements between newspapers and those offended. In most cases this implies the publication of corrections to earlier stories. If such a solution is not sufficient, the Ombudsman may bring the case before the Press Ethics Review Board, which has been set up by The Newspaper Publishers' Association, the National Press Club and The Union of Journalists. The Review Board, which consists of nine members issues statements criticizing stories which they find unfair. The newspaper publishing a story resulting in such criticism is then obliged to publish the findings of the Board. In addition, the Board can impose a fine of up to SCr. 3,000 (cf. e.g. Furhoff, 1974 b, pp. 101-102).

But, even if all the rules of the game are followed, the leeway for publication is considerable. As one journalist working for a left-wing Swedish magazine expressed it: "The publication rules are no problem. For instance, they state that you should give individuals the opportunity to comment on a story. That's very easy. You simply phone him and say, 'We have information implying that you are a crook, have you any comment on that?' He will answer that he is not a crook, and adding this short denial to the story you will have satisfied the publication norms."[2]

---

[1] For a description, cf. e.g. Hederberg (1969, pp. 204-209) and Pressens Samarbetsnämnd (1970).
[2] Jan Guillou at a meeting of the National Press Club, November 25, 1976.

This approach is part of a larger strategy which Tuchman (1972) describes as "objectivity as strategic ritual." She mentions four such rituals, viz: (1) the presentation of conflicting possibilities, (2) the presentation of supporting evidence, (3) judicious use of quotation marks, and (4) the structuring of information in an appropriate sequence.[1]

In the first case evidence from one source is confronted with evidence from another, whereas the second ritual implies "locating and citing additional 'facts', which are commonly accepted as 'truth'" (ibid., p. 667).[2] The third ritual refers to the addition of quotations to the story so that, while the reporter may sympathize with all the statements enclosed in the quotation marks, "the quotation marks [enable] the reporter to claim he had not interjected his opinion into the story" (ibid., p. 669). The fourth ritual finally, points to the custom of presenting the facts in descending order to importance: "If the newsman can claim he has led with the 'most material things', he can claim he has been 'objective'". (ibid., p. 670).

In some cases, however, the four described strategies are not enough, and the passing on of "sensitive information" has to be undertaken in another way. In this context one alternative channel is provided by satirical papers like The Private Eye and Le Canard Enchaîné, which are more daring in their publishing policy than other papers and specialize in controversial material.

---

[1] Tuchman's conclusions have been discussed by Gans (1972).

[2] An example of the first case: "X says A. Y says B." -- An example in the second case: "[He] asked for 'more objective obits' after reading an obituary which described the deceased as a 'master musician' [. . . .] He was told that, several paragraphs into the story, one learns the deceased had played with John Philip Sousa. The additional 'fact' the editor agreed, justified the term 'master musician'." (Tuchman, 1972, p. 667)

The checking of information is particularly thorough in cases of negative information: "All text with a negative tendency must be checked and rechecked and if it will be published at all, it must be accompanied by a comment by those who may be hurt by the text, and the managing editors must under all conditions be informed. It is therefore quite clear that negative texts often land in the wastepaper basket, since they imply a great deal of work in order to get them published." (Hanson, 1968, p. 62 f., my translation from Swedish.)

An example can be taken from the British newspaper The Private Eye, which in April 1976, published the following passage on the leading candidate for, and later holder of, the office of Prime Minister:

> "James Callaghan's political qualities, so the hacks inform us day by day, are similar to those of Harold MacMillan. He is, we are told, avuncular, reassuring, unflappable, wise. On the contrary, all the records show that, in office and out of it, Callaghan behaves like a nervous corporal, eager to carry out someone else's orders, and quick to panic if he is left on his own. He is also, into the bargain, prey to what is known in Westminster as 'the Maudling/Thorpe disease' -- which is caught after close association with property speculators and fringe bankers of a not altogether wholesome variety." (Private Eye, 2 April, 1976, p. 16)

Although established papers are hardly likely to be first to publish the above type of material, they publish it readily once disclosed. And, here the judicious use of quotation marks comes in: "according to the latest issue of The Private Eye, Mr. So-and-So is . . . .".

9.4 Selective Recruitment

A widely used technique to maintain stability in organisations is to apply selective recruitment, i.e. to recruit persons who fit the norms and values prevailing within the organization. This approach is to particular advantage in newspapers, where individual journalists work largely by themselves and where time pressure limits the opportunity for control. Thus, Sigelman (1973) in a participant observation study found that selective recruitment played an important role with respect to attitude promotion in newspapers.[1] As a result of this selective recruiting, Sigelman found, "newspapers appear to devote few resources to centrally insuring that new members are socialized into favourable attitudes." (Ibid., p. 138). He also discovered in his study that selective recruitment was mainly a question of self-selection. In his words: "Political criteria [.....] do play a significant role in recruitment -- but it is the recruits, not the newspapers, who actually apply them." (ibid., p. 138)

---

[1] For similar conclusions in a comparison of newspaper and TV news, cf. Warner (1971). The observation of selective recruitment made by Sigelman seems to be valid for other newspapers besides the two he studied. The same mechanism has been suggested with respect to Swedish newspapers for instance, particularly Social Democratic newspapers (cf. Tingsten, 1947 a and Söderlund, 1973, p. 22).
Studies of recruitment to Swedish newspapers include Söderström & Ahrnstedt (1959), Hadenius et al.(1968, Ch. 7; 1970, Ch. 9), and Journalistkåren i Sverige (1971).

The basic ideas behind the selective recruitment mechanism are that relatively coherent behaviour in the newspaper can be obtained and that the level of conflict can be reduced. But, there is also another side to the coin: selective recruitment involves certain risks for the creativity of a paper as the hiring staff are likely to hire people who are rather similar to themselves. In one interviewee's opinion, this process has certain implications: "They pick the average guys. They don't dare take a chance with the odd or unusual person. You get 'office guys' into the newspaper. And, then when you get people who have a creative potential they adapt." Thus, my interviewee concluded, most journalists become persons who deliver "safe stories" on time. Also contributing to this development is the training offered at different schools of journalism: "Graduates from those schools tend to write using a template. After a while they realize the difference between theory and practice. And, that creates a lot of frustration for them."[1]

A practical example of recruitment procedures can be taken from _Dagens Nyheter_. Earlier, the standard procedure in this paper was that journalists who had been working on local papers started as stand-ins at _Dagens Nyheter_ to be subsequently employed on a permanent basis. In the early seventies, however, a new system was introduced, which implies that all jobs are advertised. Applicants are then screened on the basis of submitted job specimens, references,

---

[1] Needless to say, the interviewee is not a graduate from a school of journalism. He had other types of work experience before entering journalism and has learnt the craft on the job.

The theoretical emphasis of Swedish journalism training was stressed by one interviewee, who did not consider the journalistic training at the school to be very extensive. The practical job was to produce a fictitious newspaper, but not even this was found to be very rewarding: "You feel stupid in interviewing a person for a newspaper which will never appear. -- The practical things on a newspaper you learn quite fast: you learn how to write, how to think, how to formulate headlines, etc."

A managing editor of a large newspaper also made the remark that graduates from schools of journalism are not very useful for large papers, since they need specialized journalists: "It's an advantage with a decidedly professional education, but it narrows the perspective."

and an interview with a special recruitment group comprised of
two managing editors and two journalists appointed by the local
union ("Kryt-gruppen"). The formal decision on employment is
taken by the managing editor.

This system is considered to have a number of advantages,
among them that recruitment is made from a wider group of applicants.
But, as was mentioned earlier, there is also a risk of conformity
as the different departments favour persons who are similar to themselves.[1]

In other systems of recruitment, too, specimens play an important
role. Talking about recruitment in one department of a Stockholm
daily, a journalist thus told how the paper approaches prospective
employees after following their reporting for a while: "You read
their stories. In this way you get wind of those who can develop."

Another mechanism in screening is gradual movements into the journalistic craft, i.e. both the journalist and the newspaper try it out
for a while. More than one journalist has described how they
started by delivering short notices then worked as a stand-in during
summer months, and finally ended up as a full-time journalist.[2]

There are also differences with respect to screening. In sports
departments the political attitude of the employee is considered
less important, whereas politics is of utmost importance on the
editorial page, where selective recruitment is the rule. A remark
of an editorial writer illustrates this: "Well, I worked for the
Party, and the newspaper people approached the Party asking whether
they had anyone who could join their staff of editorial writers."

---

[1] "In this way there is not much room for 'long shots'." (A managing editor)
[2] This type of recruitment seems to be particularly frequent in sports departments.

Another group for which screening is important is the group of spatially differentiated persons, e.g. correspondents. The possibilities to influence the everyday behaviour of correspondents are very limited, and the newspaper needs persons whom they can trust. This is particularly the case when the "story" to be covered is difficult to judge.[1]

Most important of all in terms of recruitment of course, is the recruitment of managing and executive editors. In many cases such positions are filled from among those already employed, which is usually a safe strategy in terms of publication norms. Now and then it happens, however, that outsiders are recruited, and such hirings are likely to have important repercussions on the editorial policy of the paper.[2]

Finally, it appears relevant to note that selective recruitment probably was more pronounced earlier, when there were a large number of newspapers. The decline in the number of newspapers can therefore be expected to have implied fewer possibilities for journalists to join the newspaper of their first choice. It is therefore not surprising that a study of Swedish journalists found that more than fifty per cent of the interviewees had once or several times worked for a newspaper with a different political opinion than their own (Journalistkåren i Sverige, 1971).[3]

---

[1] Cf. here the discussions on the Swedish radio news reporting from Portugal in 1975, or Waugh (1938).

[2] "In the paper, where I used to work, there was no discussion on policy. Changes in the paper took place only as a result of personnel changes. A shift on the job as assisting managing editor produced a new profile for the paper. We got two new young guys who made the paper fresher." (A former journalist)

[3] Similar findings have been reported in SOU 1975:78 (Journaliststudien, p. 235 ff.) and Windahl (1975, Ch. 6).

This circumstance has contributed to an increasing professionalization of journalism.[1] Professionalization implies that a great deal of the rules governing performance come from the environment. Hall (1972), for example, concludes that "the presence of professionals appears to cause a diminished need for formalized rules and procedures." (Ibid., p. 121) This conclusion in turn, implies that professionalized organizations tend to be less formalized than other organizations, and a basic reason for this is that guide lines are likely to be considered superfluous and therefore will only cause alienation (ibid., p. 187).

Newspapers do not fit completely into the above description of professional organizations: as we have seen in the earlier chapters -- and will see in the following section -- there are also a great deal of formalized rules and procedures within newspapers.[2]

9.5 Socialization

Socialization in newspapers is mainly accomplished in three ways: (1) informal contacts with more experienced newsmen, (2) the editorial conference and (3) editorial revisions.[3] These procedures

---

[1] It may be noted that Sigelman (1973), using five criteria from Greenwood (1957), finds it rather difficult to rate journalists as professionals. The criteria were: (1) a basis for systematic theory, (2) authority recognised by the group's clientele, (3) broad community approval, (4) a code of ethics regulating relations with clients and colleagues, and (5) a professional culture sustained by formal associations.

A less restrictive criterion would be to use the dictionary definition of professional: "One who has an assumed competence in a particular field or occupation" (Davies, 1970, p. 562, third entry).

Also of relevance is the work of Kornhauser (1963), who, using proportion of salaried employees as the indicator of professionalism, found journalists to be highly professionalized. But, he also found that the number of journalists have not increased to the same extent as other professionals (e.g. scientists, engineers, professors and accountants) (ibid., p. 5).

[2] Hall also concludes with regard to the findings of Blau (1968) and Blau et al. (1966) that professional organizations are likely to have limited vertical and horizontal differentiation (Hall, 1972, p. 122). In this respect, too, newspapers are "deviants" (cf. Chapter Five).

[3] Further instruments of socialization which should be mentioned are courses arranged by the company (cf. e.g. Ågren, 1970, p. 254 ff.) and internal memos (ibid., 247 ff.).

have been stressed by Sigelman (1973, p. 138) as well as by interviewees.[1]

Among the three mechanisms mentioned by Sigelman, the first, _informal contacts_ implies a process similar to the game "follow the leader", i.e. that cub journalists try to learn by watching their more senior colleagues. The need for this game probably becomes less pronounced as journalists become increasingly professionalized through formal education.[2]

The _editorial conference_ is, as Sigelman notes "surely the most organized, coherent, continuing, and centralized process" of all mechanisms for socialization (loc.cit.).[3] It is, however, "directed at veterans rather than new recruits" (loc.cit.). These veterans, in turn, influence their younger colleagues by means of informal contacts.

In the editorial conferences, decisions are taken on what should be covered and how it should be covered. In this way they constitute an important marketplace of ideas.[4] In addition, they play a significant role for front-page decisions.

The third approach to socialization, _editorial revisions_, has the basic features of quality control. In other words: there is a dilemma between the risks of accepting something that should be rejected and rejecting something that should be accepted.[5] Particularly the latter case may arouse conflict in a newspaper,

---

[1] The significance of socialization in newspapers has also been illustrated by Breed (1955) and Edelstein (1966).

[2] Cf. Hall (1972): "the more work standards he [the employee] brings with him, the less the need for organizationally based standards." (op.cit., p. 190). This thesis is debatable, however. Cf. above the critical remarks on formal education.

[3] Cf. here the opinion of an editorial writer: "Larsson talks about Herbert's conferences -- talks with disgust about the instructions and the orders which hampered and embarrassed him. The only way is to write editorials without orders and then possibly let it be examined afterwards if there is anything to discuss." (Brandell, 1976, p. 63, my translation from Swedish).

[4] But, of course, as in most oligopolistic markets there are tendencies for stalemates (cf. the kinked demand curve).

[5] These two errors are generally referred to in statistics as errors of Type I and Type II (cf. e.g. Wonnacott & Wonnacott, 1972, pp. 195-196).

The problem of quality control also occurs with respect to advertising. In that context the issue concerns whether an ad meets the standards - moral and ethical - of the paper (cf. Adler, 1971, p. 137 f.).

since questions on legality and quality are rather diffuse and rejections may therefore be considered as opinion control rather than quality control. The issue of editorial revisions and rejections is closely related to the position of the publisher, and such issues are often, as was mentioned above, a conflict between journalistic values, on the one hand, and economic or political values on the other.[1] It also has to do with the internal conflict between journalists concerning the allocation of space (cf. Chapter Eight).

A useful way of looking at the quality control process in newspapers is to see the production flow as a gatekeeper chain, i.e. a chain of successive checks of the material. (This chain has been described earlier in Chapter Three.) The main gatekeeper is the news-editor, who performs the first selection among inflowing information and assigns journalists to different stories. The next point in the chain is the individual reporter. He is usually not a gatekeeper in the sense that he accepts or refuses a story.[2] Instead, he is a gatekeeper in that he gathers certain information but leaves out other information. This selectivity need not necessarily mean that the reporter has a conscious bias in reporting, but only that a limited amount of information can be processed at a time. In addition the reporter has space problems: his stories cannot be too long.[3]

---

[1] An example is given by Ågren (1970, p. 249), who mentions the problems he experienced as editor in covering "sensations". If he permitted "gluttony" in reporting a rape, he was in conflict with journalistic norms. If he played it safe, marketing people complained that the competitor took all the marginal readers.

[2] In theory, a journalist, at least in Sweden, has the option of refusing to perform a certain job since the professional code of the Union of Journalists establishes that a journalist may not be compelled to perform humiliating jobs or to write against his conviction (cf. e.g. Hederberg, 1969, p. 208). But, as Hederberg notes most journalists do not want to appear "troublesome" in the eyes of the managing editors and prefer not to protest. In addition, their refusal may mean that another reporter is assigned to the job, (ibid. p. 155).

[3] The reporter may also change his judgement in the course of writing. This was, for instance, the case with Jim, a sports reporter at The Record, who one night entered the composing room shouting: "I have a scoop! I have a scoop!" But, half an hour later he declared: "I read through my notes and found that the story wasn't waterproof. So, I played it down a little."

The mentioned selectivity on the part of the journalist is basic to the objectivity of reporting. Here it is often argued that objectivity is an impossibility.[1] A discussion at The London Times provided a somewhat different view, however. The interviewed journalists did not consider objectivity to be a problem: "You present the facts!" This view was subsequently qualified, however, to recognize that the reporter gives as balanced a view as possible of what has happened.[2] In terms of the different types of reporter roles mentioned by Argyris (1974, p. 47) this view relates to the traditional reporter, who stresses facts in terms of the Four W:s (What, Where, When and Who). As Brucker (1972, p. 70) has pointed out, there has been a movement from this type of reporting to a reporting where the reporter plays the role as reporter-researcher or reporter-activist: "The whole development of interpretive reporting since World War I has been a reaction against news forced into the Four W-mold" (ibid., p. 77).[3]

The possibilities to work in other roles than that of the traditional reporter vary between newspapers.[4] Some papers, which hold a radical attitude and want to promote change, feature another type of journalism. Others, like evening papers, may do so

---

[1] Cf. again Berger & Luckman (1966).

[2] In order to achieve this, it is claimed that The Times strives to have reporters learn as much as possible about the object for reporting. In addition, the mentioned paper tries to send reporters whom they trust to the scene of news events. (The latter was commented on by a Times journalist in the following way as he read my notes from the discussion: "We trust all our reporters, but obviously some are better at certain stories than others. The News Editor, who is in overall charge of reporters, knows his men, and knows which one to send to a given situation. (We use a racing phrase for this: 'Horses for courses').". In relation to the above discussion it should be mentioned that a Swedish journalist in London identified a difference between the method of writing in Swedish and British newspapers: "The myth of the objectivity of the press is deeply rooted here in England."

[3] There seems to be a parallel between the three reporter roles and the distinction made by Habermas (1968) concerning different types of research paradigms: (1) a technical, (2) a hermeneutical and (3) an emancipatory.

[4] An obstacle for in-depth journalism is the competition between different newspapers. A paper being on the track of a story does not dare wait too long, since it may be beaten to it by a competitor.

now and then, because such stories may stimulate circulation.[1] Since circulation is continuously checked by comparing figures between different years, months and weeks, circulation boosts thus determine the type of journalism permitted in such papers: "They sold 80 000 extra copies on one of my stories and 50 000 on another. As a matter of fact, that means that I have earned my salary. You see, the fact that the paper sells on stories implies that you have one-hundred per cent influence over publication if you have a hot tip or a scandal. Management has an eye on circulation all the time." (An evening paper journalist)

But, irrespective of the orientation of the newspaper, there has been a tendency to do more in-depth stories than earlier. A contributing factor in this regard is that the event is often already known to the reader (cf. e.g. Nordisk Tidskrift, 1975, p. 165) so that the newspaper therefore provides commentary and background.[2]

Having written the story, the reporter is in the hands of another group of gatekeepers: the copy-editors and the night editor. They make changes in formulations, cut stories and even discard certain stories. They add headlines and sub-headlines, which are important components for the "marketing" of the different stories.

Although the Swedish interviewees considered editing important, it seems to play a less pronounced role in Sweden then in other countries. In addition, a team-work approach in editing was mentioned: "In our department we work together. All of us participate in information collection, writing and editing. It's very important that we are able to edit ourselves. It's a question of power."[3]

---

[1] For a discussion concerning the possibilities for critical journalism in an evening paper, cf. Expressen, 4 December, 1976, pp. 4-5.

[2] On some pages like the sports pages this leads to difficulties for the uninitiated reader: "You try to find the right angle. But, you take for granted that the readers know the result. Therefore, you often forget to tell the score. Sometimes you even forget to tell what kind of event you are writing about." (A sports journalist)

[3] In the department where this interviewee is working job rotation is used so that each journalist works as copy-editor for a fortnight and then as reporter the following fortnight: "There is a problem with persons who only do editing and rewriting. You should have circulating members of the staff, who understand both jobs."

The system by which a given desk edits its own material is not the case everywhere. Some Swedish newspapers have persons who do only editing. These persons seem, quite in contrast to their colleagues in the United States, to have a rather weak position: "We have a lot of stuck-up journalists who won't accept that you change a line in their manuscripts. So, persons who only do editing have quite a low status!" (A journalist)[1]

The circumstance that reporters know that their stories are going to be edited appears to have the effect, at least in the eyes of the copy-editors, that their stories are not fully worked over.[2] A contributing factor is the risk every reporter runs that his article won't make the paper of the following day: "So, why work hard on the formulations in a story, when it will just be lying in the manuscript box?"[3] Similarly, The Times generally edits manuscripts filed by external free-lance writers considerably, since they tend to send their stories to several newspapers. Doing so, they are apt to use a style which is average for all types of newspapers: "If they took the trouble to write it more carefully, they would be used more."

Headlines constitute a particularly delicate part of the copy editor's job since they can elicit strong reactions due to their condensed form and their conspicuousness. Moreover, copy-editors often try to formulate headlines with a sting, asking: "How do I puff for this? How far can I go?"

In addition to handling the copy delivered by reporters, copy editors and the night editor have to decide on stories that turn up.

---

[1] Cf. here also the remark of a former executive editor: "The copy editors constitute a forgotten group. They have difficulties in showing performance".

[2] A corollary of this is that editing will be time-consuming. This, in turn, is somewhat annoying in a production process under time-pressure.

It also happens that journalists try touchy formulations in order to "test" the watchfulness of copy editors.

[3] This circumstance also makes it possible for copy editors to retaliate against reporters. One copy editor in a national newspaper once told me: "Her story was horrible. I didn't do any editing. I just put her by-line on it and sent it to the composing room. She didn't like that."

Such decision-making can take some time, since the editors have to consider competing stories. A good example was shown at The Record as a story arrived from a local correspondent. Chris' first reaction was: "We can't take it. There's been too much nagging about it. Furthermore, it's a proposal from the Opposition. We're not made of jelly!" Only minutes later, however, he realizes that the story is of importance: "How can I get it in? Is it possible to cut somewhere? As a matter of fact not. But, I can use it if I cut it drastically." And, after some further minutes of consideration: "It has to go in. I have a feeling they want to keep it quiet. The story on the Bishop will have to wait."[1] The result was thus that the story was published, a judgement shared by Chris' colleague at The Record's main competitor, The Chronicle.[2]

Finally, in Swedish newspapers there is the decision on the news-bill. A night editor at The Record expressed his general rule for selecting stories for the news-bill: "Local and short".[3] He and the news editor also agreed that front-page stories are usually candidates for the news-bill. They consider it important that front-page as well as news-bill stories are "scoops" or "exclusives", i.e. stories the rival paper has not been able to cover.[4]

The design of the news-bill basically reflects the judgement of the news-editor and the night editor. The only exceptions are coordination

---

[1] Reading my notes, Chris exclaimed: "It sounds like I'm a schizophrenic. But, the job is like that."

[2] The latter even played it up more by putting a load on the front page.

[3] This rule seems to hold for The Record's main competitor, as well. The only stories of a non-local character that appeared on the news-bill during my visit were stories on the earthquake and the abolition of "medium-strength" beer in Sweden.

Bill, the news editor, qualified the rule, adding: "Not too local".

[4] The effects of the news-bill on sales have been discussed to a large extent at The Record, but there has not been any consensus of opinion. Particular consternation arose during a boycott, during which the news-stands refused to post the news-bill. During this period the sale of single copies increased!

between the news-room and the marketing department, when The Record has arranged certain events and contests.[1] And, in the opinion of a marketing man on this paper it should be the other way around: "The editorial office shouldn't be the one to design the news-bill. Now, it's a news thing, when it ought to be an advertisement. We should do it."[2] The news editor, of course, does not agree. In his opinion "there is no state of opposition between selling news and good news."[3] And, when the editors judge that certain stories will increase the number of copies sold, the distribution people are given notice. Another expression of this cooperation between the news-room and the marketing department is the printing of special news-bills for distribution in different areas in order to promote sales.[4]

Editorial revisions constitute an instrument for socialization of reporters. Similarly the work of copy editors is under scrutiny: formulations or selections of stories considered unappropriate are commented on by the news editor on the following day.[5] This, for example, was the case for Chris when he left out the story about the Bishop. Bill, the news editor, remarked: "That was a little unfortunate. We ought to have had him". A comment which brought Chris to remark later on: "You can't hesitate too much about the

---

[1] Another exception is the consultation with the sports department for the news-bill on Mondays.

[2] Critical remarks were also made by people working in dispatch: "There ought to be coordination between the news-room and the circulation department. Look at to-day's news-bill for instance. They carry a story from Smalltown, the same day as we have gratis distribution to all households in that town." The same person also argued for greater differentiation of the news-bills and a focus on local news: "The news-bill should carry different items in different local communities. A news-bill like the one with the earthquake won't sell more copies. People will get the news on the radio."

[3] A colleague of his expressed the opinion, however, that "there is a conflict between making a commercial product and conveying a message".

[4] A further step in this direction, which some people favour, would be to decentralize the design of the news-bills completely, i.e. to transfer it to the news-stands.

[5] The news editor, at least at The Record, reads or comments on very few of the stories in advance. His opinion is practically always communicated after the fact.

Cf. also the comment by an evening paper journalist: "The ceiling is high. You write what you like. Once or twice."

news. You have to imagine the values of the editors. If the result is good, you don't hear very much. But, if something goes wrong, you get the message".[1]

In relation to the news-bill and headlines a similar situation prevails, i.e. the only type of feed-back given is complaints: "There have been calls".[2] In addition, copy-editors now and then get feed-back from reporters who are annoyed at the copy editing and formulations of headlines. Such irritation is not seldom stimulated by reactions from the reporters' interviewees.[3]

9.6 Some Results of Publication Decisions

In order to give an impression of the outcome of the selection of news the front pages, the editorial page and the news-bills of The Record and its main competitor, The Daytown Chronicle, were studied during a ten-day period. On average the two papers presented 7.2 and 9.0 items per day, respectively, on their front pages.[4] Of these, the majority were stories with a local touch: 88.8 per cent for The Record, and 77.7 per cent for The Chronicle. In The Record, for example, national and international front-page stories were limited to events such as the earthquake, rises in the price of coffee and the Parliamentary decision to prohibit medium-strength beer.[5]

---
[1] Another example was the reaction to the location of a picture: "This is unfortunate. You get the impression that the man on the picture is either a dope dealer or a home distiller. And, he is neither."

[2] "They think that our readership consists to eighty per cent of religious spinsters!" (Remark by reporters on news editors.)

[3] The reactions may appear in later contacts with an interviewee. And, a number of critical comments may make reporters a bit cautious. Phil, for instance, considers labour union leaders most difficult to handle: "They really don't trust journalists. You can meet a union leader a fortnight after a story has been published and he remarks that a line in my story could be misinterpreted."

[4] The front pages of the two papers contained on average 3.3. and 4.0 pictures per day, i.e. forty-five per cent of the stories were illustrated.

[5] And, when an international story like the earthquake is featured, efforts are made to give the presentation a local touch. This was illustrated by the remark of Bill, the news editor, in Chapter One (Section 1A1: "Suddenly the Ground Started to Shake .... "): "What you can do is to try to do a local follow-up".

It thus seems as though The Chronicle usually presents more items per front page than The Record. It also seems to be more apt to mention national and international events. The first of these two conclusions holds, even when differences in front page sizes are taken into account.[1]

The conclusion on the dominance of local news is not valid for the editorial page, however. Here there is, as Furhoff (1963) has pointed out, a clear dominance for national news: only twenty per cent of the editorials in The Record and six per cent in the rival Chronicle discussed local problems.[2] The corresponding figures for national problems were seventy and eighty-eight per cent, respectively, leaving ten and six per cent for international problems. The domination of national issues is even more pronounced if the prime editorials are considered: only one out of ten in each paper was not on national affairs.[3]

Turning, then, to the different types of stories on the front page, the results shown in Table 9:1 were obtained.

---

[1] The size of the front page of The Chronicle is about seven per cent larger than that of The Record.

[2] Similar findings are reported by Hanson (1968, p. 29). In ten local papers he found that eleven per cent of the editorials were devoted to local problems. The corresponding figure for international and national problems were thirty-five and fifty-four per cent, respectively.

[3] The remaining editorial was a local one in The Record and an international one in The Chronicle.

Topic	The Record	The Daytown Chronicle
Labour Market, Business and Political Parties	40.3 %	22.2 %
Education, Health Care and Social Welfare	13.9 %	11.1 %
Accidents	15.3 %	20.1 %
Events and Contests Arranged by the Paper	11.1 %	2.2 %
Sports and Leisure	8.3 %	17.9 %
Criminal Cases	4.1 %	11.1 %
Environment Protection and Regional Planning	2.8 %	7.7 %
Fine Arts	1.4 %	6.6 %
Miscellaneous	2.8 %	1.1 %
	100.0 %	100.0 %

Table 9:1. Topics of Front-Page Stories in The Record and its Main Competitor.

Certain conclusions can be drawn from the table:

1. The Record stresses stories in relation to the labour market, education, health care and social welfare. It does so to a much greater extent that The Chronicle (54.2 per cent vs. 33.3 per cent).

2. The Chronicle, on the other hand, stresses "traditional news", i.e. accidents, sports and criminal cases more than The Record. These subjects make up 49.1 per cent of the front-page items in The Chronicle, compared to 27.7 per cent in The Record.

3. The Record has several stories on the front page relating to arrangements of its own. Accounting for as much as 11.1 per cent of the front-page stories, they are a clear indication of the necessity for a minor newspaper to stimulate readership.

Looking at the upper left-hand corner of the front pages of the two papers, i.e. the position considered the most read in the paper, the topics featured in the two papers coincide in three cases out of ten. All three are cases of "traditional news": two car accidents and the earthquake. A similar situation can be observed with regard to the news-bill: the items that coincide are accidents.

But, also on the news-bill, a difference in orientation between the two papers can be observed. Thus, Table 9:2 shows again that The Chronicle is more apt to feature "traditional news" (accidents, criminal cases and sports), whereas The Record stresses stories concerning the labour market, education, etc.[1] Also, The Record uses its news-bill to publicize arrangements of its own.

Topic	The Record	The Daytown Chronicle
Labour Market, Business and Political Parties	31.6 %	14.3 %
Education, Health Care and Social Welfare	21.1 %	4.8 %
Accidents	21.0 %	23.8 %
Events and Contests Arranged by the Paper	15.8 %	-
Sports	10.5 %	38.1 %
Criminal Cases	-	9.5 %
Environment Protection and Regional Planning	-	9.5 %
Total	100.0 %	100.0 %

Table 9:2. Topics of News-Bill Items[a]

Note:
[a] The figures in this table are based on only eight observations instead of ten as in Table 9:1.

The results from The Record and The Chronicle appear to indicate certain differences between the two papers. There are such differences, since the two papers have different policies as to what

---

[1] The number of items is quite stable, averaging between two and three.

they want to stress. But, comparing the two newspapers as well as newspapers in general, it is astonishing how similar the products are. The differences are more a question of _to what extent_ various types of news items are presented than of whether they should be presented. This is a sign that the different checks on publication have worked, particularly the external rules of the game and socialization. In addition, the competition among newspapers often implies something of a game of follow-the-leader (cf. Section 4.6: "Competitors").

9.7 Concluding Remarks

Basically, the publication issue boils down to the question "Who determines the contents of the newspaper?" This question has been particularly relevant in recent years as different procedures to increase industrial democracy have appeared. In Sweden this development has resulted in a law from January 1, 1977, abolishing the old rule that "the employer has the right to direct and distribute the work". Instead, the law prescribes that consultation should take place between employers and employees (cf. e.g. Bergqvist & Lunning, 1976). Some exceptions to the rule exist, however. Among the exceptions mentioned are policy issues in firms engaged in public opinion activities. (_ibid_., p. 209 § 2).[1]

In many newspapers there are trends toward increased democracy within the news-room.[2] This tendency has brought another question into the debate: Who defends the interests of the readers? Does not news-room democracy merely imply that the decisions are moved just one step down, when they should be moved down still further?

---

[1] Similar arrangements exist in West Germany and Norway (cf. Strömholm, 1975 and Stortingsmeldning no. 29, 1973-1974, p. 3).

[2] In practice, this kind of democracy seems to imply that the elected officers of the local chapter of the Union of Journalists do the day-to-day work on issues and that they gather their colleagues for short meetings in the news room now and then.

This issue has been discussed by Hadenius and Gustafsson (1975), who even suggest reader representation on the boards of directors of newspapers. Their explicit suggestion was that readers should be represented by persons nominated by organs of local government. This proposal brought a sharp reaction from newspaper publishers: How would it be possible to watch local governments, if they were able to restrict unfavourable reporting through their representation on the board?(<u>Pressens</u> <u>Tidning</u>, December 1975, p. 2).

The discussion in the present chapter has shown that even today there are a number of checks on publication. They can be summarized in Figure 9:2.

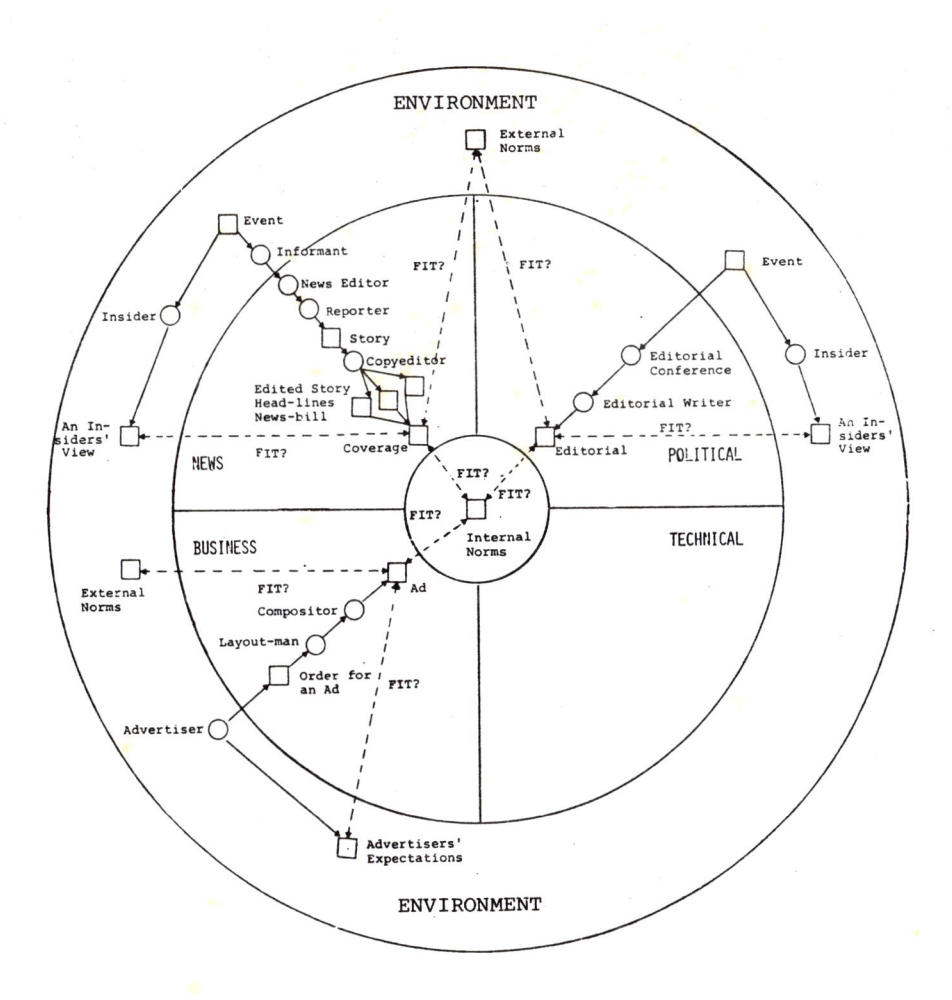

Figure 9:2. Different Processes Involved in the Publication Issue.

Explanations:
◯ = Actors
▢ = Information in Different Forms

Looking first at the upper left-hand part of the circle -- the news oriented group -- we note a screening process, in which a number of persons -- informants, news editors, reporters and copy editors -- participate. They influence, to greater or lesser degrees, the final coverage (edited story, headlines and the news-bill) of an event. This coverage, in turn, may fit or misfit the views of insiders (those involved in the event), the external norms of publication and/or the internal norms of publication. If a misfit with any of these three occurs, a publication conflict arises. Important for the limitation of the number of such conflicts is the gradual screening of the coverage of different events. This screening process, in turn, is handled internally by selective recruitment as well as by different forms of socialization of those recruited.

Similar relationships can be discerned with respect to the lower left-hand and upper right-hand parts of the circle, i.e. the business and politically oriented groups. As far as the ads are concerned, the advertiser has certain expectations on the ad, and if these are not fulfilled -- as was the case with the Neartown car dealer (cf. Chapter One, Section 1A4) -- he communicates his dissatisfaction through verbal complaints (voice) or the cancellation of advertising in the paper (exit, cf. Hirschman, 1970). But, as we have seen in this chapter, an ad can also violate external or internal norms. Production in the politically oriented group, finally, shares features in common with those identified in the news oriented group.

PART IV: NEWSPAPER COUNTRY, AU REVOIR!

"This is not the end. It is not even the beginning of the end. But it is, perhaps, the end of the beginning."

(Mr. Winston Churchill, November 10, 1942)

CHAPTER TEN. CONCLUSIONS.

10.1 Introduction

The previous chapters document a gradual penetration of newspapers as organizations by exploiting different kinds of data. In this way it has been possible to develop a framework. The study can now be summarized and conclusions can be drawn (Section 10.2). Some implications for other types of organizations will be provided in Section 10.3.

The research process has not only implied a dialectical process between different types of data. It has also implied tacking between data and theories: formulations have been confronted by data, which has led to reformulations, etc. A consequence of this technique is that the present report is merely one step along the way to penetrate newspaper country. Some indications of future activities therefore will be given in the final section.

10.2 A Quick Guide to Newspaper Country

The basis for the analysis has been the organizational model presented in Chapter One (Figure 1:1). Three important aspects of organizations were identified: TECHNOLOGY, ENVIRONMENT and PERSONNEL (cf. Figure 10:1).

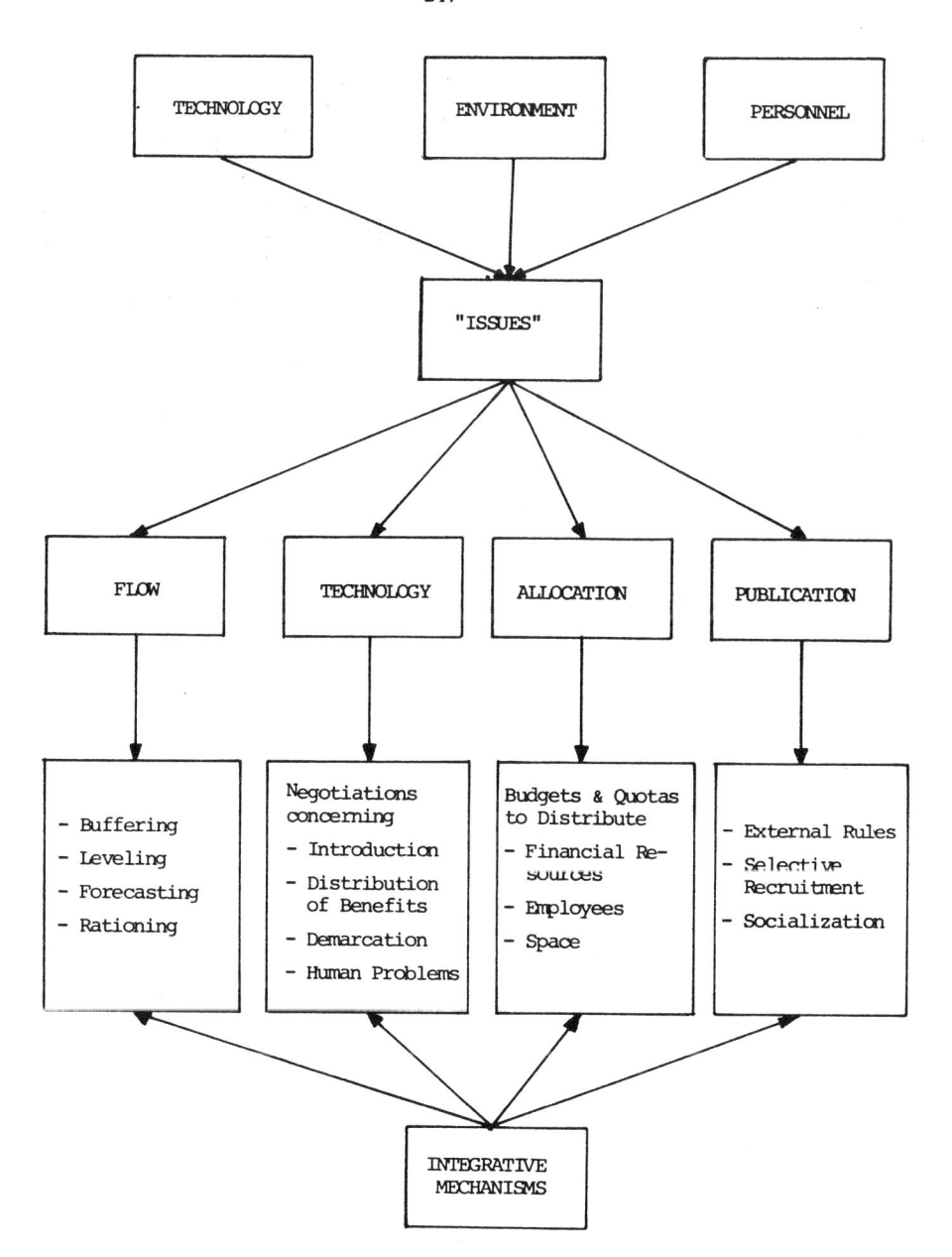

Figure 10:1. A Map of Newspaper Country

The analysis of NEWSPAPER TECHNOLOGY included four phases, i. e. those of collection, processing, reproduction and distribution. These four phases were analyzed in terms of: <u>operations</u> <u>technology</u> (automaticity, workflow rigidity and specificity of evaluation); <u>materials</u> <u>technology</u> (understandability and variability); and <u>knowledge</u> <u>technology</u> (number of exceptional cases and analyzability of arising problems). It could be concluded that newspaper technology implies a mix of a number activities with different characteristics. Therefore, it is not surprising that newspapers do not fit into a traditional classification of organizations such as the one provided by Thompson (1967). Nor, is it surprising that the mixed conditions of technology promote the occurence of different issues.

As far as NEWSPAPER ENVIRONMENT is concerned, it appears that the role of <u>owners</u> is changing as the professionalization of journalists and demands for participation increase. At the same time the role of <u>governments</u> has also changed as the economic situation of newspapers has brought different kinds of government subsidies into the industry. An important reason for this support is the belief that newspapers play a crucial role in modern democracies. In that context one can observe a movement from a libertarian to a social responsibility theory of the press.

Another important part of the environment consists of the <u>suppliers</u>, among whom the advertisers perform an extraordinary function, since they have to pay for the privilege of providing input for the newspaper. Their money offers an important financial resource for most newspapers, without which many would fold. Their input, the advertisements, also play a significant role in the attractiveness of a newspaper when ads are mixed in appropriate blends with the input from different news sources. Among the latter there are quite a few which volunteer information in order to have certain ideas communicated or to make something known. In addition, news is provided by reporters, free-lance writers and wire services.

Like the advertisers, the <u>readers</u> of a newspaper have certain
unusual characteristics. First of all, newspaper consumption is
almost always limited to one copy a day of each newspaper. Price
cuts are thus not likely to increase the consumption of those
who are readers already. Second, a newspaper can be consumed by
several persons in sequence. And, third, the brand loyalty seems
to be quite high among newspaper readers in general and readers
of subscribed newspapers in particular. These circumstances are
significant for the limited possibilities for a newspaper to increase
circulation.

A contributing factor to the situation just mentioned is that
<u>competitors</u> often play "the game of the kinked demand curve" regarding
the design of the product as well as regarding the price.
Different newspapers in a particular market, therefore, have a
tendency to ressemble each other. The dominant participant in
this game is the paper that is largest in terms of advertising
inflow or circulation. Such dominance has, in many instances, led
to the closing down of minor papers and a monopoly position for
the major paper. Several theories have been advanced in order to
explain this tendency, including the circulation spiral model and
economies of scale. But, irrespective of the theory used for analysis,
it is obvious that the economic disadvantages of minor newspapers
result in psychological disadvantages in addition to inferiority
in terms of resources.

The discussion of NEWSPAPER PERSONNEL implied the identification
of a basic structure, i. e. a differentiation between four groups
with diverse orientations. The four groups are oriented toward
news, political communication, business and technical production,
respectively. In addition to this differentiation it is also possible
to identify four types of differentiation <u>within</u> each of the
groups. First, there is a <u>horizontal</u> differentiation between
different news desks and between different departments. Second,
there is a <u>vertical</u> differentiation between individuals who are
at various levels in the hierarchies of the four groups. Third,
newspaper employees are <u>spatially</u> differentiated since some employees
work outside the newspaper building. And, finally, there
is a <u>temporal</u> differentiation because employees in the newsoriented

and the technically oriented groups work on day as well as on night shifts.

The variety of differentiation within newspapers creates differences in opinion regarding the different issues in newspapers. As a result certain requirements are put on the integration of the work and here various kinds of meetings play an important role.

The characteristics of NEWSPAPER TECHNOLOGY, NEWSPAPER ENVIRONMENT and NEWSPAPER PERSONNEL generate four main ISSUES in newspaper organizations; i. e. the issues of <u>flow</u>, <u>technology</u>, <u>allocation</u> and <u>publication</u>. Of these the publication issue is the one most specific to newspapers. But, it is also important to stress that resource allocation in general, and the allocation of space in particular, is an important overall issue on newspapers. Furthermore, the sudden technological changes in printing techniques after centuries of rather stable technology have made this issue extremely "hot" for newspapers, compared to other industries. Finally, the short production cycle implies that relatively small margins are involved in the flow issue.

As can be seen from Figure 10:1 there are a number of integrative mechanisms relating to the four issues. With respect to the flow issue newspapers use the different strategies mentioned by Thompson (1967), i. e. buffering, leveling, forecasting and rationing. The technology issue is handled through negotiations which concern the introduction of new technology, the distribution of benefits, the demarcation between different tasks, and the handling of human problems. The allocation issue is dealt with through budgets and quotas in order to distribute financial resources, employees and space, whereas the publication issues is balanced by external publication rules, selective recruitment, and socialization.

The main integrating factor, however, seems to be the fact that the different groups produce a joint product daily. This is particularly the case with respect to the flow issue. Identification with the product is an important factor enabling employees to handle variations in the production flow.

The circumstance that employees of a newspaper company produce a joint product also has consequences for the publication issue: it has become a "golden rule" in the industry to "stick together", both inside a newspaper and between newspapers. It is thus quite difficult for an outsider to win a discussion with a newspaper. Although there are internal discussions, these are not communicated outside the newspaper. The remark of a <u>Record</u> journalist is significant in this context: "Mr. B., our former editor-in-chief, was happy to discuss inside the house. But, outside, he was hard as stone. Against those outside we stood united."[1]

What then, are the normative implications of the present study? One thing that should be considered in organizing is the fact that technical dependencies in newspaper production create power bases. Just, as Crozier (1964), in his study of the French Tobacco Company, showed that maintenance people were powerful, it also is clear that the technical staff on a newspaper are strong. They obtain material from all other groups, and it is in their department

---

[1] Cf. also Woodward & Bernstein (1974), who relate an incident when it seemed as if the two reporters were wrong in their reporting: "Bradlee [the executive editor of <u>The Washington Post</u>] turned to his typewriter to write a statement for all news organizations that had been calling that afternoon for a comment [...]. After a number of false starts, he issued the following statement: 'We stand by our story'" (<u>ibid.</u>, p. 192). In a footnote the two authors also pass on Bradlee's comment on the incident later on: "I can remember sitting down at the typewriter and writing about thirty statements and then sort of saying, 'Fuck it, let's go stand by our boys.'" (<u>loc. cit.</u>)

that this material is merged into a joint product. It is also up to them that the product hits the distribution system in time. As a result, not only economic reasons are behind efforts of newspaper managements to try to "jump the composing room" by introducing new technology. Similarly, it is clear that compositors do not want to give up a powerful position and therefore fight the completely integrated technology.

The new technology is also important in another respect: it offers an opportunity to increase communication and interaction between the different groups of personnel. And, no doubt, one important practical implication of this study is the need for promotion of communication in newspapers. The new technology can do this since it makes jobs more similar and brings people together physically. Another effect of technological change is that job rotation will be more easily accomplished. This, in turn, will promote better understanding of other jobs in the paper as well as reduce the boredom in the work.

The last mentioned circumstance also stresses the need for an increased feedback to personnel from their bosses. At present this feedback is mainly of the negative type, while the need for positive feedback is great. In this context the opening up of dialogues with readers seems extremely important.

Relations with readers point to the need for continuous policy discussions inside the newspaper. These discussions should include all sorts of employees and deal with all four issues.[1] In this way the products may be gradually improved.[2]

---

[1] These policy discussions are likely to be of the type mentioned by March & Olsen (1976) as "garbage can processes", i.e. their outcome is highly dependent on the time and energy different employees are willing to invest.

[2] It should be noted that only gradual changes can be undertaken (cf. Chapter Four, Section 4.2: "Customers").

To sum up, the following points can be made in relation to practical implications:

- Technological dependencies create power bases, which have to be taken into account in organizing.
- There is a need to promote communication between different groups of personnel.
- There is a need for job rotation.
- Feedback should be increased between newspaper personnel and readers as well as between high-level and low-level employees. The need for positive feedback seems particularly urgent.
- There is a need for continuous policy discussions in order to facilitate gradual improvements of the product.

10.3 Implications Outside Newspaper Country

Thus, we have drawn some conclusions in relation to newspaper country. It should be noted, however, that some conclusions are also valid for other types of organizations. Take, for example, a university department, which has a basic differentiation between (1) employees who mainly do research, (2) those who mainly teach, and (3) those engaged in administrative work. The communication between these three groups is often limited, a circumstance which creates a number of conflicts between groups. There are discussions on scheduling (when to do what: the flow issue), on methods for research and teaching (the technology issue), on the sharing of scarce resources (the allocation issue) as well as on the subjects for research and teaching (the publication issue).[1]

A second type of organization in which similar problems arise is a theatre company with one group producing the dramatic products, another producing the "hardware" (costumes, wigs, side-scenes, etc.) and still another involved in administration. Between these groups of theatre personnel, too, the different types of issues can be identified.[2]

---

[1] An important difference between newspapers and university departments, however, is that the latter do not produce a joint end product.

[2] A study identifying such issues is Dale & Spencer (1976).

Yet another type of organization which exhibits characteristics similar to newspapers are hospitals, where a dual structure can be observed: one containing doctors and nurses, the other containing administrative employees (cf. e. g. Rhenman, 1974). Here, too, conflicting views on issues are generated by a rapidly increasing degree of differentiation in the former group as a result of an increasing specialization.

The organizations mentioned hitherto are extraordinary organizations in that the software component is crucial to production. Of course, this circumstance increases the basic differentiation and promotes conflicts around issues. But, in more hardware oriented organizations, such as manufacturing firms, too, such problems are likely to arise, even if it has to be acknowledged that they are more likely, the greater the dominance of software in the production. An organization with intensive commitments in research and development might thus be expected to experience the problems mentioned to a larger extent than an assembly plant for standardized products. A basic conclusion of this work, however, seems to be that the framework used in the present study could also be useful in the analysis of other types of organizations.

The future may show that yet further lessons can be learnt from a study of newspaper organizations. First, it should be noted that the management of different types of organizations in modern societies require more and more participative elements, i. e. the opening up of channels for expressions of a variety of goals and ideas other than those traditionally emphasized in business organizations. This situation with a mix of different goals, has for a long time been a feature of newspaper organizations Thus, as the participative elements increase in importance in other types of organizations, the latter may be facing problems which earlier have been common on newspapers. The experiences from newspapers can then be useful.

Second, newspapers in many countries have been supported by their national governments. As the goals in society tend to move toward an increased emphasis on job security, the holding down of unemployment and increased protectionism, government support seems to enter other industries as well. In this situation we again have the possibility of learning from newspapers concerning the organizational effects of public support.

10.4 One for the Road

The analysis here is presently being used for further work on newspapers. A project has been designed to study an individual newspaper in all of its different aspects. This study will make use of historical records as well as different kinds of data gathered particularly for the project. This data will then be integrated in order to provide an understanding of the situation of that particular newspaper which, in turn, may demonstrate how the framework presented here can be used as a diagnostic tool. In addition, the results may provide some insights for the paper under study as well as for other newspapers. In this manner the maps and guidebooks to newspaper country will hopefully improve.

The success of the planned project is of course very much dependent on the cooperation of newspaper employees. Plans are one thing and the realization another. As Steinbeck once said: "A journey is a person in itself; no two are alike. And all plans, safeguards, policing and coercion are fruitless. We find after years of struggle that we do not take a trip; a trip takes us. Tour masters, schedules, reservations, brass-bound and inevitable, dash themselves to wreckage on the personality of the trip. Only when this is recognized can the blown-in-the-glass bum relax and go along with it. Only then do the frustrations fall away. In this a journey is like marriage. The certain way to be wrong is to think you control it." (Travels with Charley, p. 4).

REFERENCES[1]

Adler, R., 1971, *A Day in the Life of The New York Times*, Philadelphia & New York: Lippincott.
(Cf. pp. 116, 124, 143, 146, 202, 218 and 230)

Affiliated Publications Inc., 1973, "Prospectus".
(Cf. p. 122)

Almé, B., 1974, "Norsk presses eiere", *Pressens Årsbok*, Köpenhamn: Dansk pressehistorisk selskab, pp. 86-95.
(Cf. p. 75)

Alsterdal, A., 1976, "Kollegialt", *Pressens Tidning*, 57, October, p. 19.
(Cf. p. 148)

ANPA, 1970, *The Structure and Layout of Editorial/News Departments*, Bulletin 1008 from the ANPA Research Institute.
(Cf. pp. 99 and 100)

Argyris, C., 1970, *Intervention Theory and Method: A Behavorial Science View*, Reading, Mass.: Addison-Wesley.
(Cf. p. 37)

Argyris, C., 1974, *Behind the Front Page*, San Fransisco, Cal.: Jossey-Bass.
(Cf. pp. 104, 108, 111, 153, 218 and 232)

Arvedson, L. A., 1974, *Deadlines and Organizational Behavior: A Laboratory Investigation of the Effect of Deadlines on Individual Task Performance*, Unpublished Ph. D. dissertation from the Graduate School of Business, Stanford University.
(Cf. p. 145)

Asch, S. E., 1953, "Effects of Group Pressure upon the Modification and Distortion of Judgements", In: Cartwright, D. & Zander, A., *Group Dynamics: Research and Theory*, Evanston, Ill.: Row, Peterson, pp. 151-162.
(Cf. p. 114)

Bagdikian, B., 1971, *The Information Machines*, New York: Harper & Row.
(Cf. pp. 146, 186 and 187)

Bain, J. S., 1956, *Barriers to New Competition*, Cambridge, Mass.: Harvard University Press.
(Cf. p. 93)

Bain, J. S., 1968, *Industrial Organization*, New York: Wiley (Second Edition, First Edition: 1959).
(Cf. p. 92)

---

[1] The figures below each reference refer to the pages, on which the reference in question appears in the text.

Barnard, C., 1938, The Functions of the Executive, Cambridge, Mass.: Harvard University Press.
(Cf. p. 3)

Bell, D., 1966, The Reforming of General Education, New York: Columbia University Press.
(Cf. p. 44).

Berg, C., 1967, "Miljöförändringar och konflikter - en illustration och test av några teoretiska föreställningar om konflikter i en organisation", SIAR-S 5, Stockholm: SIAR.
(Cf. p. 218)

Berg, O., & Kinell, M., 1971, "Nyhetsurvalet på en kvällstidningsredaktion", Trebetygsuppsats i administration vid Handelshögskolan i Göteborg.
(Cf. p. 54)

Berger, P. L., & Luckman, T., 1966, The Social Construction of Reality: A Treatise on the Sociology of Knowledge, New York: Doubleday.
(Cf. pp. 38, 215 and 232)

Bergqvist, O., & Lunning, L., 1976, Medbestämmande i arbetslivet, Stockholm: Liber.
(Cf. p. 241)

Billström, L., 1974, "Journalisten är agressionshämmad och behöver intensiv psykoterapi", Journalisten, 71, December, p. 21.
(Cf. p. 153)

Björk, L., et al., 1974, "Arbetsmiljö inom grafisk industri", Stockholm: PA-Rådets förlag.
(Cf. pp. 136 and 183)

Blau, P. M., et al., 1966, "The Structure of Small Bureaucracies", American Sociological Review, 31, April, pp. 179-191.
(Cf. p. 229)

Blau, P. M., 1968, "The Hierarchy of Authority in Organizations", American Journal of Sociology, 73, January, pp. 453-467.
(Cf. p. 229)

Blomé, G., 1967, "Dagspressen i Örebro 1900-1965", Seminarieuppsats från Journalisthögskolan i Stockholm (mimeo).
(Cf. p. 90)

Brandell, U., 1976, Dagbok från DN, Stockholm: Trevi.
(Cf. pp. 78, 83, 107, 136, 140, 156 and 230)

Brandes, O., 1971, Supply Models, Göteborg: BAS (Diss.)
(Cf. p. 149)

Breed, W., 1955, "Social Control in the Newsroom", Social Forces, 33, May, pp. 326-335.
(Cf. p. 230)

Brucker, H., 1972, Communication is Power, New York: Oxford University Press.
(Cf. p. 232)

Böll, H., 1974, Die Verlorene Ehre der Katharina Blum, Köln: Kiedenheuer & Witsch.
(Cf. pp. 34 and 217)

Carendi, J., et al., 1970, "Nyhetsurval på en kvällstidningsredaktion", Trebetygsuppsats i administration vid Handelshögskolan i Göteborg.
(Cf. p. 54)

Carlsson, E., 1948, "Press och ekonomi", In: Svenska Tidningsutgivareföreningen 50 år, Stockholm: TU:s förlags AB, pp. 75-90.
(Cf. p. 190)

Carstedt, G., & Isaksson Pérez, B., 1974, Företag i strukturomvandlingen, Del I-V, Studier i företagsekonomi, Umeå universitet (Diss.).
(Cf. p. 92)

Carter, R. E., Jr., 1958, "Newspaper Gatekeepers and the Sources of News", Public Opinion Quarterly, 22, pp. 133-144.
(Cf. p. 114)

Cramér, H., 1961, Sannolikhetskalkylen och några av dess användningar, Stockholm: Almqvist & Wiksell.
(Cf. p. 193)

Crozier, M., 1964, The Bureaucratic Phenomenon, Chicago, Ill.: University of Chicago Press.
(Cf. p. 251)

Cyert, R. M., & March, J. G., 1963, A Behavorial Theory of the Firm, Englewood Cliffs, N. J.: Prentice-Hall.
(Cf. pp. 3 and 83)

Dagens Nyheter
(Cf. pp. 76, 81, 123, 190 and 219)

Dale, A., & Spencer, L., 1976, "Sentiments, Norms, Ideologies and Myths: Their Relation to the Resolution of Issues in a State Theatre Company", Working Paper from Brunel University and The European Institute for Advanced Studies in Management.
(Cf. p. 253)

Dalkey, N., & Helmer, O., 1963, "An Experimental Application of the Delphi Method to the Use of Experts", Management Science, 9, April, pp. 458-467.
(Cf. p. 114)

Davies, P., (ed.), 1970, The American Heritage Dictionary of the English Language, New York: Dell (Paper Back Edition).
(Cf. p. 229)

Deutschmann, P. J., 1959, "Predicting Newspaper Staff from Circulation", Journalism Quarterly, 36, Summer, pp. 350-354.
(Cf. pp. 199 and 200)

Donohew, R. L., 1967, "Newspaper Gatekeepers and Forces in the News Channel", Public Opinion Quarterly, 31, Spring, pp. 61-68.
(Cf. p. 114)

Edelstein, A., 1966, Perspectives in Mass Communication, Köpenhamn: Handelshöjskolen i Köbehavn.
(Cf. p. 230)

Editor & Publisher, 1973, International Yearbook, New York: Editor & Publisher.
(Cf. p. 35)

Ehnmark, A., 1976, Karamellkoket, Stockholm: Norstedts.
(Cf. p. 118)

Ejvegård, R., 1976, "Grafisk industri i USA", Grafia, 7-8/76, pp. 16-17.
(Cf. pp. 182 and 183)

Ekeflo, G., 1976, "Våra grejer måste gå hem i stugorna", Aftonbladet, April 11, p. 4.
(Cf. pp. 84 and 118)

Elfving, B., 1967, "Dagspressen i Gävle 1900-1967", Seminarieuppsats från Journalisthögskolan i Stockholm (mimeo). (p. 90)

Ellis, T., & Child, J., 1973, "Placing Stereotypes of the Manager into Perspective", Journal of Management Studies, 10, October, pp. 233-255.
(Cf. pp. 66 and 96)

Engström, C., 1966, Insändaren, Stockholm: Bonniers.
(Cf. p. 118)

Engwall, L., 1973 a, Models of Industrial Structure, Lexington, Mass.: D. C. Heath & Co.
(Cf. p. 92)

Engwall, L., 1973 b, "Business Behavior: The Cigarette Case", Marquette Business Review, 17, Summer, pp. 59-72.
(Cf. p. 160)

Engwall, L., 1974 a, "Swedish Newspapers in the Post-War Period", Research Report No. 92 from the Department of Business Administration, Stockholm University (mimeo)
(Cf. pp. 39, 84 and 213)

Engwall, L., 1974 b, A Behavorial Approach to the Growth of Firms, Department of Business Administration, University of Uppsala, (mimeo).
(Cf. pp. 3)

Engwall, L., 1975, "The Structure of the Swedish Daily Press", Swedish Journal of Economics, 77, September, pp. 318-328.
(Cf. p. 33)

Engwall, L., 1976, "Response Time of Organizations", Journal of Management Studies, 13, February, pp. 1-15.
(Cf. p. 72)

Esselte Norstedts, 1973, Print 80, Stockholm: Norstedts.
(Cf. pp. 165 and 185)

Etzioni, A., 1961, A Comparative Analysis of Complex Organizations, New York: Wiley.
(Cf. p. 96)

Expressen, December 4, 1976, pp. 4-5.
(Cf. p. 233)

Fjaestad, B., & Nowak, K., 1972, Massmedia och företagen, Stockholm: SNS.
(Cf. p. 79)

Flegel, R. C., & Chaffee, S. H., 1971, "Influence of Editors, Readers, and Personal Opinions on Reporters", Journalism Quarterly, 48, Winter, pp. 645-651.
(Cf. p. 219)

FLT, 1976, Dagspressboken, Stockholm: Förenade Landsortstidningar.
(Cf. p. 40)

Fria Moderata Studentförbundet, 1974, DN - mångsidig men ensidig, Stockholm.
(Cf. p. 78)

Frick, N., & Malmström, S., 1976, Språkklyftan, Stockholm: Tiden.
(Cf. p. 220)

Furhoff, L., 1963, Pressens förräderi, Stockholm: Bonniers/Tribun.
(Cf. pp. 81 and 238)

Furhoff, L., 1967, Upplagespiralen, Stockholm: Svenska Bokförlaget.
(Cf. pp. 88 and 191)

Furhoff, L., 1969, "Tidningsdöden på elva orter - förslag till politiskt perspektiv", Statsvetenskaplig tidskrift, 72, No. 2, pp. 211-228.
(Cf. p. 90)

Furhoff, L., 1973, "Some Reflections on Newspaper Concentration", Scandinavian Economic History Review, 21, No. 1, pp. 1-27.
(Cf. p. 92)

Furhoff, L., 1974 a, "Om ägarförhållanden i svensk dagspress", Pressens årsbok, Köpenhamn: Dansk pressehistorisk selskab, pp. 96-103.
(Cf. 75 and 76)

Furhoff, L., 1974 b, Makten över medierna, Stockholm: Cavefors.
(Cf. pp. 92 and 223)

Furhoff, L., 1976, "Den nya tidningstekniken: radproducenter eller journalister", Dagens Nyheter, January 21, p. 4.
(Cf. p. 181)

Galbraith, J. K., 1967, The New Industrial State, Boston, Mass.: Houghton Mifflin.
(Cf. p. 75)

Gans, H. J., 1972, "The Famine in American Mass-Communications Research: Comments on Hirsch, Tuchman, and Gecas", American Journal of Sociology, 77, January, pp. 697-705.
(Cf. p. 224)

Gaskell, P. A., 1970, "Staff in Control of Paris Paper Carries Out 'A Quiet Revolution'", Editor & Publisher, February, p. 17 and 46.
(Cf, p. 77)

Gieber, W., 1964, "News is What Newspapermen Make It", In: Dexter, L. A., & White, D. M., (eds.), People, Society and Mass Communication, New York: Free Press, pp. 173-181.
(Cf. 114 and 219)

Greenwood, E., 1957, "Attributes of a Profession", Social Work, 2, July, pp. 44-55.
(Cf. p. 229)

Gustafson, B., 1968, Press, Stockholm: Norstedts.
(Cf. pp. 34 and 217)

Gustafsson, A., & Olsson, P., 1975, "Projekthandbok", Examensarbete utfört vid institutionen för industriell ekonomi och organisation, Kungliga Tekniska Högskolan.
(Cf. p. 139)

Gustafsson, K. E., & Hadenius, S., 1976, Swedish Press Policy, Stockholm: The Swedish Institute.
(Cf. p. 81)

Gustafsson, K. E., & Wickström, B., 1972, Alternativa system vid förmedling av annonser - en konsekvensanalys, Göteborg: BAS (1972:16).
(Cf. p. 71)

Gustafsson, K. E., 1970, Företaget och reklamen, Göteborg: Akademiförlaget.
(Cf. p. 71)

Gustafsson, K. E., 1974, The Transformation of the Swedish Advertising Agency System, London: IPA.
(Cf. p. 71)

Gustafsson, K. E., 1975, Trycksaksreklamen i informationssystemet, Göteborg: Wezäta.
(Cf. p. 71)

Habermas, J., 1968, Erkenntnis und Interesse, Frankfurt: Suhrkamt.
(Cf. pp. 42 and 232)

Hadenius, S., & Gustafsson, K. E., 1975, "Samhällsintresset och tidningsägandet", Dagens Nyheter, December 18, p. 4.
(Cf. p. 242)

Hadenius, S., & Weibull, L., 1972, Press·Radio·TV, Stockholm: Aldus (Second Edition, First Edition: 1970)
(Cf. p. 71)

Hadenius, S., et al., 1968, Socialdemokratisk press och presspolitik 1899-1909, Stockholm: Tiden-Barnängen.
(Cf. p. 225)

Hadenius, S., et al., 1970, Partipress, socialdemokratisk press och presspolitik 1910-1920, Stockholm: Rabén & Sjögren.
(Cf. p. 225)

Hadenius, S., 1968, "Upplagespiralen och den socialdemokratiska pressen", Tiden, 60, February, pp. 81-84.
(Cf. p. 92)

Hall, R. H., 1972, Organizations, Englewood Cliffs, N. J.: Prentice-Hall.
(Cf. pp. 3, 107, 229 and 230)

Hammenskog, S., 1969, Självmordet, Stockholm: Bonniers.
(Cf. pp. 83, 137, 216 and 217)

Hanson, H., 1968, Anders Persson har vrickat foten, Oskarshamn: Prisma (Verdandi-debatt XXXX).
(Cf. pp. 150, 224 and 238)

Hanssmann, F., 1961, "A Survey of Inventory Theory from the Operations Research Viewpoint", In: Ackoff, R. L., (ed.), 1961, Progress in Operations Research, Vol. 1, New York: Wiley, pp. 65-104 (Chapter 3).
(Cf. p. 149)

Hederberg, H., 1969, Press på villovägar, Stockholm: Wahlström & Widstrand.
(Cf. pp. 223 and 231)

Hein, P., 1968, Grooks II, Cambridge, Mass. & Copenhagen: MIT Press & Borgens forlag.
(Cf. p. 132)

Hellmark, C., et al., 1969, Ni har väl läst tidningen idag?, Stockholm: Wahlström & Widstrand.
(Cf. p. 114)

Henriksson-Jönsson, K., et al., 1975, Personalfrågor vid Upsala Nya Tidning", Seminarieuppsats från Företagsekonomiska institutionen, Uppsala universitet.
(Cf. p. 176)

Hernelius, A., 1961, "Tidningsdöden", Svenska Dagbladet, July 1, p. 4,
(Cf. p. 88)

Hickson, D. J., et al., 1969, "Operations Technology and Organization Structure: An Empirical Reappraisal", Administrative Science Quarterly, 14, September, pp. 378-397.
(cf. pp. 43, 46, 51 and 52)

Hirschman, A. O., 1970, Exit, Voice and Loyalty, Cambridge, Mass.: Harvard University Press.
(Cf. p. 244)

Hofstede, G. H., 1967, The Game of Budget Control, Assen: Van Gorcum.
(Cf. p. 188)

Holmberg, P., 1963, Arbete och löner i Sverige, Solna: Rabén & Sjögren.
(Cf. p. 160)

International Comprint, 1971, Forecast of Long-Term Business and Technological Trends in Graphic Arts, Geneva: International Comprint.
(Cf. p. 185)

Johnson, K. M., & Garnett, H. C., 1971, The Economics of Containerization, London: Allen & Unwin.
(Cf. p. 175)

Journalisten
(Cf. p. 179)

Journalistkåren i Sverige, 1971, Stockholm: Gebers.
(Cf. pp. 76, 225 and 228)

Judd, R. P., 1961, "The Newspaper Reporter in the Suburban City", Journalism Quarterly, 38, Winter, pp. 35-42.
(Cf. p. 114)

Knoph, H., 1974, Strukturendring i norske aviser. Del I. Moderne satsproduksjon, Bergen: Chr. Michelsens Institutt.
(Cf. pp. 165 and 185)

Kornhauser, W., 1963, Scientists in Industry, Berkeley, Cal.: University of California Press.
(Cf. p. 229)

Krogh, T., 1974, "Information i medarbejdereje", Pressens Årsbok, Köpenhamn: Dansk pressehistorisk selskab, pp. 39-51.
(Cf. p. 76)

Larsson, L. O., 1976, "2 av 5 tidningar trycks i offset", Pressens Tidning, 57, November, p. 17.
(Cf. p. 157)

Lawrence, P. R., & Lorsch, J. W., 1967, Organization and Environment, Homewood, Ill.: Irwin.
(Cf. p. 3)

Le Monde, 1975, "Rapport des gerants de S.A.R.L. Le Monde au assemblée generale ordinaire du 23 mai 1975".
(Cf. p. 190)

Legris, M., 1976, "Le Monde" tel qu'il est, Paris: Plon.
(Cf. p. 77)

Leigh, R. D., (ed.), 1947, A Free and Responsible Press, Chicago, Ill,: University of Chicago Press.
(Cf. p. 79)

Lewin, K., 1947, "Channels of Group Life", Human Relations, 1, pp. 143-153.
(Cf. p. 54)

Likert, R., 1961, New Patterns of Management, New York: Mc Graw-Hill.
(Cf. p. 145)

Lo-Johansson, I., 1954, Stockholmaren, Stockholm: Bonniers.
(Cf. p. 118)

Lund, E., & Thomsen, N., 1974, "Ejer- og kontrolforhold i dansk presse", Pressens Årsbok, Köpenhamn: Dansk pressehistorisk selskab, pp. 104-131.
(Cf. p. 75)

Lyons, L. M., 1947, "A free and responsible press", Nieman Report, April 1947.
(Cf. p. 79)

Lyons, L. M., 1971, Newspaper Story. One Hundred Years of the Boston Globe, Cambridge, Mass.: The Belknap Press of Harvard University.
(Cf. p. 122)

March, J. G., & Simon, H. A., 1958, Organizations, New York: Wiley.
(Cf. pp. 3 and 39)

March, J. G., & Olsen, J. P., 1976, Ambiguity and Choice in Organizations, Oslo: Universitetsforlaget.
(Cf. p. 252)

Marris, R. L., 1964, The Economic Theory of "Managerial" Capitalism, London: The Free Press of Glencoe.
(Cf. p. 75)

Matejko, A., 1967, "Newspaper Staff as a Social System", Polish Sociological Bulletin, 1, pp. 58-68.
(Cf. p. 40)

McDonald, I., 1975, <u>A Man of The Times</u>, London: Hamish Hamilton.
(Cf. p. 148)

Mirror Group, 1975, "Development Plan, June 10, 1975".
(Cf. p. 175)

Mitroff, I. I., 1974, <u>The Subjective Side of Science</u>, Amsterdam: Elsevier.
(Cf. pp. 36 and 41)

Mumford, E., & Pettigrew, A., 1975, <u>Implementing Strategic Decisions</u>, New York: Longmans.
(Cf. p. 166)

Mumford, E., 1968, "Planning for Computers", <u>Management Decision</u>, 2, pp. 98-102.
(Cf. p. 169)

New York Times Co., 1973, "1972 Annual Report".
(Cf. p. 124)

Nielsen, B. H., 1974, "A/S Dagbladet Politiken's overgang til fondseje 1973", <u>Pressens Årsbok</u>, Köpenhamn: Dansk pressehistorisk selskab, pp. 67-75.
(Cf. p. 76)

Nilsen, A., 1975, <u>Strukturendring i norske aviser. Delrapport Nr. 2. Konsekvenser for økonomi, sysselsettning, arbeidsmiljø og organisasjon</u>, Bergen: Chr. Michelsens Institutt.
(Cf. p. 185)

Nixon, R. B., & Hahn, T., 1971, "Concentration of Press Ownership: A Comparison of 32 Countries", <u>Journalism Quarterly</u>, 48, Spring, pp. 5-16.
(Cf. p. 75)

<u>Nordisk Tidskrift</u>, 1975, "Massmedierna i Norden", 51, No. 3, p. 165.
(Cf. p. 233)

Nussberger, U., 1971, <u>Die Mechanik der Pressekonzentration</u>, Berlin: De Gruyter.
(Cf. pp. 92 and 191)

Nycop, C.-A., 1970, <u>Bära eller brista</u>, Stockholm: Bonniers.
(Cf. pp. 34 and 147)

Nycop, C.-A., 1971, <u>Nyfiken med sting</u>, Stockholm: Bonniers.
(Cf. pp. 34 and 134)

Nystrom, P. C., et al., 1976, "Interacting Processes as Organizational Design", In: Kilman, R. H., et al.(ed.), 1976, <u>The Management of Organization Design</u>, Vol. I, New York: North Holland, pp. 209-230. (Cf. p. 70)

Ortmark, Å., 1969, <u>De okända makthavarna</u>, Stockholm: Wahlström & Widstrand.
(Cf. p. 217)

Pearsall, M., 1970, "Participant Observation as a Role and Method in Behavorial Research", In: Filstead, W. J., (ed.), 1970, <u>Qualitative Methodology. Firsthand Involvement with the Social World</u>, Chicago, Ill.: Markham, pp. 340-352.
(Cf. p. 41)

Perby, M.-L., 1976, "Arbetets innehåll och mening - en förhandlingsfråga", <u>Grafia</u>, 3/76, pp. 15-17.
(Cf. pp. 170 and 183)

Perrow, C., 1967, "A Framework for the Comparative Analysis of Organizations", <u>American Sociological Review</u>, 32, April, pp. 194-208.
(Cf. pp. 46, 51 and 52)

Peter, L. J., & Hull, R., 1969, <u>The Peter Principle</u>, London: Souvenir Press.
(Cf. p. 107)

Petersson, K., 1966, <u>Presskontakter</u>, Stockholm: Bonniers.
(Cf. pp. 73 and 114)

Pettersson, U., 1974, "Problem vid simulering av tidningsföretag", <u>Uppsats till konferensen "Management Science i Sverige"</u>, Stockholm, October 1974. (Cf. p. 166)

Pettigrew, A., 1973, <u>The Politics of Organizational Decision-Making</u>, London: Tavistock.
(Cf. p. 166)

Polich, J. E., 1974, "Predicting Newspaper Staff Size from Circulation: A New Look", <u>Journalism Quarterly</u>, 51, Autumn, pp. 515-517.
(Cf. pp. 199 and 200)

Pondy, L. R., 1969, "Effects of Size, Complexity and Ownership on Administrative Intensity", <u>Administrative Science Quarterly</u>, 14, No. 1, pp. 47-61.
(Cf. p. 191)

Pressens samarbetsnämnd, 1970, <u>Spelregler för pressen</u>, Stockholm.
(Cf. p. 223)

<u>Pressens Tidning</u>
(Cf. pp. 81, 164, 177, 179 and 242)

<u>Private Eye</u>, April 2, 1976, p. 16.
(Cf. p. 225)

Pugh, D. S., et al., 1969, "The Context of Organization Structures", <u>Administrative Science Quarterly</u>, 14, No. 1, pp. 91-114.
(Cf. p. 51)

<u>På Stan</u>, 25-30 October, 1975, p. 5,
(Cf. p. 152)

Radnitzsky, G., 1970, <u>Contemporary Schools of Metascience</u>, Göteborg: Akademiförlaget, Part I & II (Sec. Rev. Ed., First Ed.: 1968)
(Cf. p. 42)

Ramström, D., 1971, "Småföretagen och framtiden", In: Ramström, D., (ed.), Mindre företag - problem och villkor, Stockholm: Prisma, pp. 169-181.
(Cf. p. 92)

Rasmussen, L., 1975, "Informationsselektion", Inslag i radioprogrammet OBS!-Kulturkvarten, August 6.
(Cf. p. 84)

Ray, R. H., 1952, "Economic Forces as Factors in Daily Newspaper Concentration", Journalism Quarterly, 29, Winter, pp. 31-42.
(Cf. p. 93)

Reddaway, W. B., 1963, "The Economics of Newspapers", Economic Journal, 73, June, pp. 201-218.
(Cf. pp. 71, 87, 137 and 191)

Rhenman, E., 1974, Managing the Community Hospital: Systems Analysis of a Swedish Hospital, Farnborough: Saxon House (First Swedish Edition, 1969: Centrallasarettet, Lund: Studentlitteratur).
(Cf. p. 254)

Rifbjerg, K., 1974, Du skall inte vaere ked af det Amalia, Haslev: Gyldendal.
(Cf. pp. 115 and 217)

Ring, S., 1976 a, "Inget bly: inga typografer?", Dagens Nyheter, February 13, p. 4.
(Cf. p. 174)

Ring, S., 1976 b, "Inlägg i radioprogrammet 'Vår grundade mening'", April 14, 1976.
(Cf. p. 181)

Rivers, W. L., 1965, The Opinionmakers, Boston, Mass.: Beacon Press.
(Cf. p. 82)

Robinson, E. A. G., 1931, The Structure of Competitive Industry, Cambridge: Cambridge University Press.
(Cf. p. 92)

Rosse, J. N., 1967, "Daily Newspapers, Monopolistic Competition and Economies of Scale", American Economic Review, 57, May, pp. 522-533.
(Cf. p. 92)

Royal Commission on the Press, 1976, The National Newspaper Industry, London: HMSO. (Cf. p. 81)

Rühl, M., 1969, Die Zeitungsredaktion als Organisiertes Soziales System, Bielefeld: Bertelsmann Universitätsverlag.
(Cf. pp. 40 and 96)

Sandgren, E., 1968, Blaskan, Stockholm: Bonniers. (Cf. pp. 34 and 217)

Scherer, F. M., 1970, Industrial Market Structure and Economic Performance, Chicago, Ill.: Rand McNally.
(Cf. p. 93)

Schwoebel, J., 1968, La presse, le pouvoir et l'argent, Paris: Seuil.
(Cf. p. 77)

Siebert, F. S., et al., 1956, Four Theories of the Press, Urbana, Ill.: The University of Illinois.
(Cf. pp. 79 and 80)

Sigal, L. V., 1973, Reporters and Officials. The Organization and Politics of Newsmaking, Lexington, Mass.: D. C. Heath & Co.
(Cf. pp. 40, 82, 114, 124, 126, 146 and 202)

Sigelman, L., 1973, "Reporting the News: An Organizational Analysis", American Journal of Sociology, 79, July, pp. 132-151.
(Cf. pp. 225, 229, 230)

Smith, A., 1977, Subsidies and the Press in Europe, London: PEP, vol. XLIII, No. 569.
(Cf. p. 2)

Smythe, D. W., 1960, "On the Political Economy of Communications", Journalism Quarterly, 37, Fall, pp. 562-563.
(Cf. p. 93)

SOU 1965:22, Dagspressens ekonomiska villkor, Stockholm: Esselte.
(Cf. p. 80)

SOU 1968:48, Dagspressens situation, Stockholm: Bonniers.
(Cf. pp. 80, 92 and 205)

SOU 1974:102, Svensk press. Presstödet och tidningskonkurrensen, Stockholm: Allmänna förlaget.
(Cf. p. 38)

SOU 1974:34, Grafisk industri i omvandling, Stockholm: Allmänna förlaget.
(Cf. pp. 167 and 185)

SOU 1975:11, Svensk press. Tidningar i samverkan, Stockholm: Liber.
(Cf. p. 84)

SOU 1975:78, Svensk press. Pressens funktioner i samhället, Stockholm: Allmänna förlaget.
(Cf. pp. 79 and 228)

SOU 1975:79, Svensk press. Statlig presspolitik, Stockholm: Allmänna förlaget.
(Cf. pp. 44, 79 and 80)

Springel, J., van, 1965, "Diagnosis and Therapy of Daily Press Management", Gazette, 11, No. 4, pp. 297-322.
(Cf. p. 88)

Stangerup, H., 1975, "Pressens kris har flera dimensioner", Svenska Dagbladet, November 10, p. 2.
(Cf. pp. 72 and 74)

Statistisk Årsbok, 1914-   , Stockholm: Statistiska Centralbyrån.
(Cf. p. 161)

Steinbeck, J., 1963, Travels with Charley, New York: Bantam
Books (Paper Back Edition, First Edition Published in 1962
by the Viking Press, New York).
(Cf. p. 255)

Stortingsmelding Nr. 29 1973-74.
(Cf. p. 241)

Strömholm, S., 1975, "Västtysk paragraf 32", Dagens Nyheter,
September 9, p. 2.
(Cf. p. 241)

Swartz, C., 1965, Med röda gullband, Strängnäs: Seelig.
(Cf. p. 92)

Söderlund, G., 1973, Redaktör(S), Stockholm: Rabén & Sjögren.
(Cf. p. 225)

Söderström, H., & Ahrnstedt, P., 1959, "Svenska dagstidnings-
journalisters utbildning, rekrytering, attityder m. m.",
Seminarieuppsats från Statsvetenskapliga institutionen vid
Uppsala universitet.
(Cf. p. 225)

Sörmark, S., 1971, På Aftonbladet, Stockholm: Bonniers.
(Cf. pp. 70, 83 and 108)

Talese, G., 1970, The Kingdom and the Power, New York: The World
Publishing Co., (Paper Back Edition, First Edition: 1969).
(Cf. pp. 34 and 124)

Teste, S., 1976, "Alla strejkar vid Washington Post men tidningen
kommer ut", Journalisten, January, p. 27.
(Cf. p. 170)

Thompson, J. D., 1967, Organizations in Action, New York: Mc
Graw-Hill.
(Cf. pp. 3, 51, 66, 67, 119, 139, 147, 149, 150, 154, 248, 250)

Thomsen, N., 1968, "Recension av Furhoff L., Upplagespiralen,
1967 och andra skrifter", Statsvetenskaplig tidskrift, 50,
pp. 320-329.
(Cf. pp. 92 and 191)

Tingsten, H., 1947 a, "Tidningsmannens frihet", Dagens Nyheter,
January 19, p. 6.
(Cf. pp. 75, 218 and 225)

Tingsten, H., 1947 b, "Den moderna pressen: 'Monopolistiska ten-
denser', politiskt inflytande", Dagens Nyheter, January 17,
p. 5.
(Cf. p. 75)

Tingsten, H., 1971 a, Mitt liv 3: Tidningen 1946-52, Stockholm:
PAN/Norstedts (Paper Back Edition, First Edition: 1963)
(Cf. pp. 34, 189 and 218)

Tingsten, H., 1971 b, Mitt liv 4: Tio år 1953-63, Stockholm: PAN/Norstedts (Paper Back Edition, First Edition: 1964)
(Cf. pp. 34, 75 and 218)

Tollin, S., 1960, Dagspressekonomi - en analys av 95 bokslut,
(Cf. p. 190)

Tollin, S., 1972, "Tollstads tidning. En tidningsekonomisk essä", In: Furhoff, L., et al., 1972, Massmedieekonomi, Stockholm: Almqvist & Wiksell, pp. 49-63. (Cf. p. 190)

Torbacke, J., 1972, Dagens Nyheter och demokratins kris 1937-1946, Stockholm: Bonniers.
(Cf. p. 84)

TS-boken, 1942- , Solna: Tidningsstatistik AB.
(Cf. p. 213)

Tuchman, G., 1972, "Objectivity as Strategic Ritual: An Examination of Newsmen's Notions of Objectivity", American Journal of Sociology, 77, January, pp. 660-679.
(Cf. pp. 222 and 224)

Tuchman, G., 1973, "Making News by Doing Work: Routinizing the Unexpected", American Journal of Sociology, 79, July, pp. 110-131.
(Cf. pp. 40, 147 and 148)

Vallinder, T., 1971, Press och politik, Falköping: Gleerups (Second Revised Edition, First Edition: 1968).
(Cf. p. 80)

Vår grundade mening, April 7, 1976.
(Cf. p. 183)

Wahlgren, C., 1970, På skilda fronter, Malmö: Sydsvenska Dagbladet.
(Cf. pp. 111 and 172)

Warner, M., 1971, "Organizational Context and Control of Policy in the Television Newsroom: A Participant Observation Study", British Journal of Sociology, 12, September, pp. 283-294.
(Cf. p. 225)

Waugh, E., 1938, Scoop, Washington, D. C.: Little.
(Cf. p. 228)

Weick, K. E., 1969, The Social Psychology of Organizing, Reading, Mass.: Addison-Wesley.
(Cf. pp. 43 and 96)

Westman, U.-S., 1974, "Ägoförhållanden i finländsk press", Pressens Årsbok, Köpenhamn: Dansk pressehistorisk selskab, pp. 76-85.
(Cf. p. 75)

Whisler, T. L., 1970, *Information Technology and Organizational Change*, Brooks-Cold: Wadsworth.
(Cf. p. 169)

White, D. M., 1950, "The 'Gatekeeper'" A Case Study in the Selection of News", *Journalism Quarterly*, 27, Fall, pp. 383-390.
(Cf. p. 54)

Wildavsky, A., 1964, *The Politics of the Budgeting Process*, Boston, Mass.: Little, Brown & Co.
(Cf. p. 188)

Windahl, S., 1975, *Professionella kommunikatörer - en explorativ studie*, Lund: Studentlitteratur (diss.).
(Cf. pp. 116 and 228)

Winsbury, R., 1975, *The Technology and the Press. A Study of the Experience in the United States*, London: HMSO.
(Cf. pp. 141, 157, 158, 160, 164, 168, 170, 171, 174, 176, 180, 181 and 186)

Wonnacott, T. H., & Wonnacott, R. J., 1972, *Introductory Statistics for Business and Economics*, New York: Wiley.
(Cf. p. 230)

Woodward, B., & Bernstein, C., 1974, *All the President's Men*, London: Quartet Books.
(Cf. pp. 34, 42, 82 and 251)

Ågren, S., 1970, *Sanning till 90 %*, Stockholm: Askild & Kärnekull.
(Cf. pp. 83, 84, 108, 229 and 231)

SUBJECT INDEX

advertisers   71, 248
allocation data   38-39
allocation issue, defined   188
allocation issue, summarized   208-212
allocation of financial resources   188-194
allocation of providers   194-201
allocation of space   201-208
authoritarian theory of the press   79

budgeting   188-191
buffering   140-141
business oriented group, defined   98-99
buyers of other printed products   72

case studies   6-8, 11-32
circulation spiral model   88-92
collection phase   54-57
competitors   83-95, 249
continuing news   147-148
cooperation   83-84
customer-propelled growth   159

deadlines   142-146
demarcation problems   178-181
developing news   148
dialectics   42
differentiation   96-103, 249-250
distribution of benefits   174-178
distribution phase   63-64

economies of scale   92-93
environment, defined   3-5
environmental communication links   114-120

external publication rules   222-225

feedback of interviews   36-38
financial flow   4
financiers   75-78
flow issue, defined   133-139
flow issue, summarized   135, 154-156
forecasting   147-149
further work   255

generalization   2, 42-44
governments   79-82, 248

hierarchy   103-108
hiring policies   195, 225-229
horizontal differentiation   99-102, 249
hospitals, implications for   253
human relations aspects   151-154, 182-183

integration   103-120, 250-252
interviews   34-38
issues   9-10, 133-244, 250

knowledge technology   51-52, 248

lateral contacts   109-113
leveling   142-146
libertarian theory of the press   79

manning   174-178
materials technology   51-52, 248

news oriented group, defined   98-99
newspaper environment   9, 69-95, 248-249
newspaper personnel   9, 96-131, 249
newspaper technology   8, 46-68, 248

operations technology   51, 248

organization charts, examples   122-131
ownership   75-78, 248

participant observation   40-41
personnel, defined   3-5
physical flow   4
politically oriented group, defined   98-99
pressure for new technology   159-166
procedure of introduction   166-173
processing phase   57-59
productivity   198
promotion policies   104-105
provider-propelled growth   159
providers, defined   3-5
public support   2, 80-81, 248, 254-255
publication issue, defined   215-221
publication issue, summarized   221, 241-244

rationing   149-151
readers   69-70, 249
reproduction phase   60-62
research methods   33-44

selective recruitment   225-229
social responsibility theory of the press   79
socialization   229-237
Soviet Communist theory of the press   80
spot news   148
stocking of material   140-141
strategies to handle pressure for growth   159-166
suppliers   73-74, 248

technically oriented group, defined   98-99
technology, defined   3-5

technology development 185-187
technology issue, defined 157-158
technology issue, summarized 184
technology profiles 57, 59, 63, 64, 65
temporal differentiation 102-103, 249-250
theatre company, implications for 253

university department, implications for 253

variations in input 136-139
vertical differentiation 104-108, 249

written material 34

PN 4734 .E54